Explore the World

NELLES GUIDE

BRAZIL

Authors:
Anton Jakob, Fernanda Cordoe
Claus Jäke

*An Up-to-date travel guide
with 131 color photos
and 18 maps*

Dear Reader: Being up-to-date is the main goal of the Nelles series. Our correspondents help keep us abreast of the latest developments in the travel scene, while our cartographers see to it that maps are also kept completely current. However, as the travel world is constantly changing, we cannot guarantee that all the information contained in our books is always valid. Should you come across a discrepancy, please contact us at: Nelles Verlag, Schleissheimer Str. 371 b, 80935 Munich, Germany, tel. (089) 3571940, fax. (089) 35719430, e-mail: Nelles.Verlag@T-Online.de

Note: Distances and measurements, including temperatures, used in this guide are metric. For conversion information, please see the *Guidelines* section of this book.

LEGEND

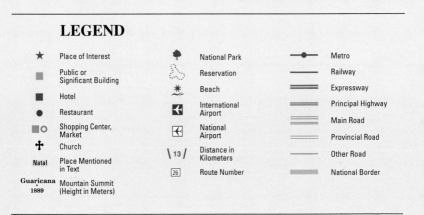

★	Place of Interest	♠	National Park	●──	Metro
■	Public or Significant Building		Reservation	────	Railway
■	Hotel	☀	Beach	═══	Expressway
●	Restaurant	⬉	International Airport		Principal Highway
■○	Shopping Center, Market	⬇	National Airport		Main Road
✝	Church				Provincial Road
Natal	Place Mentioned in Text	\13/	Distance in Kilometers		Other Road
Guaricana 1889	Mountain Summit (Height in Meters)	26	Route Number		National Border

BRAZIL
© Nelles Verlag GmbH, D-80935 München
All rights reserved

First Edition 2000
ISBN 3-88618-053-0
Printed in Slovenia

Publisher:	Günter Nelles	**Photo Editor:**	K. Bärmann-Thümmel
Managing Editor:	Berthold Schwarz	**Translator:**	Robert Nusbaum
Project Editor:	Anton Jakob	**Cartography:**	Nelles Verlag GmbH
English Edition		**Lithos:**	Priegnitz, Munich
Editor:	Chase Stewart	**Printed By:**	Gorenjski Tisk

- X02 -

CONTENTS

Imprint / Legend 2
List of Maps 6

LAND AND PEOPLE

History and Culture 13
Geopolitical Overview 34

TRAVELING IN BRAZIL

THE MAGIC TRIANGLE

The Southeastern Region 45
Rio de Janeiro 48
GUIDEPOST: Hotels, Restaurants, Sights 69
São Paulo 73
GUIDEPOST: Hotels, Restaurants, Sights 80
Minas Gerais 83
Belo Horizonte 83
Diamantina 85
Ouro Preto 87
Mariana 92
Congonhas do Campo 93
São João del Rei 95
Tiradentes 96
GUIDEPOST: Hotels, Restaurants, Sights 96

THE SOUTH

The Southern Region 101
Rio Grande do Sul 101
Santa Catarina 105
Paraná 110
Cataratas do Iguaçu 113
GUIDEPOST: Hotels, Restaurants, Sights 118

THE MIDWEST

The Midwest 125
Brasília 125
GUIDEPOST: Hotels, Restaurants, Sights 131
Pantanal 133
GUIDEPOST: Hotels, Restaurants, Sights 137

THE NORTHEAST

The Northeastern Region 141
Bahia 142
Salvador da Bahia 142
Recôncavo 155
Southern Bahia 158
GUIDEPOST: Hotels, Restaurants, Sights 160
Pernambuco 163
Recife 163
Olinda 166
João Pessoa 170
Natal 172
Fortaleza 173
São Luís 175
GUIDEPOST: Hotels, Restaurants, Sights 177

THE NORTH – THE AMAZON

The Northern Region 183
The Amazon River 183
Pará 187
Belém 190
Santarém 194
Amazonas State 196
Manaus 197
GUIDEPOST: Hotels, Restaurants, Sights 201

FEATURES

The Rain Forest 208

Indigenous Peoples 216

Music 223

Eating and Drinking 228

Literature 232

GUIDELINES

Before You Go 234
    Climate / Best Time to Travel 234
    What to Wear 235
    Entry Requirements 235
    Airport Taxes 235
    Currency / Changing Money 235
    Staying Healthy 236

Traveling in Brazil 237
    By Air 237
    Brazil Airpass 237
    By Rail 237
    By Long-Distance Bus 237
    By City Bus 238
    By Ship, By Car 238
    Car Rental 238

Practical Tips from A to Z 238
    Accommodation 238
    Banks 239
    Beaches 239
    Bribery 239
    Business Hours 239
    Carnival 240
    Customs 240
    Drugs 240
    Electricity 240
    Embassies (Brazilian) 240
    Embassies (Foreign) 241
    Holidays 241
    Medical Services, Pharmacies 241
    Phone Calls 241
    Photography 242
    Postal Services 242
    Security 242
    Shopping 243
    Taxis 243
    Television 243
    Time 244
    Tipping 244
    Weights and Measures 244

Glossary 244
Useful Words and Phrases 245
Authors / Photographers 249
Index 250

LIST OF MAPS

Brazil 6-7

Southeastern Region 46-47

Rio's Beaches. 50-51

Rio de Janeiro 60-61

The Rio Area 66-67

São Paulo 74

Minas Gerais 85

Ouro Preto 86-87

Southern Brazil 102-103

Iguaçu. 113

Brasília. 127

Pantanal 132

Bahia 143

Salvador 147

The Salvador Area 153

The Northeast. 166-167

Amazonas. 184-185

Manaus. 196

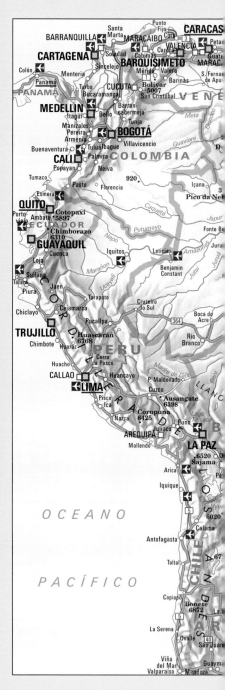

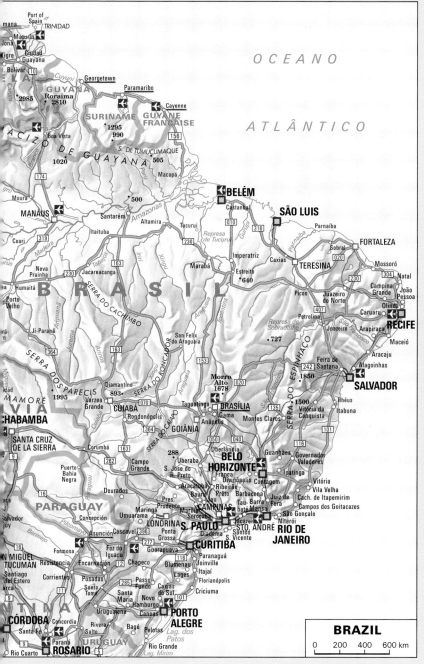

HISTORY AND CULTURE

On April 22, 1500, a 13-ship, thousand-man Portuguese armada under the command of Pedro Álvares Cabral landed on the coast of Brazil near Porto Seguro. Cabral had been dispatched by the crown to trade in the Indies, but having been instructed by Vasco da Gama to avoid the coast of Africa, he strayed into a current that carried him all the way to Brazil – although Spanish explorers had previously sailed along the same coast prior to Cabral's "discovery." With Cabral was a government official named Pero Vaz de Caminha, and it is to him we owe the first written history of Brazil. In a letter dated May 1, 1500, he reported the discovery to his king, Dom Manuel I:

"The men here are handsome, with skin painted black and red, and checked patterns on their torsos and legs. There is no doubt that they make a favorable impression. Among them were four or five young women, who, like the men, wore no clothes. The impression they made was not unfavorable either. One among them had painted one of her thighs with black paint from the knee up to the hip and buttocks, leaving the natural skin color showing elsewhere. Another of them had painted the fronts and backs of her knees, as well as the backs of her feet. Her private parts were completely naked and were displayed with such innocence that there was not the slightest trace of shame. Another young woman was carrying an infant on her breast, fastened there with a cloth in such a way that all that was visible of him were his little

Previous pages: Music, dancing and lust for life are vital to the Carnival. Numerous nature parks offer opportunities to explore Brazil's rich flora and fauna. Left: Amazonian Indian in festive body paint.

legs. Not a single raiment was to be seen on either the mother's legs or her torso...

"As they (the Portuguese scouts) told us later, after walking a good half-mile, they came to a village with nine or ten houses, each of which was about as long as our flagship. These houses are made of wood, with walls made out of boards, and roofs of thatch. Though these dwellings are quite high, they have only a single room with no dividing wall of any kind, only numerous wooden posts from which hammocks that serve the inhabitants as beds are suspended at a good distance from the earthen floor. Beneath these hammocks they light fires for warmth. Each house has an entrance with a low doorway in each of two opposing walls. In each of the dwellings live 30 to 40 people from whom the scouts received food, principally manioc and other roots that grow in this land and which the inhabitants eat.

"They have nothing made of iron, and they cut wood and tree trunks with wedge-shaped stones affixed securely to wooden handles so that they do not come loose. They do not sow seeds, nor do they raise animals. There are neither cows nor goats, nor sheep nor chickens here, nor any other animal accustomed to living together with humans. They live off manioc roots, which are plentiful here, as well as from the seeds and fruits that spring forth naturally from the earth and forests. They are far stronger and better nourished than we, in spite of all our wheat and vegetables. These people seem to me to be so radiantly innocent that I am sure if we understood their language and they ours, they would soon become Christians."

Unfortunately, this letter, as well as other relatively unbiased Portuguese accounts of the New World, were not published during this period, thus leaving the image that Europeans formed of Brazil to be decisively influenced by men such as Amerigo Vespucci and Hans Staden.

Vespucci, who undertook a voyage to South America for the Portuguese crown in 1501, wrote the following in a letter to Lorenzo di Medici:

"This land is inhabited by totally naked people, both male and female. While living and sleeping amongst them for 27 days, I have conducted an intensive study of their way of life. They have neither laws nor any kind of religious faith. They live according to nature and know nothing of the immortality of the soul. They own nothing, for everything is owned in common; they have neither provinces, kingdoms, nor boundary lines, and there is no king who rules over them. What perplexed me most with respect to their incessant wars and the cruelty attendant upon them was that I could not find out from these people to what purpose they wage war upon each other, for they have neither objects of value nor kingdoms,

Above: The glowing red color of brazilwood gave the country its name. Right: Ceramics from the Marajoara (Museu Goeldi, Belém).

and know nothing of the desire for power or the wish to have dominion over others. When we bid them explain the cause, they could only make reference to the distant past: they seek revenge for the death of their ancestors. This is a bestial thing. One of them even spoke of having eaten two hundred human bodies."

Hans Staden, a German cannoneer who served in the Portuguese navy, undertook lengthy journeys to Brazil for the Portuguese crown in 1547-1548, and again in 1555. The book he wrote about his experiences, *A True History and Description of a Landscape of the Savage, Naked, and Horrible Cannibalistic Men Living in America in the New World*, was published in 1557 and became a best-seller throughout Europe.

High Cultures of Unknown Origin

Just who these indigenous peoples called "Indians" by the Europeans really were has not been definitively explained. It is relatively certain, however, that approximately 35,000 years ago hunters followed their game from the Asian continent across the frozen Bering Straits. Although the area that is now Brazil is thought to have been completely settled as early as 12,000 years ago, there are conflicting estimates regarding the size of the indigenous population at the time of the arrival of the Europeans. Most experts speak of an unevenly distributed two to three million people, with more settlements in coastal and fluvial areas, and fewer numbers of inhabitants elsewhere – in other words, a demographic situation similar to that of modern-day Brazil. The were also regions that were completely uninhabited.

The population was divided into four main language groups: *Tupi-Guarani, Jê, Aruák* and *Karíb*, all of whom practiced animistic religions. Some groups were hunter-gatherers, while others cultivated beans, manioc, gourds, sweet potatoes

and corn. They made ceramic vessels, but knew nothing of either iron or writing. They were sometimes warlike and, for religious reasons, cannibalistic as well.

Archaeologists have found pre-Columbian mounds of mussel shells called *sambaquis* all up and down the Brazilian coastline. One such discovery near Belém by the Brazilian researcher Mário Simões caused a considerable stir, as the pottery from the site dated from 5500 B.C. This find was welcomed by experts who supported the theory that the Amazon region was at one time inhabited by an advanced civilization that did not originate with hunters from Asia. Researchers subsequently found persuasive evidence that a Marajoara culture flourished on an island in the Amazon Delta from 400 B.C. to 1300 A.D.; that is, for 1,700 years without interruption. Near Lago Arari in the northeastern corner of this island (now called Marajó) the traces of about 400 man-made earthen hills, called *tesos*, were discovered. These hills provided protection from the Amazonian flood waters, and served as a safe, dry place for the construction of houses of adobe. The theory that the island of Marajó was continuously inhabited is substantiated by the discovery of elaborately painted pottery, including burial urns as tall as 100 centimeters, in which upper-class *Marajoarans* were buried. Anna Roosevelt, a North American archaeologist, estimated that the inhabitants must have lived in groups numbering approximately 10,000 people each, and that the total population of the island was about 100,000. The *Santarém* culture, after which the eponymous city on the Amazon River is named, flourished for five hundred years, from the 11th to the 16th century A.D. The *Santarém* lived mainly from the cultivation of corn, and made ceramic vessels as well.

Papal Arbitration

Contact with the Europeans was initially peaceful and, until 1532, harmonious. Portugal's primary interest in controlling the profitable spice trade led it to devote most of its attention to India, Southeast Asia and the Far East.

The new possession was at first regarded merely as a way station. It was originally called *Terra de Vera Cruz*, but was soon renamed Brazil, after brazilwood (*pau brasil*), in which commodity the colony abounded and whose reddish color was reminiscent of glowing coals (*brasa*). This wood was put to profitable use as a dyestuff in the European textile industry. The handful of European traders doing business in the colony needed the natives' help in obtaining the wood, which, in addition to parrots and monkeys, the Indians traded for such items as knives, axes, scissors, fish hooks, glass beads and mirrors.

This harmonious phase was short-lived, however. As early as 1502, Portugal granted the prosperous merchant Fernão de Loronha the island of São João (today called Fernando de Noronha) as a fiefdom, along with certain trading privileges. In exchange, Loronha agreed to build a fort and to explore 500 kilometers of coastline annually. The process of taking possession of the new land was gradual, but as the tempo of exploration increased, so did resistance from the original inhabitants.

Portugal was not the only European power with colonial designs on newfound places, however. The French, for example, refused to honor the Treaty of Tordesillas that had been signed in 1494 by Spain and Portugal. The treaty modified the line of demarcation, promulgated in 1493 by Pope Alexander VI, that had divided the New World (excluding Brazil, which had not yet been discovered) between the two Catholic countries of Spain and Portugal. The line of demarcation coincided with the 48th parallel – meaning that it fell between the mouth of the Amazon and the *capitania* of São Vicente, south of the present-day state of São Paulo. All regions to the west of this line were deemed Spain's, and all those to the east Portugal's.

The existence of this treaty failed to prevent French pirates and merchants from seeking gain along the coast of Brazil, however, and when Portugal protested, François I responded by claiming ignorance of this "testament of Adam" that granted the kings of Spain and Portugal equal shares of the known world. The Portuguese King João III sent out a number of military expeditions, and in 1532, Martim Afonso de Sousa founded the first settlement, São Vicente, with royal support.

The Capitanias

The era of the *capitanias* is regarded both as the turning point in Portugal's colonial policy toward Brazil, and as Portugal's first step towards the establishment of European settlements and a colonial administrative infrastructure. In 1533, the first sugar mill was built in São Vicente for the purpose of increasing sugar production. Only one year later, the King divided Brazil into 15 hereditary captaincies, or fiefs, extending 50 leagues along the coast and an indefinite distance inland. These areas were distributed to persons favored at court, who took the name of *donatário*. They were granted extensive rights and privileges over these domains, including the power to make laws, and military and political powers. As executors of the King's commands, the donatários also enjoyed the privilege of immunity, but were nonetheless kept on a short leash by court officials. Although the task of granting land fell to the donatários, defending the land was left to the settlers. Outside the walls of their settlements, they engaged in two types of agriculture: clear-cutting for the

Right: Brazil's exotic animal world fascinated Europeans – 19th-century watercolor of parrots.

cultivation of beans, rice, manioc and corn; and the cultivation of sugar cane, cotton and tobacco on large plantations called *fazendas*.

The capitania system had worked well on the Atlantic island of Madeira and in the Azores primarily because these places, unlike Brazil, were uninhabited when the Europeans arrived in them. But in Brazil, the indigenous peoples reacted to the Europeans' appropriation of land and institution of forced labor and enslavement by fleeing into the interior, where they established new settlements. Many fought with the settlers or simply refused to work, although some Indians managed to adapt to the white man's ways, even making alliances; some with the Portuguese, and others with the French.

Twenty years after establishment of a colonial infrastructure, only two of the capitanias – Pernambuco and São Vicente – were successful, owing to the profits they earned from sugar cane. All the others failed, which led to further changes in colonial policy. The capitanias remained in place until the mid-18th century, although with substantially reduced powers. By 1549, the colony had a central government: after the capitania of Bahia was overrun by the Tupí-Guaraní, the King bought it back and appointed Tomé de Sousa Brazil's first Governor-General. Sousa was an experienced colonial governor, having already cut his administrative teeth serving the crown in Africa and India. He founded the city of Salvador da Bahia, which remained the seat of the Portuguese colonial government until 1763.

Competing Colonial Powers

Portuguese colonial policy until the middle of the 17th century comprised the suppression of Indian uprisings; the defense of Portuguese interests against French and Dutch encroachment; the settlement of disputes among various competing groups of colonists; the attempt to put an end to unregulated trade in in-

17

creasingly scarce brazilwood; and the fostering of missionary work among the indigenous peoples, as well as settlement of the colony itself.

Inasmuch as sugar-cane production was highly profitable, other European nations took a much greater interest in this activity than in harvesting brazilwood. The French, for example, had been trying to gain a foothold on the Brazilian coast since early in the 16th century. In 1555, Nicolas de Villegaignon, a Maltese knight in the service of Henry II of France, took possession of the Bay of Guanabara (near present-day Rio de Janeiro) with a group of Huguenot settlers and established the colony of *La France Antarctique*. The Portuguese then wanted to expel the French from Brazil, a task that was entrusted to Estácio de Sá. In 1565 he succeeded, and two years later founded Rio de Janeiro, which became the capital of Brazil in the 18th century.

Portugual and Spain claimed to derive their right to colonize other peoples from the Vatican's *auctoritate apostolica*, which stated that the mere act of spreading the Christian faith among "heathens" justified the means by which this was done. The crown and the colonial government provided the Church in Brazil with most of its financial support, at the same time giving it free rein to carry out both its religious and "civilizing" task of spreading Portuguese cultural values throughout the colony. By 1549, the first Franciscan missions had been built. In 1551, the first bishopric was established in Salvador, and the first Jesuit college was founded in São Paulo in 1554. The Jesuits were for many years the only Europeans who condemned the colonists' crimes against the indigenous peoples. However, like the Benedictines, Carmelites and Dominicans who came after

Right: A settlement of the Dutch West Indies Company in Brazil (17th-century watercolor).

them, the Jesuits unwittingly contributed to the catastrophic mortality levels among the indigenous peoples by spreading contagious disease.

The decimation of the indigenous populations by murder, war, epidemics, and the extensive cultivation of sugar cane for the European market gave rise to a shortage of manpower, which was overcome by the introduction of African slaves into Brazil, beginning in 1574.

In 1580, owing to a crisis in the ruling dynasty of Portugal, Philip II of Spain became ruler of the Portuguese motherland. This joint reign of a Spanish and Portuguese king lasted until 1640. In principle, Portugal was allowed to continue acting as an independent political power. However, while little outward change occurred in colonial administrative policies, all of Portugal's colonies became the property of the Spanish crown. During this period, Portugal gradually came to resemble a Spanish province, and as a result was gradually drawn into Spain's foreign policy misadventures. For example, in 1588 Portugal lost many of her ships when she was forced to participate in the "invincible" Spanish armada's naval campaign against England. Portugal's colonial empire was then attacked by France, England and Holland, who were Spain's enemies. These unfortunate events also had serious consequences for Brazil: the port of Lisbon, previously one of the most important ports in Europe, was henceforth off limits to ships from countries that were adversaries of Spain, which made it very difficult for Brazilian merchants to sell their goods. Even the slave trade was affected, as the British, French and Dutch became competitors for the lucrative three-way commerce.

Brazil's port cities were increasingly plundered by pirates, and the weakened motherland was in no position to come to the colony's defense. In 1587, the British tried unsuccessfully to take Salvador, and

pillaged Santos and Recife several years later. In 1612, the French founded the city of Saint Louis in Maranhão, but three years later the Portuguese won it back and changed its name to São Luis. The Portuguese then hastily built a series of forts, among them Fortaleza and Belém (1616), the latter of which also served the interests of Spain, as it was located at the mouth of the Amazon, from which entry into the gold-rich Spanish colony of Peru could be controlled.

The Dutch Invasion

In 1621, the truce between Spain and Holland that had lasted for 12 years finally came to an end. This in turn paved the way for the decline of the joint Spanish-Portuguese monarchy, which had been the dominant naval and economic power in Europe during this period. Portugal's overseas colonies were not spared involvement in the ensuing military conflicts. With the founding of the Dutch West Indies Company in 1621, the Dutch began making a concerted effort to become the preeminent power throughout the Americas, the Caribbean and along the west coast of Africa. The financial resources needed to pay for the Company's maritime plundering was acquired as a result of high-seas robberies carried out by the Dutch admiral Peter Heyn. In 1628, he gained possession of the priceless silver treasures of the Spanish-Mexican navy, thereby providing the Dutch with the means to mount a full-scale invasion of Brazil. They attacked Pernambuco first, as it was not only the wealthiest of the Brazilian capitanias, but also provided safe anchorage for Dutch ships en route to the East Indies. By 1630 the Dutch had occupied both Olinda and Recife, and eventually gained control of the whole northeast coast of Brazil. In the hinterlands of Brazil, however, resistance to Dutch domination persisted until 1637, when Count Moritz arrived in Recife to take command of "New Holland."

This German aristocrat and seasoned soldier of the Thirty Years' War ex-

19

tended Dutch control from Rio São Francisco to Fortaleza. Moreover, in order to keep his South American enclave well supplied with slaves, he also took numerous fortified positions on the coast of West Africa. But in 1638, his attempt to occupy the colonial capital of Salvador da Bahia failed, just as his predecessor's had 14 years earlier.

Moritz von Nassau was a visionary statesman who instituted wise policies based on mutual understanding: he supported scientific research and artistic endeavor, and tried to promote religious tolerance as well. During his rule of Calvinist New Holland, both Portuguese Jews and Brazilian Catholics were encouraged to settle in Recife. But the more conspicuous Nassau's power became, the more the petty-minded "shopkeepers" of the Dutch West Indies Company distrusted him – especially because, in their view, the investments in Brazil were not sufficiently profitable. In 1644, weary of the constant bickering with the Dutch, he resigned his post. And inasmuch as none of his successors had anything approaching his diplomatic skills and statesmanlike stature, conflicts soon erupted among the colony's various religious and cultural groups.

Nassau's successors, intent on using their position to enrich themselves, failed to earn from Brazilians the loyalty and respect Nassau had enjoyed. Several isolated violent confrontations with the authorities soon grew into a full-scale insurrection against the Dutch, which was quickly suppressed. Portugal, which had cut its ties to Spain in 1640 but was still dependent on Holland's good will, publicly denounced the revolt while clandestinely supporting it. In 1645, Recife came under siege, but the Dutch were able to bring about a military stand-off, and several times brought reinforcements into the beleaguered city by sea.

In 1648, and again in 1649, the Dutch suffered decisive defeats in battles fought on the slopes of Guararapes, south of Recife. England's declaration of war against Holland in 1652 was decisive, owing to the fact that, with their forces engaged in protecting sea lanes into Portugal, the Dutch lacked the resources to retake Pernambuco. On January 26, 1654, Recife finally capitulated. Within a few months, all Dutch citizens left the coastal areas of Brazil, and the hold of the West Indies Company on Brazil was broken forever. In signing the Peace of The Hague, Holland accepted Portuguese rule over Brazil. Portugal, for its part, was forced to pay the West Indies Company compensation of "cash money, salt, sugar and tobacco" for the next 16 years. Portugal, having established its dominion over Brazil, would never again face a serious challenge from another European colonial power.

Nonetheless, minor military conflicts with France and Spain continued into the 18th century. French pirates tried to establish bases along the coast between Maranhão and Rio de Janeiro. They also took over the Atlantic island of Fernando de Noronha, and pirates under Dugnay-Trouin gained control of Rio de Janeiro, for whose ransom Brazil was forced to pay a handsome sum. It was only with the help of Britain, which meanwhile had become the world's dominant naval power, that the French were driven away from the coast and out of Fernando de Noronha.

The Slave Republic

Historians now put the number of West Africans who worked as slaves on the plantations of the New World at 9.6 million. Of those 9.6 million, 3.6 million – seven times the total number of slaves who worked in the southern United

Right: It was the work of slaves brought from Africa that allowed the colonial economy to prosper.

States – were brought to Brazil. Unscrupulous slave traders were able to earn enormous profits from this commerce. They acquired their human cargo from West African tribes, such as the Yorùbá, Wolof or Bantu, who were continually at war with one another, in exchange for cheap European wares or – at a later stage – poor quality Brazilian tobacco.

Conditions on the plantations were exceedingly hard for the slaves, who first were taken away from their families and then forced to convert to Christianity. Moreover, their lives were often made intolerable by ill-tempered overseers who, suspecting African rites of harboring the seeds of rebellion, used draconian measures to prevent the Africans from practicing their religions. This led the slaves to disguise their gods as Catholic saints, and to develop clandestinely the *capoeira*, a ritualized dance of self-defense much feared by the Europeans.

Throughout the 17th century, an increasing number of slaves succeeded in escaping and in establishing backwater settlements in remote areas called *quilombos*, where they could practice their religions and live according to their traditional values. Many ex-slaves either helped their fellow sufferers to escape, pillaged and burned the estates of their former tormentors, or abducted slave-owners' women.

As a result of these escapes, the labor shortage on the *fazendas* soon became so acute that the colonial government began sending out expeditions to bring the slaves back by force. The poorly-armed escapees were seldom able to put up much resistance. The *quilombo* of Palmares, which was as large as today's federal states of Pernambuco and Alagoas combined, did nonetheless survive as a functioning settlement from 1630 to 1694. It was founded in the Garanhun highlands north of Bahia by 40 escaped slaves. By the end of the 17th century 30,000 Africans were living in a clandestine "state" with a total area of about 27,000 square kilometers protected by palisades and moats that withstood over

40 attacks by colonial troops. But the governor finally put an infamous *bandeirante*, Domingo Jorge Velho, in command of a force of about 10,000 soldiers and ordered him to remove this "disgrace" from the colony. After a 22-day siege the attackers destroyed the capital city of the slave republic and massacred its inhabitants, many of whom committed suicide rather than be taken by the enemy. Zumbi, the last high chief of Palmares, was stabbed by a traitor in 1695, and November 20, the anniversary of his death, is still celebrated by Afro-Brazilians as a "day of black consciousness."

The Bandeirantes

A crisis in the mainstays of the colonial economy, sugar cane and the slave trade, began putting increasing pressure on in-

Above: Growing demand in Europe created a market for tobacco. Right: The arduous task of mining precious stones cost countless slaves their lives.

digenous Brazilians, while at the same time two groups began exploring the backlands. One was the *Paulistas* – Jesuits from São Paulo – and the other was comprised of inhabitants of the area around that city (*bandeirantes*). The two groups eventually came into conflict with one another. Military-style expeditions called *bandeiras* set out under a *bandeira* (banner), employing as guides acculturated Indians or *caboclos* – mulattos – who helped them push their way into the hitherto unexplored hinterland. The bandeirantes were to some extent romanticized as popular heroes, although they were for the most part unscrupulous adventurers motivated by the desire for wealth, or interested in obtaining cheap labor for their plantations. Nor did they shrink from attacking and plundering Jesuit missions, which were easy prey, inasmuch as the priests had few weapons.

Nonetheless, the bandeirantes did a great deal to extend Brazil's borders beyond what they had been: to the south to Rio de la Plata, to the west to the Paraná and Paraguai rivers, and to the north, beyond the Amazon region. In addition, their months-long campaigns in effect nullified the Treaty of Tordesillas. After 1640, Spain was too weakened by its involvement in other conflicts to take any military action to enforce compliance with the papal line of demarcation. This remained a diplomatic sticking point until 1752, when Spain signed the Treaty of Madrid recognizing the new boundaries, which later became those of present-day Brazil. In exchange, Portugal made concessions in Africa, and renounced its claims to Colónia do Sacramento (present-day Uruguay).

By the end of the 16th century, the bandeirantes had mended their ways, and no longer constituted bands of ruthless scoundrels out for whatever booty they could plunder: they became instead the King's troops, questing for yearned-for riches. But it was only in the late 17th century that they succeeded in uncovering treasures in the earth, first finding gold and diamonds in Minas Gerais, and later in Goías, Mato Grosso and Bahia. These discoveries set off a gold rush, as prospectors from every corner of Brazil, as well as from Portugal, converged on the mining areas, often with their slaves in tow. This lead to the enactment of immigration laws that also set annual quotas for slaves.

Gold prospecting gave rise to numerous conflicts, as the Paulistas tried to defend their property against encroachments by newcomers, especially the Portuguese. The crown interceded by taking over the newly-founded capitanias of Minas, Goías and Mato Grosso, and placing the mining and sale of gold under its jurisdiction. All gold was brought to the royal smelter, where it was assayed, melted down into ingots and then sold, with the crown retaining a *quinto*, i.e., one fifth. Despite rigorous surveillance and exorbitant fines, gold and diamond smuggling flourished. For slaves, such activities represented a chance for them to buy their freedom. The most famous example is that of Chico Rei, an enslaved tribal prince who bought freedom for himself and his friends with gold dust that the women of his tribe smuggled out of the mines concealed in their hair.

Brazil under the Braganças

Under the Bragança Dynasty (1640-1853) a new political ideology came into existence, one strongly influenced by Jesuit political thinking, in which sovereign interests and the common good became the watchwords. Despite the fact that Portugal was an absolute monarchy at this time, the King's personal power now took a back seat to the well-being of his subjects. In politics, business and everyday life, the public realm began to take precedence over the private sphere. Owing to the fact that Portugal had lost

its colonies in Africa and the Far East, Brazil became the colonial power's most precious overseas possession and consequently was granted a *conselho ultramarino* (overseas council), which was the highest instance of colonial government. This body decided upon such matters as military policy, tax laws, immigration, health, education, and the rights of slaves and aboriginal Brazilians.

In order to prevent the spread of tobacco and sugar monoculture, it also promoted the cultivation of corn, manioc and beans, encouraged independent freemen to emigrate from Portugal to Brazil, and supported livestock raising in the interior. The aim of these policies was to transform economically self-sufficient Brazil into a bread basket for the mother country, as well as for Portugal's other colonies and the King's navy. Exports were shipped on Portuguese vessels only, and new companies were founded along lines similar to those of Dutch companies. But the ire of the colony's landowning classes and political elite was

23

aroused by the laws that had been passed providing for protection of Indians and slaves, as well as by the monopolistic practices of trading companies and the increasingly high taxes being levied by the mother country. In the absence of active enforcement, these laws were largely ignored, but opposition to Portuguese rule was nonetheless on the rise.

Mining became an agent of significant change, as migration caused the population to grow, and people from various cultures entered into relationships ranging from business partnerships to marriage. Continuing exploration of the interior regions of Brazil led to the building of roads. Meanwhile, other branches of the economy, such as food processing, livestock raising and trades, also experienced rapid growth. In addition, increased economic activity in Minas Gerais integrated many isolated settle-

Above: The first expeditions began exploring the Amazon region at the end of the 18th century.

ments into the colonial infrastructure. As a result, economic and political power shifted from the northeast to the southeast, leading, in 1763, to the designation of Rio de Janeiro as capital.

Life in 18th-century Brazil strongly reflected the growing power and monarchism of the Braganças (the Portuguese royal family), particularly after 1750, when the enlightened but autocratic Marquês de Pombal became Prime Minister. Pombal tried to strengthen Brazil's economic position by governing the colony more efficiently and promoting manufacturing in Portugal. The new Prime Minister also encouraged immigration to the Rio Grande do Sul area in the south, and made a concerted effort to promote economic growth in the hitherto undeveloped Amazon basin.

Having lost the spice trade in the Far East to the Dutch, the Portuguese crown attempted to promote the cultivation of pepper, cloves and cinnamon in the Amazon, but with little success, since only cocoa beans grew well enough for com-

24

mercial purposes. The first scientific expedition into the region, led by the naturalist Alexander Rodrigues Ferreira from 1783 to 1792, investigated the economic potential of Amazonian flora and fauna. This resulted in the indigenous population once again being forced inland, although the Europeans also relied heavily on the natives' knowledge of the rain forest for the success of the expedition. In 1755, the enslavement of Indians was outlawed, and marriages between Europeans and indigenous peoples were encouraged. However, increased contact with Europeans gave rise to epidemics and illnesses among the native Americans. This, along with the Europeans' often violent behavior towards them, led to a steady decline in their numbers. And in 1759, Pompal banished the Jesuits, who were the indigenous peoples' only defenders, but whom he feared were creating a "state within a state."

The Independence Movement

The expulsion of the Jesuits wrought catastrophic changes in Brazil's educational system, due to the fact that upper class families began sending their children to schools in Portugal and France. However, one consequence of this change was that the ideas of the Enlightenment, and later the French Revolution, wended their way back to Brazil, where they were reinforced by the example of the American colonies' independence from England. Rising discontent with hated royal officials and monopolistic trading companies also contributed to the growth of an independence movement, which initially took root among the intellectual and upper classes, but quickly spread down the social ladder. Tax increases and the arrogance of colonial officials also constituted tinder to the already dry straw of discontent. When gold production took a sudden downturn, the crown demanded continued payment of

the *quinto* (i.e., 20 percent), and the colony's debts soared. Insurrections that broke out against Portuguese tax officials in Minas Gerais, Bahia and Pernambuco were all put down by force.

The first serious attempt to achieve independence from Portugal, the *Inconfidência Mineira* (Minas Conspiracy), was led by a dentist, José da Silva Xavier, known as *Tiradentes* (Tooth Puller). The insurrection began in Ouro Preto in 1789 among a group of rebels from a cross section of Brazilian society, including government officials, military officers, priests and judges, as well as ordinary citizens, all calling for Brazilians to resist the power of the colonial government. The uprising ended when the rebels were betrayed, arrested, and in a trial that lasted until 1792, found guilty of conspiracy. Tiradentes, condemned to death by guillotine, became a national hero after his head was put on public display in Ouro Preto. Most of the other conspirators were sent into exile in the African colonies, and several were set free. In 1798, a group comprised of tradesmen, soldiers, mulattos, Muslims, slaves, and freemasons staged an insurrection in Bahia. They opposed the power of the clergy and demanded the abolition of slavery, a republic instead of a monarchy, and the introduction of free trade. This conspiracy was also betrayed, and its leaders executed.

Events in Europe at the beginning of the 19th century had a pronounced dampening effect on revolutionary ferment: Owing to her alliance with England, Portugal refused to participate militarily in Napoleon's continental blockade against the British, whereupon French troops occupied Portugal. In January 1808, the British helped evacuate the royal family and the court of King João VI to Rio de Janeiro, at which point Brazil effectively ceased to be a colony (although this did not become official until 1815), for the mother country was now being governed in exile, from Rio. Maria I, who was suffering from melancholia, abdicated in 1792, and her son, Crown Prince João VI, was made ruler in her name, becoming Prince Regent in 1799. In 1810, with the help of Portuguese and English troops, Wellington expelled Napoleon from Portugal. But the Prince Regent chose not to return to the mother country and instead, in 1815, founded the Kingdom of Portugal, Brazil and Algarve, established its capital in Rio de Janeiro, and after his mother's death in 1818, was crowned King.

One of João's first official acts was to open all of the country's harbors, which meant that Brazil, instead of carrying out trade through Lisbon, could now sell goods directly to other countries. João also founded the country's first university (in Salvador), military academy, art school, library, government printing office and newspaper; promoted scientific research and manufacturing; and invited European scientists, engineers and artists to settle in Brazil. As a result, Rio soon became a cosmopolitan city, while Portugal, which was now being governed by the British, was reduced to the status of a colony, a state of affairs the Portuguese found intolerable. In 1821, a revolution forced the King to return to Europe, and Crown Prince Dom Pedro remained in Brazil as regent. But the Portuguese parliament made a demand (which was not acceded to) that the regent, too, return to the mother country, and that Brazil once again be granted colonial status.

Independence

Brazil was now divided between proponents and opponents of independence. Bahia and Pará remained loyal to Portugal, while Pernambuco and Ceará demanded independence and the procla-

Right: An 1832 lithograph of Emperor Pedro I of Brazil.

mation of a republic. The powerful Southeastern Region, however, favored the more moderate solution of creating an independent Kingdom of Brazil. A year of insurgencies and counterinsurgencies followed, but the country managed to avoided descending into violent factionalism. On September 7, 1822, upon the advice of his wife, Leopoldine of Habsburg, the Prince Regent declared Brazil's independence in São Paulo with the Ipiranga Proclamation: "Independence or Death." One month later, the Prince Regent was named Emperor Pedro I of Brazil, and later that year had himself officially crowned amidst much pomp and ceremony. Pedro, however, was a disappointment, for he turned out to be just another old-fashioned autocrat. He dissolved the Constitutional Assembly, and in 1824 promulgated a constitution of his own devising that granted wide-ranging powers to none other than his royal self. The result of this action was to leave the Parliament and Senate with little say in the country's policies, and only relatively few citizens with the right to vote, which at the time was granted on the basis of income (in 1872, only 13 percent of Brazilians were enfranchised).

This autocratic monarch was quite successful in the area of foreign policy, however. In 1824, the United States recognized Brazil, and one year later, following the signing of a peace treaty with Portugal, the former mother country followed suit. This treaty cost Pedro I a great deal of support, however, as it called for the return of confiscated Portuguese property, as well as the payment of war reparations. The three-year-long war with Argentina over the province of Cisplatina also eroded support for the Emperor. The conflict, which ended in 1828, led to heavy losses for Brazil and brought about the creation of Uruguay. In addition, Brazilians begrudged Pedro I his failure to properly appreciate his wife, Leopoldine, the daughter of Franz I of

Austria, and her death in 1826 at the age of 29 was deeply mourned. João VI died that same year in Portugal. Pedro I regarded himself as his successor, and even promulgated a new Portuguese constitution. On April 7, 1831, he abdicated in favor of his five-year-old son Pedro d'Al-Cântara and returned to Portugal, where he died three years later.

The Regency

For 10 years, until the crowning of the successor to the throne (who had not yet reached his majority), Brazil was ruled by a triumvirate regency, and from 1834 on, by the aristocrat Araújo Lima, which led to a power vacuum as well as insurrections in the South and Northeast. However, by forging alliances with large landowners from other provinces, the coffee barons managed to maintain a status quo that rested on the twin pillars of slavery and a landed elite.

The 15-year-old prince was declared Emperor Pedro II in 1541, well before reaching his majority. He responded to separatist insurgencies with military force, and in 1849 royal troops put down the last unrest in Pernambuco.

Owing perhaps to his Habsburg roots, the young Emperor had (in contrast to his father) developed a love of the arts and sciences. He spoke classical as well as modern foreign languages, and had what was reputed to be a model relationship with his wife, Teresa Cristina of Sicily. His own political ideas were more forward looking than those of the advisers and court officials who helped him govern. He was, for example, responsible for building the country's first railroad, as well as its first streetcars and telegraph lines. In 1872, the first census was taken, and an underwater cable was laid between Brazil and Europe.

The Argentine dictator Rosas forced Brazil into another war, this time over Uruguay, which Brazil won in 1852 under the leadership of General Caxias. But there was also trouble along the country's southern borders. Solano

27

López, an ambitious Paraguayan dictator, attempted to transform his small country into a large empire with the help of 100,000 French-trained troops, which led to a war of five years' duration (1865-1870), which Paraguay lost – along with half of its population. A peace treaty ending the conflict, the bloodiest ever fought in South America, was signed in 1872.

In 1850, pressure from England forced Brazil to prohibit the importation of new slaves, and beginning in 1871, all children born to slaves were legally free. In 1885, all slaves over 60 years of age were freed, although Pedro II had previously granted freedom to the slaves he himself owned. A surprising fact revealed by the census was that 30 percent of Brazil's population at this time consisted of slaves. Finally, on May 13, 1888, Pedro II's superstitious daughter Isabel proclaimed the *Lei Aurea* (Golden Law) banning slavery in Brazil forever. To compensate for the resulting labor shortage, the government promulgated the *Lei das Terras* (Land Act), requiring the registration of all privately-owned land. All other available land, however, was regarded as public property, and could be freely acquired. Institution of this law gave rise to massive immigration from Europe, where, due to political crises and industrialization, there was large-scale unemployment.

The abolition of slavery created huge resentment towards the monarchy among large landowners, as well as among graduates of military academies, who felt themselves to be at an economic and political disadvantage. As a result, Republicans began gaining support, which increased owing to both the lack of a male successor to the Emperor and the fact that the power elite did not want an

Right: Descendants of African slaves make up a large proportion of Brazil's population, though many are members of the lower socio-economic classes.

Empress who was well-disposed towards the Catholic Church. In November 1889, Marshal Deodoro da Fonseca dissolved the King's cabinet and formed a provisional government. The Emperor, wishing to avoid a bloodbath, abdicated and went into exile with his family in Paris, where he died two years later. The Republicans rebelled against the monarchy, which had no roots in South America, but they did not rise up against Pedro II, whose many accomplishments are honored in Brazil to this day. Among the Emperor's many achievements were keeping the large country unified in the face of secessionist movements and territorial claims from abroad; beginning the process of creating a national consciousness; developing a transportation infrastructure; and laying the groundwork for the process of industrialization that was yet to come.

The "Old Republic"

The Constitutional Assembly passed a new constitution in 1891, naming Marshal Deodoro de Fonesca first President of what was later referred to as the "Old Republic." Brazil became a federalist state patterned after the United States, with a constitution modeled on that of both America and France. Legislative powers were divided between the Chamber of Deputies and the Senate, the latter body being comprised of three senators from each Brazilian state. The President was granted broad powers and was to be elected to a four-year term by popular vote. However, Brazil's authoritarian society paid little heed to the new ideas contained in its constitution. In 1891, faced with growing opposition to his policies, Fonseca dissolved parliament and handed over the reigns of power to his vice-president, Marshal Peixoto, who crushed several insurrections and as a result went down in Brazilian history as the "Iron Marshall." His successor, Prudente

de Morais (1894-1898), became Brazil's first civilian President. He re-established peace in the country, which earned him the byname *O Pacificador* (The Peacemaker). He is especially remembered for his campaign against the *canudos,* religious fanatics in Bahia who were defeated only after a fourth expedition was sent out against them in 1897. The author Euclides da Cunha wrote a book about these events called *Os Sertões* (1902).

Federalism soon became a threat to the republic owing to the central government's inability to curb the unlimited power of the oligarchies over the federal states, whereby family members or close associates of office holders were placed in important and influential positions. This nepotism, which is still common practice in Brazilian politics today – particularly in the less developed Northeast of Brazil – is called *coronelismo*; *coronel* being a respectful term of address for landed gentry and large landowners. Under this system, in exchange for loyalty and obedience, the *coronel* supports the material and social aims of his supporters and inferiors, while a kind of private militia called the *jagunços* does away with opposition by violent means.

In the state of São Paulo, overproduction of coffee brought on an economic crisis, to which the government responded by instituting price supports that were financed by large foreign loans – a policy which brought about a dramatic increase in the young nation's foreign debt. As security for one large loan, Rothschild & Sons took over control of one of the country's most important shipping centers. Until World War I, mainly British companies invested in Brazil, and after the war, the United States became the leading source of foreign capital.

In 1903, Brazil again expanded its borders – on one hand as a result of its victory over Bolivia in a war over the Acre region, and on the other owing to the diplomatic successes of Baron Rio Branco in a major territorial dispute with British Guyana and in border disagreements of lesser magnitude with neighboring

Peru and Columbia. Between 1870 and 1920, the country's population rose from 10 to 30 million, nearly three million of whose numbers were comprised of European immigrants. Growing industrialization gave rise to an urban proletariat of factory workers. In the absence of labor laws, companies determined working conditions, which were usually substandard: low wages, 14-hour days, and even less pay for women and children. In 1907, the Labor Party (founded in 1893) mobilized 2,000 workers for a strike in support of the eight-hour day. The government responded with repressive measures; six months later a law was passed making foreigners who disturbed the public order subject to deportation.

In 1922, the centennial of Brazilian independence was celebrated in Rio with an arts festival and industrial exposition. In the same year, Brazil's Communist Party (PCB) was founded, and Luís

Carlos Prestes, a former military officer, was named Chairman. He organized a protest march, the *Coluna Prestes*, which attracted a great deal of public attention as 1,500 people walked from the south to the north of Brazil demonstrating in favor of land reform. In São Paulo, the *Tenentismo* (Lieutenants' Movement) also received broad-based support for challenging the power of the oligarchy.

Vargas, the New State and Populism

The global economic crisis of the 1920s had a profound effect on Brazil as well. Within a period of only two years the price of coffee on world markets dropped from 22.5 to eight cents per pound. By 1930, Brazil, for whom coffee represented two-thirds of its total exports, was bankrupt. A purportedly fixed election provided a pretext for a putsch, which received broad support from the military and resulted in Getúlio Vargas becoming provisional president. He remained in office until 1945; from 1934

Above: Folkloric group in Treze Tílias: immigrants keep their traditions alive to this day.

by election, and from 1937 as "emergency" president, though he was accused of being a dictator. Vargas was nationalistic, anti-communist and not in the least beholden to the powerful coffee barons in São Paulo. He attempted to create a strong central government that he hoped would become the driving force behind dynamic economic and social policies. Most of his appointees to high state government positions were members of the Lieutenants' Movement. He instituted regulation of the most significant sectors of the economy, as well as of activities of state-owned firms such as those responsible for alcohol and sugar production.

The ensuing insurrections that broke out among the oligarchs, communists and fascists were suppressed by Vargas and used as a pretext for dissolving political parties and parliament. He created a "New State" (*Estado Novo*), which was strongly influenced by the example of Italian Fascism. Under this new regime, what Vargas termed "the national interest" reigned supreme. With the help of the army, opposition was suppressed and the press censored. The federal states lost much of their autonomy, and the central government took over management of their budgets and finances. The bulk of government investments went into the metallurgical, energy and transportation sectors, and the development of large privately-owned industrial concerns was fostered through protectionism.

The Ministry of Labor, which was established in 1931, instituted Brazil's first labor code, whose provisions included a guaranteed minimum wage and paid vacations. Workers' standard of living was improved by these and other measures, including an eight-hour work day, protection from arbitrary firing, and price controls on staple food items. To be sure, the social net still left many workers unprotected. Moreover, many companies found ways to circumvent the labor laws, which were inadequately enforced by

slow and overworked courts. Nonetheless, the new regulations did bring about enormous improvement in the miserable conditions that workers had previously endured. Both agricultural exports – an indispensable source of foreign currency – and the manufacture of processed food for export markets were given stronger government support. Smallhold farmers received land grants, which allowed them to produce low-cost (and partially subsidized) food staples such as rice, beans and corn for the domestic market.

During World War II, Brazil was initially neutral, but all German schools in southern Brazil were ultimately ordered closed in anticipation of the advent of Hitler's expansionist policies in the Amazon region. In 1942, owing to massive diplomatic pressure from the U.S., Brazil declared war on Germany and Italy, and thereby became, with Mexico, one of two Latin American countries to participate in the conflict. In 1944, a contingent of 25,000 soldiers was sent to Italy, and the coastal city of Natal and island of Fernando de Noronha became U.S. military bases. Although Brazil was on the winning side, the end of the war and the worldwide democratization that followed marked the end of the Vargas regime. The army forced the President to resign, and ex-Minister of War General Gaspar Dutra won the next election.

But Vargas retained his seat in the House of Deputies, and with it his close ties to the centers of governmental power. He also remained highly popular even while out of office, and became President again in 1950. As soon as he took power, he began instituting policies designed to promote industrialization; founding the state-owned petroleum company *Petrobrás*, as well as the national power company *Electrobrás*. It was later said that he laid the groundwork for the policies of his successors. Vargas's life ended melodramatically: In 1954, following an unsuccessful attempt by members of his presidential guard to assassinate one of his most outspoken critics, he committed suicide amidst a firestorm of criticism from both the press and military. Getúlio Vargas was dead, but not his policies, which to some extent were perpetuated by his successors, presidents Quadros and Goulart, under the banner of *Getulismus*.

Juscelino Kubitschek – Creator of Brasília

Vice-President J. Café Filho succeeded to the presidency following Vargas' death. In the election of 1955, all political parties supported former state governor Juscelino Kubitschek. The right-wing military officers, who had brought about Vargas' downfall, tried to prevent the "communist" Kubitschek from taking office, but were thwarted by a counter-coup led by General Teixeira Lott.

Kubitschek devised a five-year plan, called the *Plano de Metas*, whose goal was to modernize the Brazilian economy by attracting private and foreign investment to the industrial, food-processing, transportation and energy sectors. The rallying cry of the plan was "Fifty years of progress in five years." The government promoted development of both the industrial triangle of São Paulo-Rio-Belo Horizonte, and the infrastructure of the inland regions of the country. Unfortunately, northeastern Brazil was not included in this investment program, and by way of compensation a special development office called SUDENE was established for this disadvantaged region. One of its pet projects, an idea dating back to colonial days, was to transfer Brazil's capital to the geographical center of this large area. In just four years, the new futuristic seat of government, Brasí-

Right: Juscelino Kubitschek, founder of the futurist capital city of Brasília, looks out upon his life's work.

lia, was wrested from the arid Goiás plateau, a thousand kilometers away from Brazil's coastal cities.

Kubitschek's policies transformed the country within a period of only five years. He succeeded in laying the foundations for the development of a modern industrialized economy, but at the cost of a sizeable foreign debt, rising inflation, and a huge gap between production and wages, which led to increasing poverty among large segments of the population. The recession of 1960-62 exacerbated Brazil's social problems to such an extent that unrest spread, leaving the way open for the military to step in once again.

The Military Dictatorship

The impetus for the coup came from João Goulart, who had served as Vice-President under Jânio Quadros and then President when the latter resigned. Goulart, an influential cattle rancher and close personal friend of Getúlio Vargas, had also held the postition of Labor Minister under Vargas. In the parliamentary elections of 1962, left-wing parties made substantial gains, a development frowned upon by policy makers in the U.S. This led to a CIA-backed coup that was planned by a group of anti-communist, industrial and military leaders. The imminent legalization of the Communist Party, the entry of Brazil into the ranks of the nonaligned states, and an agrarian reform law introduced into parliament on March 15, 1964, gave hard-liners all the justification they needed to swing into action. The die was cast when, on March 31, "in the name of God and the Fatherland," the state of Minas Gerais promulgated the *Pronunciamento*, seceding from the central government. The affluent neighboring states of São Paulo and Rio Grande do Sul soon followed suit.

Goulart went into exile in Uruguay, and for the next 20 years a group of only five generals maintained a permanent

state of emergency in Brazil. The old political parties were disbanded, and two new ones were founded – ARENA (*Ala Renovadora Nacional*) and a travesty opposition party, MDB (*Movimento Democratico Brasileiro*). "National security" provided a perfect pretext for repressive and dictatorial policies, including frequent attacks on left-wing parties, universities and the press. One occurrence typical of this pattern was the government's response to demonstrations calling for the re-establishment of democracy that took place in December 1968. These demonstrations resulted in a "Fifth Amendment" being added to the constitution, which authorized the government to send the entire parliament on an indefinite holiday and granted the head of state power to rule by decree.

It was not long before opposition surfaced. Brazilian students, influenced by the student rebellions in Europe, protested, and a guerrilla movement emerged. In 1970, in an attempt to pressure the government into letting their comrades out of prison, guerillas kidnapped the German ambassador. The cruelest actions of this 20-year period were carried out under the five-year dictatorship of General Médici (1969-1974). The reign of terror of the secret police and its infamous death squads led to massive protests domestically, and to Brazil's isolation from the international community. The first signs of a return to democracy and a lessening of repression came in 1978 under German-born President Ernesto Geisel, and then during the Figuiredo era (1979-1985). Amnesties were granted to political prisoners, exiles could be repatriated without fear of imprisonment, and press censorship abated.

In 1984, the final year of the dictatorship, the Brazilian populace abruptly and inexplicably abandoned its traditional role of passive victim and began taking the political initiative – a turn of events that took even the opposition by surprise. The Labor Party organized *diretas já*, a campaign designed to bring about direct elections, and during the summer holiday

(January) of 1984 the movement caught on throughout the country. Women wore protest buttons on their bikinis, and for the first time in decades, political issues were integrated into Carnival by, for example, samba groups, who attracted huge crowds with grotesque, oversized puppets that poked fun at the leaders of the regime.

However, there was a general sense of disappointment over the outcome of these events. In April 1984, the parliament made a typical Brazilian "horse trade," whereby Tancredo Neves, a well-known political figure, was named as Brazil's first civilian President after two decades of military dictatorship. Significantly, the new political leadership refrained from demanding restitution of any kind from the military, which for unexplained reasons was not held accountable for the grave human rights abuses, corruption and financial scandals that had marked its 20 years in power. Neves also maintained strong ties to the military by appointing as Vice President José Sarney, whom the military trusted.

But the long-awaited transition to democracy was marked by tragedy. On the evening before he was to take office, the president-elect became seriously ill and died a week later. As a result, Sarney, who had not been democratically elected, became interim president until the first popular elections in 29 years were held on November 15, 1989. In 1988, a new democratic constitution had been promulgated by the legislature, setting the stage for the March 1990 election of Collor de Mello, who defeated his opponent, the labor leader Lula, and thereby became (at age 40) the youngest president in the history of Brazil. He did not complete his mandate, however, as he was driven from office two years later following revelations of corruption and influence peddling.

His successor, Itamar Franco, attempted to bring about reconciliation within Brazilian society. These efforts have been intensified since 1995 by Franco's successor, the former Finance Minister Henríque Cardoso, who has tried to reduce both inflation and the country's foreign debt, and has also instituted a long overdue program of land reform.

GEOPOLITICAL OVERVIEW

Brazil is the world's fifth-largest country in population and land area, larger than all the other countries in Latin America combined and over 92 times the size of Portugal. The longest distance from east to west is the equivalent of the distance between Moscow and Marrakesh. The southern tip of the country at the border with Uruguay lies at 33°S, and the northern tip on the border with Venezuela at 5°N, which is approximately the equivalent of the distance between Lisbon and the North Pole. Brazil's 7,400 kilometers of Atlantic coastline stretch from French Guyana in the north to Uruguay in the south.

With about 160 million people living in a land area of 8,511,996 square kilometers, Brazil has a population density of 18 per square kilometer – one of the lowest in the world. Moreover, its annual birth rate of 1.8 percent means that the country's population is not growing at a significantly rapid rate. Population distribution is uneven, with 60 percent of the populace living in southern and southeastern Brazil, and only about five percent residing in the Midwest. Fifty-three percent of the population is caucasian, 34 percent is mulatto or mestizo, 11 percent is of African descent and the remaining two percent includes approximately 300,000 aboriginal peoples and one million citizens of Japanese extraction. The language spoken in Brazil is Portuguese,

Right: Three generations of Brazilians on a pilgrimage to the Bahian church of Bom Jesus da Lapa pose for a souvenir photo.

with no dialects, but with some typically Brazilian elements. There are, in addition, some 180 languages spoken by the various indigenous groups. Eighty-five percent of Brazilians are professed Catholics, but many also practice Afro-Brazilian religions such as Candomblé.

Officially called República Federativa do Brasil, the country is divided into 26 states plus the Federal District of Brasília. The legislature is made up of a Congress consisting of 513 deputies elected to four-year terms, and a Senate with 81 senators (three for each state, including Brasília), who serve for eight years. The President has broad powers and is chosen by popular election every four years.

Brazil is comprised of three large geographic regions. To the north lies the mostly unexplored mountainous area of Guyana, where Brazil's highest peak, Pico da Neblina (3,014 meters), is located. South of this region lies the Amazon basin, which accounts for over a third of the country's land area. It is also the world's largest continuous forest, containing one-fifth of the earth's fresh water. Most of Brazil consists of highlands, with medium-sized mountain ranges extending to the sea. Thus, a typical coastal mountain range like the Serra do Mar stretches from Salvador da Bahia to Porto Alegre. Only about three percent of the entire country is over 900 meters above sea level.

Politically and historically the country is divided into five regions, and this classification system is adhered to in this book. The Europe-like Southern Region encompasses the states of Rio Grande do Sul, Santa Catarina and Paraná, the latter containing one sight that should not be missed, the spectacular waterfalls at Iguaçu. The Southeastern Region, though small, is a microcosm of Brazil, with the highest per capita income, the most extensive *favelas* (shantytowns), and the highest crime rate. São Paulo, Minas Gerais and Rio de Janeiro, on the other hand, form a "magic triangle," while the small state of Espirito Santo is also part of the Southeastern Region.

35

Brazil's Midwest is very thinly populated (excepting of course the federal district of Brasília), probably because it is
the only region lacking a coastline. What
it has instead are the "great forests" of
Mato Grosso and Mato Grosso do Sul,
which provide pasture land for large
herds of cattle, as well as food and safe
haven for countless flocks of birds, mil-
lions of caimans and numerous species of
mammal. Also located in this area are the
Goiás highlands, which prospectors for
precious stones have been frequenting
since colonial times.

The Northeastern Region forms a
"bump" that extends in the direction of
Europe. It is in this place that the first
Europeans landed, the first major settlements were founded, and slave ships
arrived loaded down with Africans. Encompassing nine states from Bahia to
Maranhão, the region has rich and fertile

*Above: The Sertão suffers from severe
droughts. Right: Favelas in Manaus –
"dwellings" for uprooted peasants.*

soil along the coast, but is arid and unin-
habitable inland: for example, it often
happens that there is no precipitation
whatsoever for years in the Sertão. Thousands of kilometers of beaches, exclusive
seaside resorts and colonial grandeur
exist in sharp contrast to appalling poverty and misery. There is more African
culture here (especially in Bahia) than in
all the rest of South America, and more
exoticism, joy of life, musicality, and
spirituality than anywhere else in Brazil.

The Northern Region, with a land area
of 3.5 million square kilometers, is Brazil's largest, comprising seven states: the
small state of Tocantins in the south; Pará
with its colonial city of Belém; Amapá on
the border with French Guyana; Roraima, whose border with Guyana and
Venezuela is home to the largest concentration of Yanomamis in Brazil; Acre,
which was originally part of Bolivia, in
the west; and Rondônia, where extensive
tracts of forest have been cut down. The
largest state in Brazil is Amazonas,
whose capital city of Manaus is at the Rio

Negro and which is home to the world-renowned *Teatro Amazonas*.

Brazil – Land of the Future?

In 1995, the anthropologist and former Brazilian cabinet minister Darcy Ribeiro published a book by this title that posed the question: Does this huge nation have a future in an era of globalization of world markets? In terms of gross national product the answer is yes – Brazil ranks ninth, ahead of even Spain. Arms and aircraft exports account for its relatively strong position in international trade, of which an increasingly large proportion is in the area of heavy industry: in the mid-1990s exports of industrial products were five times 1965 levels.

Brazil is a typical developing country in that it is highly industrialized and produces a wide range of manufactured goods. However, no more than a third of the population benefits from this activity, while the vast majority struggles to survive in the gray (unofficial) economy or ekes out a bare and impoverished existence on the margins of a society that is rife with socio-economic inequality.

In an essay he contributed to Ribeiro's book, the President of Brazil, Fernando Henríque Cardoso, listed several reasons for this unfortunate, if not untenable state of affairs: In 1960, 10 percent of all Brazilians earned 35 percent of total gross household income. Thirty years later, the latter figure was 48 percent. The country's preternaturally rapid development created a modern infrastructure in the areas of transportation, energy, communications and industry that primarily benefited – and continues to benefit – the Southern Region. The statistics on education are also revealing. Only 40 percent of Brazil's industrial workers have more than eight years of formal education, 30 percent are functionally illiterate, and the remaining 30 percent are unable to implement written work orders.

Owing to the structure of Brazilian society today, the country's resources are used inefficiently and are apportioned in

37

a highly unjust manner. Brazil ranks first among the world's sugar and coffee producers and second in cocoa and soy beans. The export of soy beans for animal feed to industrialized nations has transformed vast tracts of land in southern Brazil into monocultures, which has damaged the environment and significantly disrupted the ecology of these areas, thereby contributing to the destruction of the conditions that would allow smaller farms to survive. The cultivation of sugar cane in the Northeast has created an ecological and economic disaster in the field of energy production. Oil imports have been reduced, but at the same time cultivation of black beans, which is a staple for much of the population, has been severely cut back, and the price of this commodity has quadrupled. In the

Above: Large projects like this dam on Rio São Francisco have made Brazil the ninth most industrialized nation in the world. Right: What does the future hold for children growing up in favelas?

1960s, the government deferred to the wishes of the automobile industry by building roads instead of railroads, which has led to the severe traffic problems and auto pollution so characteristic of modern-day Brazil.

Sociologists fault the Brazilian upper classes for living unproductive lives devoted chiefly to managing inherited wealth – an activity they are prone to pursue even more vigorously during periods of inflation. In addition, too many academic and professional disciplines have little relevance to the country's needs: Brazilian plastic surgeons are world-renowned, but large segments of the population lack adequate medical care. Trained engineers are more interested in implementing state-of-the-art Western technologies than in installing much-needed infrastructures in Brazilian villages that would deliver such basic amenities as running water and sewage pipes. These unglamorous projects are relegated to church organizations and developmental aid projects. The National

Conference of Bishops has good reason to find fault with the decline of, and crisis in, moral and ethical values: "The survival of the fittest is becoming a moral principle... The 'me first' society knows no ethical limits." The proverbial passivity and resignation of the Brazilian population – *povo sofrido mas paciente* ("the suffering but patient people") – is often pushed to the limits, although there have never been any mass revolutionary movements in Brazil.

The Misery of Brazil's Children

Seven million children live in the streets, three million children work, and two million Brazilian girls under the age of 15 are prostitutes. These statistics come not from tabloid newspapers but from reputable sources. One-third of the population of São Paulo lives in *favelas* (shanty towns) or in dilapidated housing on the verge of collapse. In cosmopolitan Rio, approximately 50 percent of Cariocas live in 400 favelas. Men who have fathered numerous children frequently refuse to support their families, often leaving their wives on their own to care for a brood of six or more, who are forced either to help their families struggle to survive, or to leave their families and live on the street and fend for themselves. Thus, in an economy with poverty of this magnitude, it is small wonder that only about 20 percent of school-aged children (7-14) manage to complete the first eight years of school. For black children the statistics are even worse: they attend school for an average of 3.3 years.

Many of these children contribute to their family's income by selling inexpensive goods or flowers on the street, or by shining shoes or delivering newspapers. Child farm laborers aged five to 14 work up to 12-hour days on orange, cotton, sisal or sugar-cane plantations for miserable wages, or even for no wages at all. For them, crushed fingers, eye in-

juries from thorns, and snake bites are everyday occurrences. Their lack of education condemns them to a life of menial labor, or forces them to engage in illicit activities. A study conducted by the University of São Paolo documented 80,000 cases of outright slavery, half of which were children, although the real figure is in all likelihood far greater. UNICEF and a coalition of church organizations have devised a program whose goal is to eliminate this kind of slavery in Brazil.

In 1997, the government began a campaign against sex tourism. Arriving passengers at airports are warned in several languages "Be careful: Brazil is keeping an eye on you!" This measure was taken after publication of a UNESCO study that listed Brazil as the third most popular country (after Thailand and the Dominican Republic) among European, North American and Japanese "sex" tourists. The increase in cases of AIDS is also a matter of concern to many of Brazil's political leaders.

39

THE MAGIC TRIANGLE

Samba, Industry and the Baroque

RIO DE JANEIRO
SÃO PAULO
MINAS GERAIS

THE SOUTHEASTERN REGION

It is fitting that the travel section of this book begins with the states of **Rio de Janeiro**, **São Paulo** and **Minas Gerais**, for at least one of these *estados* is sure to be included on the itinerary of almost every visitor to Brazil. Rio, along with a fourth state, Espírito Santo, makes up the *Região Sudeste*, the economically powerful Southeastern Region, one of five the country is divided into.

People love to call **Rio** "The Beauty," despite its extensive industrial areas. **São Paulo** likes to see itself as a business and financial hub, with its feet securely planted in the present – the significant role it has played in Brazil's history notwithstanding. And Minas Gerais, a region that abounds in history, art and culture, has as its capital city **Belo Horizonte**; a town that was founded only a hundred years ago. But what might at first glance appear to be contradictions within the region are in fact symptomatic

Previous pages: View from the rocky peak of Corcovado in Rio de Janeiro – for many, "the most beautiful city in the world" – with Sugar Loaf in the distance. Carnival is all about samba. Left: The imposing statue of Christ the Redeemer on Corcovado stands watch over the Cariocas.

of modern-day Brazil in general – a nation full of contrasts.

The short distances – for a country this large – between the points in the "magic triangle" comprised by these three metropolises, which are the largest in Brazil, break down as follows: Rio is "only" 430 kilometers from São Paulo; the latter is 440 kilometers from Belo Horizonte; and São Paulo is a "mere" 590 kilometers from Belo Horizonte – 40 minutes by plane or six hours by bus. And indeed, this is not much when compared to the 2,340 kilometers and 35 to 40 hours by bus that separate Rio from Recife!

With 300 inhabitants per square kilometer, Rio is the most densely populated state in Brazil. But São Paulo and Minas Gerais, with 125 and 27 inhabitants per square kilometer respectively, still significantly exceed the national average of 18. The fifth-largest country in the world in land area, Brazil is statistically one of the least populous. However, because the bulk of the financial and economic power of Brazil is concentrated in these three mega-cities, they exert an irresistible pull on the economically disenfranchised rural populations. Mining, industry and agriculture play important roles here, as do the service sector and tourism.

Though the Presidential Palace and the Parliament Building stand in the capital

45

city of Brasília, a distance of 1,000 kilometers from Rio and São Paulo, most important business and financial decisions are made in the two latter urban centers, where until the mid-20th century the power elite chose the Brazilian head of state according to the *café con leite* (coffee with milk) system, i.e., either from coffee-growing São Paulo or dairy farming Minas Gerais.

In Portuguese, *Minas Gerais* literally means "general mines," a term that reflects the overwhelming importance of gold, diamonds, and emeralds for this state. Since the colonial era of the 17th and 18th centuries, uncountable riches have been amassed here, and this wealth has been used to promote the arts and culture: the great masters of the Brazilian Baroque came from Minas Gerais. Heavy industry (e.g., Mannesmann), automobile manufacturing (Fiat) and agriculture (dairy products and coffee) are the economic mainstays of this state, of which Belo Horizonte is the urban center.

The still-dominant car industry, as well as nearly three-quarters of Brazil's high-tech companies (laser technology, computers, optics and fine chemicals) have their centers of operation in São Paulo, and half the computers used in Brazil are to be found here as well. In addition, 77 percent of Brazil's export products are manufactured in this megalopolis; they are exported from the country by ship from Brazil's largest port, Santos, or by plane from its busiest airport, Guarulhos.

The state of Rio de Janeiro provides employment opportunities in the area of tourism, but there are far more jobs available in industry and the service sector (e.g., banking and insurance), as well as in the export trade.

The three states described below are not only commercial hubs, but are hotbeds of athletic ardor as well: the largest outdoor stadiums in this country of passionate soccer fans are located in their capital cities.

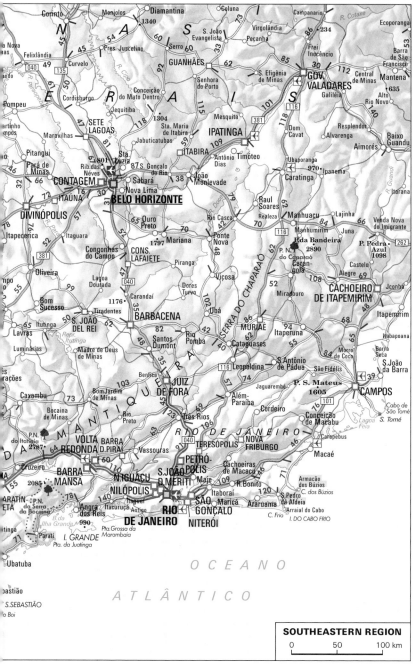

SOUTHEASTERN REGION

| 0 | 50 | 100 km |

RIO DE JANEIRO
An Adventure for the Senses

The most gorgeous beaches with women and men to match, the most renowned samba schools, the largest soccer stadiums, the most corrupt policemen, and the most millionaires – *Cidade Maravilhosa* (Marvelous City) is what the inhabitants of Rio call it. "A city where love makes life more enchanting, where one can die more easily from love" is how the poet Vinicius de Moraes describes his native city.

Cari means "white" and *oca* "house": "White Man's House" is what the original inhabitants of this region, the Tamoio, called the dwellings of the first European settlers. The name stuck, and inhabitants of Rio have been called *Cariocas* ever since.

Above: Smaller samba schools wear simpler costumes, but display as much enthusiasm as the larger ones. Left: Nearby Flamengo Beach is a popular place in the sun.

On January 1, 1502, a Portuguese expedition sailed into Guanabara Bay, which its leader André Gonçalves mistook for the mouth of a river, leading him to name the place after the date: "Rio de Janeiro" means "January River." The city was only officially founded by the Portuguese in 1565, after the French, having in the meantime gained a foothold on the coast, were expelled. Greatly aided by the introduction of black slaves, sugarcane plantations were soon thriving in the hinterland. Rio's natural harbor prospered as a center for the export of sugar and, in the 1800s when gold fever came to Minas Gerais, for the beguiling yellow metal as well. In 1763, Rio was named the state capital, retaining this status until 1960. From 1808 to 1821 the city also basked in the limelight for being the site of the royal residence of the Kingdom of Portugal.

Today, Rio has a population of over six million in an area measuring slightly under 1,200 square kilometers; the population of metropolitan Rio exceeds 10

million. The city has many peaks, ridges and hills, the highest of which, Pico da Tijuca, rises to 1,022 meters. Typical of Rio are the bare and hump-like formations called *morros*, the most famous of which is Corcovado (The Hunchback), atop whose summit a statue of Christ presides.

"Why does Christ hold his hands wide open? He's waiting for the day the *Cariocas* start working so that he can applaud..." This joke, which *Paulistas* (inhabitants of São Paulo) love to tell, is emblematic of the contrast between São Paulo, Brazil's business metropolis, and Rio, the capital of Carnival. There is some evidence of envy of the Cariocan joie de vivre in this joke as well, since visitors are attracted in droves by the Cariocas' seemingly inexhaustible capacity for acting as though enjoyment of the full complexity of life was all that mattered.

More than anything else, this city's setting makes it one of the loveliest in the world. Rio is idyllically nestled between the tropical vegetation of the Serra do Mar and the glistening waters of Guanabara Bay. Internationally-renowned architects have provided Rio with buildings that other industrialized nations would be proud to have in their capital cities. Especially in the southern part of town, one never has the feeling of being in a monstrously-big metropolis.

A good way to begin seeing Rio is from the place where locals and tourists always come together: the expansive beaches. However, when strolling along the sands of the *praias,* as well as elsewhere in Rio, visitors should bear firmly in mind that certain basic precautions are in order (see the section on "Security" on page 242 in the *Guidelines* section), because the glitter of the city has its dark side too: Rio is rife with pickpockets, con artists and muggers.

Flamengo, Botafogo and Urca

The northernmost beach close to downtown, **Praia do Flamengo**, is mostly frequented by poorer people from outlying areas, and is therefore relatively unsafe for tourists. In addition, owing to its proximity to numerous factories, as well as the port, the water at this beach is not particularly clean. On Sundays, however, it does attract numerous sports enthusiasts, as the wide street adjoining it is reserved for bicycling, roller skating, and other activities of this nature.

Like Flamengo, the name of **Praia do Botafogo** has become well known outside of Brazil due to the existence of a soccer team that goes by the same name. This smaller beach is not very clean either, but as compensation it offers a superb view of Sugar Loaf and the yacht harbor.

To the west of Sugar Loaf on Botafogo Bay lies **Praia da Urca**, a beach only 100 meters in length that is frequented primarily by residents of Rio's small Urca quarter.

Praia Vermelha

Few tourists visit the "red" beach, although many swimmers favor it, probably because it rarely has the very high breakers common to most of Rio's sandy venues. Moreover, it is clean and safe into the bargain, as it is surrounded by a military post. And because it is located right at the base of Sugar Loaf peak, swimming and sunbathing on Praia Vermelha can easily be combined with a sudorific gondola-trip to this world-famous chunk of Rio rock – especially recommended during the Brazilian summer (December to February).

Praia do Leme

Here, at the beginning of the famous Copacabana Beach, behind Morro da Babilónia, the beach called Praia do Leme extends from Ponta do Leme to Avenida Princesa Isabel, i.e., to the Meridien Hotel. Years ago, it was known as the "cleanest beach in Rio." Although,

like Copacabana, Leme is adjacent to **Avenida Atlântica**, it is less frequented, but is as good a locale to enjoy a stroll or a beer as its more famous neighbor. In the evenings, fishermen come down to the bay to try their luck amidst the high breakers. And visitors who decide to spend either December 8 or New Year's Eve here will have the opportunity to witness the African *Umbanda* ceremony, during which young women dig holes in the sand into which they place bottles containing lit candles, sugar-cane spirits, or flowers. They then walk barefoot into the sea in their long dresses and implore Yemanjá, goddess of the sea, to grant them blessings such as happiness in love (cf. p. 226).

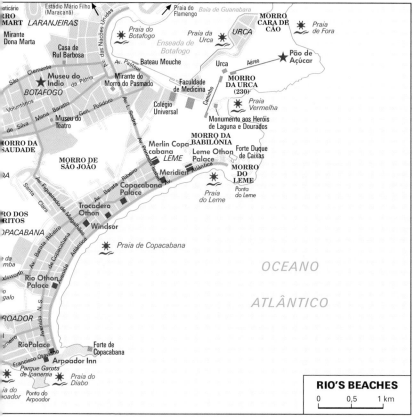

RIO'S BEACHES

0   0,5   1 km

Copacabana

The most famous neighborhood in Rio: a synonym for the Brazilian attitude towards life; beautiful beach and classic tourist trap. No visitor to Rio can resist the temptation of coming here at least once for a stroll or a swim, to go shopping or out to eat. This most densely populated piece of real estate in Brazil, lying between the morros São João and Dos Cabritos and the sea, is said to be home to some 600,000 Cariocas – not the upper class, either, although Pelé, too, owns a penthouse here: its residents stem mainly from the lower middle class, many of them living four to a room in exchange for the status conferred by a "Copa" address. And while numerous hotels are found here, the Copa is no tourist ghetto. The newly-renovated **Copacabana Palace**, the first luxury hotel on the beach, is worth seeing.

The name of the most renowned beach in South America is derived from a word in an Indian language called Aymara, which was spoken in the distant Bolivian highlands. During the 18th century, traders from the Andes brought a statue here that was revered by pilgrims, "Nossa Senhora de Copacabana," whose byname was derived from the words *kgopa* and *kgwana*, which together mean "the ridge from which one sees." In 1746, to thank God for having been rescued from a shipwreck, a bishop had *Igrejinha de Nossa*

51

Senhora de Copacabana built at the tip of the small cape where **Forte de Copacabana** now stands. The vestiges of an earlier way of life can still be observed in and around the bay in the form of fishermen who sail far out into the Atlantic by night in small boats and return to shore at dawn, where they sell their catch to local housewives and domestic servants.

The four-kilometer-long beach that extends from Leme to Copacabana offers a host of activities for active vacationers, including volleyball, exercise machines, soccer on sandy terrain, and extensive bicycle paths.

When swimming in the sea here visitors should exercise extreme caution, as waves many meters in height, rough breakers, and a treacherous undertow endanger countless tourists each year. The efficient rescue service that patrols the

Above: Copacabana, Rio's four-kilometer-long beach. Right: Soccer, volleyball and surfing are some of the most popular activities on Rio's beaches.

beach is often called upon to fish swimmers in distress out of the sea – which it does from a helicopter with a large net!

Like Ipanema and Leblon, Copacabana has consecutively numbered comfort stations. These *postos*, which make ideal meeting points, provide thirsty sun worshippers with inexpensive cold refreshment from vending machines, as well as toilets and showers. Posto No. 1 is in Leme, No. 6 is by the fishing boats, and so forth.

Although a good distance from the beach, the **Copacabana Quarter** is bursting with energy – in other words, it is authentically Brazilian! The shore avenue, Avenida Atlântica, runs parallel to **Avenida N.S. de Copacabana**, which is the neighborhood's second-busiest thoroughfare and a lively shopping street. The "leading" striptease establishments can be found in the cross street, **Avenida Princesa Isabel**, across from the Hotel Meridien. A busy fruit and vegetable market is held on Saturday mornings in the adjacent street.

Praia do Arpoador

Ipanema

Almost any Rio afficionado will tell you: First comes Copacabana, and then comes Ipanema. But before the latter comes "Harpooners' Beach" and most important of all Arpoador Peak, from which vantage point visitors can "ooh" and "ah" at a superb panorama encompassing Rio's southern beaches, complete with morros as well as Sugar Loaf and Corcovado peaks. Unfortunately, the observation platform itself is not very clean and should be avoided after dark.

Barril 1800, a bar located at the intersection of the shore avenue and Rua Gomez Carneiro, is an inviting spot to stop off at for a light meal or snack. But the Barril, for all the right reasons, does not live primarily from the tourist trade; it is that rare kind of place – so seldom found in busy tourist areas – where patrons can sit undisturbed on a cozy terrace enjoying the sparkling sights and sounds of the beach without being annoyed by the drone of traffic.

The spectacular success of the bossa nova song *The Girl from Ipanema* by the late Antonio Carlos Jobim, who died in 1994, has made this district world famous. Habitues of Ipanema are no less obsessed with the Body Beautiful than are patrons of Copacabana; but the Ipanemans appear to be a notch or two "higher" on the socio-economic scale. In any case, the price of admission – free as on all Rio's beaches – is not affected by this difference.

Founded in the late 1960s when flower power was at its height, a *Feira Hippie* (Hippie Fair) is held at **Praça General Osório** on Sundays from 9 a.m. to 7 p.m. Today's visitors will find not hippies but craftspeople, painters, sculptors and junk dealers. There are many tourists among the clientele – not only foreign ones, but many southern Brazilians as well: for *Paulistas* and *Gauchos* (inhabitants of Rio Grande do Sul) a trip to Rio is always a treat.

On Fridays a large open-air market is held on **Praça N.S. da Paz,** featuring a large variety of stands selling tempting tropical fruits and spices. A stone's throw from the marketplace are the main retail outlets of two large jewelry manufacturers, Stern and Amsterdam Sauer, although visitors are strongly advised to review the state of their finances before entering the premises.

Leblon

The borderline between Ipanema and Leblon is formed by a canal linking the Atlantic Ocean and **Lagoa Rodrigo de Freitas**, a lovely lagoon on whose banks a rowing club and an amusement park are to be found. The neighborhood around the lagoon, which is somewhat smaller, more exclusive and more elegant than Ipanema, is said to have been named for a

Above: Weekly markets offer troves of tropical fruits year-round. Right: Traveling by gondola to the top of Sugar Loaf.

Frenchman called "Le Blond" who once lived here. On Sundays, one lane of the street adjacent to Ipanema and Leblon is given over to the exclusive use of bicyclists and joggers. Every Tuesday evening there is an organized bicycle trip (participated in by many Cariocas) from Leblon to Flamengo.

Modest-sized **Vidigal Beach** on Avenida Niemeyer is primarily frequented by guests of the Sheraton, which has direct access to it. The Sheraton is Rio's only luxury hotel that has its own beach – although Vidigal is not private, as private beaches are (fortunately) expressly prohibited by the Brazilian constitution.

Praia de São Conrado

Only a few years ago there were almost no buildings near Praia de São Conrado. But of late, numerous tall modernist structures have been springing up all along this white sand beach just south of Leblon. The beach is safe and never overrun, however, and visitors can watch hang-gliders make the 900-meter descent from the top of the Gávea Massif to the sand below. If you want to try tandem hang-gliding, arrangements can be made directly with the pilots on the beach. More earth-bound visitors can opt for a sojourn to the nearby Gávea Golf Club, whose course experts regard as one of the most beautiful in the world.

Barra da Tijuca

The southernmost and longest (18 kilometers) beach in Rio lies somewhat off the main tourist route, but it is magnificent and, even on a Sunday at the height of the tourist season, never crowded.

Pão de Açúcar – Sugar Loaf

It is thought that the name Pão de Açúcar is derived from the Indian word *paudaçuqua* (peaked mountain), from which the Portuguese, perhaps struck by the resemblance of this now illustrious lump of granite to a loaf, may have construed the similar-sounding *pão de açúcar*, which means "sugar loaf."

The peak was climbed as early as 1817 by an Englishman, and in 1912 an aerial railway began transporting visitors to the top of the 395-meter-high bell-shaped peak. In 1972, Italian-made gondolas with capacity for up to 75 passengers began shuttling between Praça General Tibúrcio (Urca quarter) and the summit, with a change of cars at the middle station, 230-meter **Morro da Urca** (operating hours: 8 a.m. to 10 p.m.). The ten-minute trip abounds with magnificent vistas. There is also a restaurant at Morro da Urca, which can only be recommended for the view. From the **observation platform** on Sugar Loaf, visitors can feast their eyes on Guanabara Bay, the port, the city, the beaches and Corcovado – all in one uplifting panorama.

From here a stairway leads directly down to *Rampa Joven*, an enchanting

footpath frequented primarily by Carioca couples with their minds mainly on love. Confirmed romantics should not miss the trip up to Sugar Loaf by moonlight and starshine. With the play of light on the surface of the sea below, and the starlit southern sky above, who can help but be entranced? Caution is in order on the return trip, however, because the taxi drivers at the valley station tend to overcharge!

Corcovado

No visitor to Rio should miss the trip up the "Humpback" – although the weather is a crucial factor, due to the fact that Rio's skies are not always as blue as picture postcards would have visitors believe. In fact, owing to its relatively high elevation of 709 meters and its situation in the middle of the Tijuca Forest, thick clouds often accumulate around the peak, hiding it from view. The rule of thumb best followed is: If there are no clouds around Corvocado, go up the mountain immediately. If the statue of Christ is covered in clouds, you'd better wait; your patience will be rewarded!

In 1931, five years after it was begun, this 38-meter-high reinforced concrete monument was consecrated, and has since attained the status almost of an urban icon. Christ rises 30 meters into the air, with his hands spread 28 meters apart. The statue weighs a total of 1,145 tons. Inside the pedestal is a chapel in which mass is said on Sundays at 11:30 a.m. Even anything-but-spry Pope Paul II climbed the 220 steps to the top of Corcovado during his visit to Brazil in 1991. The peak affords a panorama of Guanabara Bay, including Sugar Loaf, the city center, Maracanã Stadium, Lagoa Rodrigo de Freitas, and the most beautiful beaches.

The 3.8-kilometer trip in the Swiss-made **cog-wheel railway** (operating hours: 8:30 a.m. to 6 p.m.) is an experience rendered unforgettable, especially for nature-lovers, by the abundance of secondary growth, coffee and banana plants, and citrus fruits and orchids that are glimpsed along the way.

Visitors who make the trip by car or taxi have the opportunity to descend the mountain by way of Estrada do Redentor, which passes through **Tijuca Forest**, the most extensive continuous green area of any large city in the world. Cariocas owe its existence to Emperor Dom Pedro II, who in the 19th century ordered the entire site (at the time a huge coffee plantation) reforested.

Largo do Boticário, one of Rio's last remaining colonial architectural treasures, is located approximately 200 meters north of the cable railway station at Corcovado. Here, lovingly restored buildings are tastefully arrayed on a small cobble-stoned square girdled by fan palms and bamboo.

Right: Soccer fans at Maracanã, the world's largest outdoor stadium.

Jardim Botânico

"Here one finds everything that the jungle contains, without its terrors, its endlessness, its inaccessibility, its dangers." Thus, in *Brazil: A Land of the Future*, did author Stefan Zweig describe this 141-hectare 7,000-species-strong botanical garden that was founded in 1808 by Prince João. Walking down avenues lined with 30-meter-high royal palms, the visitor cannot help but be affected by the magical atmosphere of these exotic plants. Those not planning a trip up the Amazon can admire here, at their leisure, such tropical wonders as *Vitória Régia*, which measures two meters across; brazilwood trees, which were once used only as a dyestuff; as well as spices, coconut palms and other flora. Visitors should not expect troves of color, however, since with the exception of orchids and bromeliads, few tropical plants sport vividly hued blossoms.

After being very poorly maintained for some time, the gardens were restored to their former elegance in time for the "Rio 1992" environmental conference.

Maracanã Stadium

Located in the eponymous quarter, **Estádio Mário Filho**, which is named after the world-renowned soccer player, was built (within a space of two years) especially for the 1950 World Cup playoffs. The facility was to have been honored by becoming the site of Brazil's victory in the World Cup. But with its 2-1 victory over the favorites in the final game, Uruguay, Brazil's diminutive neighbor, made short and humiliating shrift of these dreams of grandeur and glory. No one has depicted this event more movingly than a retired stadium employee named Isaias Ambrosio whose dramatic monologue about the suffering of a Brazilian football fan is an unforgettable experience for sports enthusiasts – even for

those who do not understand a word of Portuguese!

The stadium, which can accommodate up to 165,000 cheering Cariocas, is already five decades old, but its elliptical shape gives it a decidedly modernistic look. Experiencing the atmosphere at Maracanã during an important *Flamengos* game or at a rock concert by a megastar like Tina Turner will certainly turn out to be the highlight of any stay in Rio. Maracanãzinho, the indoor facility next door, can seat up to 20,000, and is used for volleyball and basketball games, as well as for concerts.

The City Center

Although vacationers seldom include it in their sightseeing plans, downtown Rio is definitely worth spending at least a morning or afternoon in. Indeed, visitors whose favorite holiday pastime is wandering through museums and old churches might even want to consider devoting two full days to exploring Rio's rich historical and architectural heritage, still fascinating despite the politically and economically motivated destruction brought about by 200 years of "progress." The **Old City** is comprised of the Centro and Lapa quarters, and extends roughly from the Church of São Bento to the modern Catedral de São Sebastião. Many structures in the historic center of Rio have been superbly restored, and new paving stones have been laid in the streets and squares. The area has a fresh sheen to it that even extends to the centuries-old building materials, whose stately qualities are now much more in evidence.

The **City** can be reached by taking the Metro at Botafogo Station and getting off at the sixth stop, **Carioca**. Begin your walking tour of the area at lively **Largo da Carioca** (right outside the Metro station) by first taking the stairway to **Morro Santo Antônio**.

From the square in front of **Convento Santo Antônio** you can take the pulse of life in the city, and at the same time gar-

café (modeled on the famous Pastelería Ferrari in Lisbon), guests can savor salads, cakes or ice cream in an elegant atmosphere. Hardly a tourist haunt, the café's clientele is comprised of workers from nearby office buildings, and for the most part elderly, elegantly dressed men and women from high society.

At this point, the city presents the visitor with a choice between "Sahara" and "Wall Street" – the former being the Carioca appellation for the adjoining streets, from **Rua Ouvidor** to **Avenida Presidente Vargas**, in which goods of every description are sold by merchants of Middle Eastern descent; and the latter referring to **Avenida Rio Branco**, on which most banks and currency-exchange offices are located and where, from Monday through Saturday, visitors can experience the big city undistilled, in the form of cars, buses, mopeds and pedestrians jockeying for space. During Carnival, the lesser-known samba schools parade through these streets.

ner a first impression of its contrasting architectural styles. The two Franciscan churches are places for quiet meditation amidst the urban hubbub. Two children of the popular Empress Leopoldine, who died in 1826 at the age of 29, are buried in the crypt of **Santo Antônio**, the larger of the two churches. Of greater interest is the smaller of the two structures, the 18th-century **Igreja da Ordem Terceira de São Francisco da Penitência**, which is right next door. Noteworthy are the partially gilded wood carvings by the Portuguese masters Manuel and Xavier de Brito, as well as the ceiling frescos by Caetano da Costa Coelho, both exquisite examples of late Brazilian Baroque art.

From here, several superb colonial edifices – among them **Confeitaria Colombo** (No. 32-36) – can easily be reached by crossing Largo da Carioca and entering Rua Gonçalves Dias. In this Art Nouveau

Facing the harbor at the intersection of Avenidas Branco and Vargas (two of Rio's main commercial arteries) is **Nossa Senhora da Candelária**, one of the city's largest ecclesiastical structures. It could easily be overlooked today, however, owing to the towering skyscrapers above and the noisy traffic below. Huge paintings inside tell how a flickering candle prevented a ship and its crew from going to the bottom. Afterwards, the sailors whose lives were saved decided to build a church in honor of the Holy Virgin. Work began in 1775, but the huge dome was not consecrated until 1898.

Igreja de São Bento can be reached by taking **Rua 1° de Março** northward to the eponymous morro. Visitors who come by taxi can begin their exploration of the extensively restored Old City from here. This former Benedictine monastery, founded as early as the 16th century but for the most part constructed during the 17th, now houses an elite boarding

Above: This Franciscan convent is in the center of town. Right: At churrascarias you can eat your fill of excellent meat.

school for boys, and is regarded as the preeminent ecclesiastical structure in Rio. The Baroque church is richly appointed with dark Brazilian rosewood and gilding; the choir paintings by Frei Ricardo do Pilar are also noteworthy. To return to the center of the city, go back down Rua 1° de Março, a street name that commemorates Rio's official founding on March 1, 1565.

At the corner of Tocantins stands the **Centro Cultural do Banco do Brasil**, a typical modern Rio building only one wing of which is used for business, the main section being given over to art exhibitions, theatrical and video performances, and a permanent exhibition of old coins. Just behind this edifice, on Rua Visconde de Itaborai, can be found the **Post Office Cultural Center**, a venue that, like the aforementioned bank's, is utilized for art and theater, as well as for the stamp section of the main post office.

Other churches on Rua 1° de Março include the 18th-century former cathedral, which, as the Royal Palace stands diagonally across from it , was used by members of court as a place of worship during the 19th century. Since being extensively restored, the **Paço Imperial** (built 1735), which is usually identified as "Palácio dos Vice-Reis" on city maps, has become one of the most popular sightseeing attractions in the historic center of Rio. The palace is located on **Praça 15 de Novembro**, and was originally the seat of power at which the drama of courtly life was played out. Beginning in 1743, the Portuguese Governor-General resided there, and after Rio supplanted Salvador as capital in 1763, seven viceroys in succession occupied it. Following the defeat of Napoleon in 1808, King João VI and his retinue moved from Portugal into the Brazilian palace. On September 7, 1822, his son Pedro declared Brazil's independence from Portugal and had himself crowned Emperor – whereupon the structure was renamed *Paço Imperial*. Until 1815, the royal mint operated in one wing of this structure; the coin-minting machinery and Emperor's apartments can both be viewed. The remainder of the palace is currently a *Centro Cultural*, with a café in the inner courtyard where visitors can take a break from the bustle of the city over a cup of *cafezinho*.

Cultural centers and museums generally make for excellent havens of quiet on weekdays. These institutions are also open on Sundays, which is Rio's only day of rest: offices and businesses are closed, as is the subway, which runs Monday through Saturday only. Just across from the palace on the Rua da Assembléia stands the imposing Parliament Building, the former **Assembléia**. Prior to becoming (in 1792) a martyr to the cause of Brazilian independence, Tiradentes, having called for the overthrow of the Viceroy, was imprisoned here.

The entrance to the ferry terminal for boats to Niteró is at Praça 15 de Novembro, from which visitors can view the Neo-Gothic "fairy-tale palace" from 1880, which is located on the **Ilha Fiscal** and is an architectural curiosity dating back to the waning years of the monarchy. Shortly before the end of his reign, and nine years after the palace was completed, the Emperor held one final celebration in this light blue construction, which today stands in the middle of the port like a spectral apparition.

From here, walk down Avenida Erasmo Braga to Avenida Presidente Antônio Carlos (you will pass several government ministry buildings on your way) until you arrive at **Santa Luzia**, a small church with two towers whose blue façade stands out amidst the surrounding gray colossi. Behind the church looms the **Palace of Culture**, originally the Ministry of Education, which was built according to a model by Le Corbusier, and with the participation of Oscar Niemeyer. It was completed in 1943 when much of Europe had been reduced to rubble and ash. The *azujelos* (tiled murals) by Paulo Rossi on the façade are similar to those on the Niemeyer church in Belo Horizonte (see p.

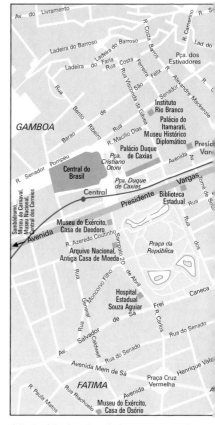

84). Inside the church there are some intriguing sculptures.

The most attractive route from this point is to walk down Rua Pedro Lessa to **Praça Floriana** and **Cinelândia**, which houses cinemas, restaurants and bars. Four neighboring buildings are also worth viewing: City Hall, the Opera, the National Library and the Museum of Fine Art. The core of the collection held by the Museu Nacional de Belas Artes consists of works that King João brought with him from Portugal. On display as well are a number of works by 17th- and 18th-century European and 19th-century Brazilian painters.

The 19th-century **Teatro Municipal** is modeled after the Paris Opera, but was

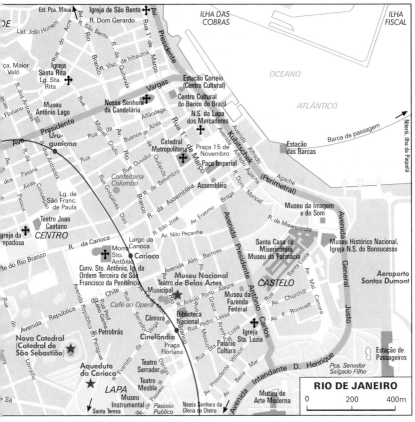

built on a smaller scale. Today, it is the scene of operas and concerts, as well as performances by touring orchestras from around the world. A visit to the Café do Opera – really more of a restaurant – is heartily recommended for its Assyrian-style dining room, reminiscent of the scenery in Verdi's *Aida*.

City Hall stands directly on Praça Floriana facing the **Biblioteca Nacional**. Founded in 1810, the national library now houses a collection of over two million books and manuscripts, including many priceless first editions.

To return to **Largo da Carioca** where this walking tour began, either take the subway from City Hall (Cinelândia Station), or wend your way down Avenida 13 de Maio to expansive Avenida Republica do Chile. Putting the library at your back and following Rua Senador Dantas in the direction of the eminently visible Petrobás Building takes you directly to the terminal on Rua Professor Lélio Gama, where you can catch the streetcar to **Santa Teresa**, a neighborhood featuring steeply climbing streets and venerable old buildings, now inhabited primarily by artists. Cariocas affectionately call this old-fashioned streetcar from bygone days **Bondinho**. It is recommended that visitors who decide to get around Santa Teresa via Bondinho take it only as far as **Dois Irmãos**. Cameras and other valuables should not be brought along on this or other "safe" streetcar lines. Special ex-

cursions are available for photo and video buffs, however, and the conductor at the terminal will gladly provide information about them.

Bondinho peregrinates across the 270-meter-long and 64-meter-high **Aqueduto da Carioca** (Arcos da Lapa), which supplied settlers with potable water during colonial times. Across from the stop on Av. República do Chile is a remarkable ecclesiastical edifice, the **Catedral de São Sebastião** (1976). This 80-meter-high trapezoidal structure by Andrade Fonesca is supposed to recall a Mexican pyramid, but in fact evokes an upside-down flower pot. During the Pope's 1991 visit, 20,000 worshipers gathered inside the church, which measures 106 meters across. Impressive in the interior are the monumental windows, which recount the history of the Church in four different co-

Above: The Carioca Aqueduct with the modern Catedral and Petrobras Building in the background. Right: A beautiful samba dancer wearing a fanciful headdress.

lors: in green over the portal, the unity of the Church; in blue over the entrance, mankind and race; to the right, in red, the Evangelists; and to the left, in yellow, the Apostles. One additional church nearby is worthy of mention, if only for its photogenic location: **Nossa Senhora da Glória do Oteiro** on Morro da Glória in the **Glória** quarter. This Baroque edifice was built in the 18th century on a double octagon plan, and can be seen from as far away as Flamengo. Of primary interest are its blue glazed tiles (*azulejos*) and exquisite wood-carved altarpieces.

The temple of Carnival- and samba-lovers known as **Sambódromo** is open to the public when Carnival is not in progress. To get there, take the subway to Praça Onze, walk a few hundred meters back towards the city center to Avenida Marqês de Sapucai, and you will find yourself standing before a huge elementary school building with 200 classrooms and space for 15,000 pupils. This complex, designed by Oscar Niemeyer and built in 1984, is the quintessence of Carioca ebullience. During the school year children are educated in it, which proves that the enormous construction costs were not merely for the benefit of a two-day-long once-yearly extravaganza, as the international media at the time claimed was the case.

At parade time, the classrooms become dressing rooms for the 18 top samba schools, whose members snake their way past an estimated 90,000 spectators on Easter Sunday and Easter Monday in two groups. Each school's 4,000 or so actors, 3,500 male and female dancers, and 500 drummers perform for about 90 minutes: anyone still in their seat after this would have to be clinically dead! The names of the samba schools – e.g., *Beija-Flor* ("Flower Kiss" or hummingbird) and *Imperatriz Leopoldinense* (Empress Lepoldine) – are as imaginative as the songs associated with them, the most popular of which often become hits. In 1996, for example, the *Mangueira* samba school made a recording of *A Esmeralda do Atlântico*, ("The Emerald of the Atlantic"), which became a chart topper.

Ilha de Paquetá

Located in northeastern Guanabara Bay, this island, which consists of only one square kilometer, can be reached by ferry from Praça 15 de Novembro (every two or three hours from 5 a.m. to 11 p.m.). Horses and bicycles are the primary means of transportation on this island, the nostalgia of whose colonial architecture invites visitors to savor long, leisurely walks. However, those yearning for the peace and quiet of a lonely stretch of white sand should bear in mind that when the weekend rolls around, the island's beaches tend to be thronged.

Costa Verde

Its tropical vegetation, bizarre mountains, and incomparable beaches have

made the **Costa Verde**, Rio's southwest coast, a favorite destination of Cariocas and tourists alike. The "green coast" highway, **Estrada Rio-Santos** (BR 101), is one of Brazil's most beautiful stretches of road, as well as the most scenically rewarding route for the drive from Rio to São Paulo.

A little-known and perhaps useful fact about Brazil is that there are a few nude beaches. One of them, **Abricó**, is to be found along this expanse of coast, 40 kilometers southwest of Rio.

The Costa Verde also offers numerous jumping-off points for boat excursions to offshore islands. To reach the coast itself, the best route to take is Avenida das Américas to Baía de Septetiba via Barra de Tijuca. After passing through the industrial zone of Santa Cruz and Itaguaí, you arrive in **Itacuruçá**, a fishing village from which sailboats make the crossing to Septetiba Bay, a trip that can also be booked in Rio as a day excursion. Outings to privately-owned **Ilha São Bernardo** – especially worthwhile for

visitors staying in Rio – can be arranged through Rio Sightseeing. The somewhat more expansive **Jaguanum** and **Itacuruçá** islands contain several small hotels. Well worth making an effort to be present for is the cavalcade of ships held off Itacuruçá on June 29, the feast day of Saints Peter and Paul, a day on which many other coastal communities also stage similar pageants.

Boats to **Ilha Grande**, a nature reserve featuring fascinating fauna and splendid beaches, depart from **Mangaratiba**, about 100 kilometers from Rio. The adjoining 60-kilometer stretch of the coast highway offers magnificent views of bay and islands. Enticing beaches and seafood restaurants also dot this landscape.

Angra dos Reis is better known for its nuclear power plant (the only one in Brazil) than it is for the countless superb

Above: Serra do Mar, the green backdrop for Paratí, the "Pearl of the Colonial Era." Right: In Paratí, time seems to have stood still.

beaches scattered across its dozens of bays and 370 islands. The city, whose name means "Royal Bay," has a population of 90,000 and is the largest town on the Costa Verde. Favorite holiday activities in Angra include golf at Hotel do Frade, as well as harpoon and deep sea fishing.

Paratí

From Angra, Highway 101 winds around Baía da Ilha Grande until it reaches the Bay of Paratí, which offers visitors a trove of beaches and islands. The Guaiana, who supplied the first European sailors with brazilwood and spices, were the original inhabitants of **Paratí**, the "Pearl of the Colonial Era." In the 19th century the town was an entrepôt for the export of gold from Minas Gerais, and later coffee from the Vale do Paraí. But after independence was declared, the gold remained in the region. Roads were built, though the harbor proved to be too shallow for large vessels, and Paratí was

more or less forgotten – a fortunate occurrence, in the opinion of many enchanted inhabitants and visitors! Car traffic is banned in most of the colonial town center, which has changed little since the 18th century and is a protected national monument.

No one ever forgets Paratí, with its picturesque winding streets, which, as one strolls through them, reward the alert visitor with occasional brief but almost heart-rendingly beautiful glimpses of the bay against the the luminous backdrop of the densely forested **Serra do Mar**, whose peaks rise to a height of 1,600 meters. Many corner beams of the town's two-story colonial structures are embellished, and colorfully painted window frames and doors abound. The museum of religious art in the church of **Santa Rita de Cássia** (1722) is well worth a visit, too. During colonial times only whites were allowed to worship in it, and blacks consequently built their own *Nossa Senhora do Rosário dos Homens Pretos* three years later.

Demand for sugar-cane spirits called *pinga* used to be strong enough to keep 150 sugar refineries and distilleries busy. Today, however, only *Engenho do Vapor* is still in operation, but it is not open to the public.

Niterói

Niterói, until 1975 capital of the state of Rio de Janeiro, lies opposite Rio on Guanabara Bay. In that same year, the states of Guanabara and Rio de Janeiro were merged into a reorganized state under the latter's name, and Rio became the capital. Niteró, founded in 1573 as São Lorenzo, has a population of 600,000, and can be reached either by ferry or over Ponte Presidente Costa e Silva, which was built in 1964. This 15.5-kilometer-long bridge shortens the trip by 100 kilometers, and is 60 meters above the water's surface, thereby allowing cargo and cruise ships to pass underneath. A ferry makes the trip from the center of Niterói to downtown Rio in 30

65

minutes; boats depart from Praça Quinze every 15 minutes between the hours of 6 a.m. and 11 p.m. While on board, visitors can marvel at and photograph the panoramic Rio skyline, which constitutes the high point of a visit to Niterói. **Itaipu**, an eminently recommendable beach favored by surfers, can be reached by taking a bus from the stop adjacent to the harbor.

Petrópolis

In 1854, British engineers constructed the first railway line between Rio and **Petrópolis**. Today, the BR 040 highway traces breathtaking curves at a climatically cozy 840 meters above sea level, affording numerous opportunities to appreciate the natural beauty of the Serra do Mar and Guanabara Bay – that is, providing the thick ocean fog doesn't roll in and spoil the view. Petrópolis, once home to the Emperor, is only 66 kilometers away from Rio, and is therefore a favorite day-excursion destination for Brazilians.

Petrópolis is also only eight kilometers from the huge **Quitandinha Complex**, which opened as a casino in 1944 but became redundant when the national lottery was introduced. In the mid-1990s, the world of finance decided that the palace-like hotel would make a good investment, and Cariocas in need of a break from the rigors of urban life can now relax in the refurbished 400-suite facility, complete with shopping center and health club.

Petrópolis (population 300,000) was founded by German immigrants, coming to prominence in 1843 when Emperor Pedro II had his summer residence built here to take advantage of the 6°C difference in temperature between Petrópolis and Rio. The Emperor liked the city so much he named it after himself. Today, his former summer home, the **Palácio Imperial**, bears the name **Museu Imperial**, and is a place where visitors don felt slippers, glide over parquet floors made of the finest woods, and

marvel at the royal regalia and crown jewels. Opposite the palace on Av. 7 de Setembro stands the royal guest house, which is inhabited to this day by descendants of the Braganças, the former Brazilian royal family. The Emperor is buried in the Neo-Gothic cathedral of **São Pedro de Alcântara**, completed in 1884. On Praça de Confluência stands the **Palácio de Cristal**, a steel and glass affair whose components were brought over from France. Regarded as ultra-modern in its day, it served as the Emperor's redoubt. A short distance away on Rua do Encanto stands **Casa de Santos Dumont**, now a museum but originally the home of the eponymous Brazilian aeronautic pioneer.

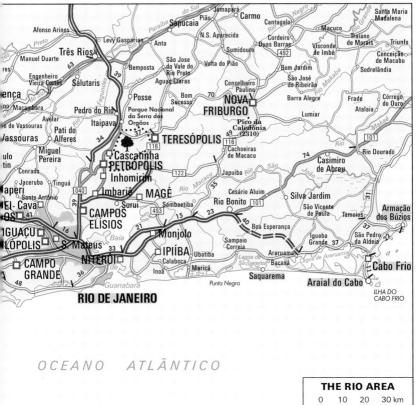

Afonso Arinos — Preto — Três Rios — Manuel Duarte — res — Engenheiro Vieira Cortes — Sálutaris — ença — no — Macambara — o de Vassouras — Avelar — Pati do Alferes — /assouras — ulo — tin — Miguel Pereira — Conrado — Jaceruba — Tinguá — aperi — Santo Antônio — EI- Cava — GS — 41 — IGUAÇU — LÓPOLIS — S. Mateus — CAMPO GRANDE — 48 — NITERÓI — Inoã — Guanabara — Baía — de — Punta Negra

Levy Gasparian — Anta — Bemposta — 63 — 39 — Posse — Pedro do Rio — Itaipava — 34 — 37 — Cascatinha — PETRÓPOLIS — Inhomirim — Imbariê — MAGÉ — Surui — CAMPOS ELÍSIOS — Sambaetiba — Monjolo — 21 — IPIÍBA — Calaboça — Maricá — 36

Paraiba — do Sul — Jomaparã — Pião — Sapucaia — N.S. Aparecida — São Jose do Vale do Rio Preto — Volta do Pião — Aguas Claras — Bom Sucesso — 70 — Parque Nacional da Serra dos Orgãos — 116 — TERESÓPOLIS — 116 — 122 — Japuiba — Rio Macacu — 35 — Cesário Aluim — Rio Bonito — 101 — 23 — 15 — 493 — Ubatiba — Sampaio Correia — 40

Carmo — Cantagalo — Cordeiro — Duas Barras — Sumidouro — 492 — Bom Jardim — Conselheiro Paulino — São José do Ribeirão — NOVA FRIBURGO — Barra Alegre — Lumiar — Pico da Caledônia — (2310) — Cachoeiras de Macacu — São João — Silva Jardim — São Vicente de Paula — Boa Esperança — Araruama — Lagoa de Araruama — Bacaxá — Saquarema — Lagoa de Saquarema

Negro — Santa Maria Madalena — Macuco — Visconde de Imbé — Traiano de Morais — Triunfo — Conceição de Macabu — Sodrelândia — Frade — Córrego do Ouro — Atalaia — 101 — Rio Dourado — 74 — Casimiro de Abreu — Tamoios — Iguaba Grande — 37 — São Pedro da Aldeia — Armação dos Búzios — Cabo Frio — Araial do Cabo — ILHA DO CABO FRIO

RIO DE JANEIRO

OCEANO ATLÂNTICO

THE RIO AREA

0   10   20   30 km

Sadly, the town has no monument to the self-exiled Austrian writer Stefan Zweig, who took his own life in 1942, and who wrote the well-received book, *Brazil: A Land of the Future,* while living far from the capital, in Petrópolis.

Teresópolis

This picturesque town, 900 meters above sea level and nestled at the foot of the Serra dos Orgãos (Organ Mountains) is 91 kilometers from Rio. It was named after Empress Teresa, but was only founded two years after she went into exile. **Teresópolis** is a good jumping-off point for a visit to the Parque Nacional da Serra dos Orgãos. The **Dedo de Deus**

(Finger of God), a peak that rises to 1,692 meters, is clearly visible from as far away as Rio, as is the highest point in the park, the 2,263-meter **Pedra do Sino** (Bell Rock). The **Cascata do Imbuí** waterfall puts on a misty non-stop performance six kilometers west of town on the road to Petrópolis.

Nova Friburgo

Nova Friburgo, 150 kilometers northeast of Rio, enjoys a temperate climate owing to its moderate elevation (850 meters above sea level). Founded in 1819 by immigrants from the Swiss canton of Fribourg (whence its name), the city has a population of 200,000 and is six kilo-

67

meters from the 2,310-meter **Pico da Caledónia**, a jumping-off point – literally – favored by hang-gliding enthusiasts.

Beaches East of Rio

Beyond Niterói lies Rio's "lake district," a series of lagoons with irresistible beaches and gorgeous recreational areas. Highly recommended are **Ponte Negra** beach near **Maricá**, 60 kilometers east of Rio, and **Saquarema**, an additional 40 kilometers east. From both, a small church that is often depicted in paintings can be seen. Surfers flock to this stretch of shoreline for its powerful breakers.

A short way from the opening of the lagoon into the Atlantic lies **Cabo Frio**, a city of 50,000 inhabitants that was founded by Jesuits in 1615 and is now the most populous community in the lagoon area. Salt is processed from the surrounding marshes, although those who throng

Above: The Neo-Gothic cathedral of Petropólis, which served as a royal burial church.

here are probably attracted not by salt but sand. Worth seeing are the very well preserved **Forte São Mateus** (1616), and **Nossa Senhora da Guia**, a chapel sailors used to take their bearings by. Six kilometrs southwards, visitors can climb **A Dama Branca** (The White Lady), a large sand dune.

Arraial do Cabo is a well-kept Rio secret. Situated on the tip of Cape Frio, the slight drawback of offering only small hotels is more than made up for by its perfect swimming beaches located on a bay whose high breakers make for ideal surfing. Arraial is also a divers' paradise, and a delight for gourmets who love freshly-caught fish. Visitors should take time out to experience the light blue waters of the underwater grotto **Gruta Azul** on **Ilha do Cabo Frio**. Locally-owned boats provide transportation and excursions to the smaller islands.

From here it's just under 40 kilometers to **Armacão dos Búzios**. The Portuguese discovered Búzios (as it is usually called) in the 16th century and along with it the entire Atlantic coast of Brazil. In a sense, Brigitte Bardot did the same for the international jet set and the mass tourism that followed in its wake by vacationing here on two occasions in the 1960s. During high season, the town's year-round population of 15,000 mushrooms. However, Búzios has retained its charm by passing strict zoning ordinances, a necessary measure in the face of increasingly frequent visits by foreign tourists on fast-paced package tours. Beaches are within easy walking distance of town, though the more distant ones, such as Tartaruga, Brava and Forno, are also the most beautiful and are reachable by bicycle, rented car, dune buggy or boat. Dollars can easily be spent on shopping streets such as **Rua das Pedras**, or in the town's many restaurants and bars. Visitors who relish seaside locales like the Côte d'Azur and don't mind relatively high prices will feel right at home in Búzios.

RIO DE JANEIRO
Area Code 021
Accommodation

An *EXPENSIVE* double room costs from US $120 to 300; *MODERATE* US $80 to 140; *BUDGET* US $35 to 80. During Carnival, you can count on paying double or triple these rates.

EXPENSIVE: **Caesar Park**, Ipanema, Vieira Suuto 460, tel. 287-3122, fax 227-7441. Currently the best in the city. Pool, sauna, room safes, superb restaurants; **Copacabana Palace**, Av. Atlântica 1702, tel. 255-7070, fax 235-7330. Authentic "grand hotel," also a national monument but it has been renovated. Large pool with a terrace for sunbathing. Sauna, fitness and business center; **Inter-Continental**, São Conrado, Av. Pref. Mendes de Morais 222, tel. 322-2200, fax 322-5500. 10 km from downtown, shuttle bus, large garden with huge pool, nicer and less crowded beach beyond the riverside road, sauna, disco, fitness center, four restaurants, three bars; **Meridien**, Av. Atlântica 1020, tel. 275-9922, fax 541-6447, centrally located between Leme and Copa, roof-top restaurant with delicious food, pool with terrace, sauna, room safes; **Rio Othon Palace**, Av. Atlântica 3264, tel. 521-5522, skyscraper at Copa. Pool, sauna, room safes; **Rio Palace**, Av. Atlântica 4240, tel. 521-3232, fax 227-1454, best location on Copacabana, lively neighborhood. Pool, sauna, bars, restaurants, room safes; **Sheraton**, Vidigal, Av. Niemeyer 121, tel. 274-1122, fax 239-5643, between Leblon and São Conrado. The only beachfront hotel. Shuttle bus. An oasis of relaxation with two pools, sauna, fitness center, three restaurants, room safes.

MODERATE: **Gloria**, R. do Russel 632, tel. 555-7272, fax 555-7282. 630 rooms, one of the largest and oldest hotels, abounds in faded charm, central, pool; **Leme Othon Palace**, Av. Atlântica 656, tel./fax 275-8080, good location, room safes; **Marina Palace**, Leblon, R. Delfim Moreira 630, tel. 259-5212, fax 294-1644. Good location, on the small side, fine restaurant; **Merlin Copacabana**, Av. Princesa Isabel 392, tel. 542-6239, fax 541-3043. Noisy because of its location in front of the tunnel to Botafogo. Small roof-top pool, sauna, room safes; **Praia Linda**, Av. Sernambetiba 1430, tel. 494-2186, fax 494-2198. Far from downtown (in Barra), but near the beach, good for water-sports enthusiasts; **Trocadero Othon**, Av. Atlântica 2064, tel. 257-1834. At Copa's beachside promenade, room safes; **Windsor Palace**, R. Domingos Ferreira 6, tel. 235-0098, fax 257-9373. In the middle of Copa, parallel to Atlântica but reasonably quiet.

BUDGET: **Arpoador Inn**, R. Francisco Otaviano 177, tel. 247-6090, fax 511-5094. 50 rooms, some with a view of Arpoador beach; **Canadá**, Av. N.S.

de Copacabana 687, tel. 257-1864, fax 255-3705. Located on a busy Copa thoroughfare, small; **Flórida**, Flamengo, R. Ferreira Viana 81, tel. 285-5242, fax 285-5777. Popular with travelers on tight budgets; **Guanabara Palace**, Av. Pres. Vargas 392, tel. 253-8622, fax 516-1582, very centrally located, quite noisy, not far from the port, between Av. Branco and Sambódromo; **Majestic Rio Palace**, R. 5 de Julho 195, tel. 255-2030, fax 255-1692, in the middle of Copa. Does not live up to its name; **San Marco**, R. Visconde de Pirajá 524, tel. 239-5032, in the middle of posh Ipanema. 40 rooms with safes.

Restaurants

Italian, Chinese, and Japanese restaurants are quite prevalent in Rio.

CHURRASCARIAS: **Barra Grill**, Ministro Ivan Lins 314, tel. 493-6060. A typical churrascaria, i.e., a large, noisy and hectic place where you can eat your fill of (top quality) meat; **Jardim**, Copa, Rep. do Peru 225, tel. 235-3263. In existence for 50 years, live music; **Marius**, various branches in Rio's better neighborhoods, an "in" place for the nouveau riche – Av. Atlântica 290, tel. 542-2393 (Leme), pretty view of the ocean, R. Francisco Otaviano 96, tel. 287-2552 (Arpoador); **Plataforma**, Leblon, R. Adalberto Ferreira 32, tel. 274-4022. The famous samba show is on the ground floor.

BRAZILIAN: **Casa da Feijoada**, Ipanema, R. Prudente de Moraes 10, tel. 267-4994. You can try the famous dish *feijoada* here, traditionally eaten on Saturday; **Chalé**, Botafogo, da Matriz 54, tel. 286-0897. Famous for fine country cooking for over 30 years; **Yemanjá**, Ipanema, R. Visconde de Pirajá 128 A, tel. 247-7004, traditional Bahian cuisine.

SEAFOOD: **Candido's**, Pedra de Guaratiba, R. Barros de Alarcão 352, tel. 417-1630. Open 12-7 pm, Sat until 11, 45 km south of Rio. Very popular and exclusive seafood restaurant; **Garden Grill**, Leblon, Tuas Ferreira 571 A, tel. 239-8387. Specializes in grilled fish; **Príncipe das Peixadas**, Av. Atlântica 974 B, tel. 275-3996. Next door to the Meridien in Leme, known for rich seafood dishes made from the freshest catch; **Satyricon**, Ipanema, R. Barão da Torre 192, tel. 521-0627. Elegant and expensive, renowned for its delectable oysters; **Shirley's**, Leme, R. Gustavo Sampaio 610. Shoebox-sized seafood place where there's a line to get in after 8 pm; **Sol e Mar**, Botafogo, Nestor Moreira 11, tel. 295-1896. Across from Sugar Loaf, superb atmosphere, not cheap but good.

INTERNATIONAL: **Ponto de Encontro**, Barata Ribeiro 750 B, tel. 257-7927. A popular Copa eatery; **The Lynx**, Ipanema, R. Terceira de Mello 31 C, tel. 227-9796. Near the hippy market; **Via Farme**, Ipanema, Farme de Amoedo 47, tel. 227-0743. Large selection of meat, fish and pasta.

Sights

Maracanã-Stadion, guided tours available when no matches are scheduled, Mon-Fri 9 am to 5 pm; **Nossa Senhora da Glória do Oteiro**, Mon-Fri 1 to 5 pm, Sat-Sun 9 am to noon; **Pão de Açúcar**, Praça General Tibúrcio, tel. 541-3737, 107 bus, aerial railway runs 8 am to 10 pm every 30 minutes, more often when necessary, capacity 75 persons; **Helicopter Sightseeing Flights**, depart from Morro da Urca (middle station on Sugar Loaf) and Lagoa Rodrigo de Freitas; US $45 per person to go around Corcovado, longer flights cost more - Vega-Helicopters, tel. 220-5000; **Corcovado**, Rua Cosme Velho 513, tel. 285-2533. Buses: 180, 422 and 581. Daily 8 am to 10 pm by car and 8:30 am to 6 pm by cog railway, which runs every 20-30 min. and takes ca. 20 min; **Botanical Gardens**, enter from Rua Jardim Botânico 920 or Rua Pacheco Leão 915, tel. 274-8248, 583 bus, open daily 8 am to 5 pm; **Paço Imperial**, Praça 15 de Novembro, tel. 232-8333. Take the subway to Carioca, various busses also go there, Tue-Sun 11 am to 6:30 pm; **Quinta da Boa Vista**, take the subway to São Cristóvão, tel. 264-8262, open Tue-Sun 10 am to 5 pm. Large park with former Emperor's residence, lakes, grottos, a zoo and a natural history museum.

Museums

Museu Nacional, in Quinta da Boa Vista. Over a million objects on display – archaeology, ethnology, zoology and botany; **Museu Histórico Nacional**, Praça Marechal Âncora, tel. 240-9529. Subway to Cinelândia. Tue-Fri 10 am to 5 pm, Sat, Sun and holidays 3 to 5 pm. Old coins, religious art, permanent exhibition on colonial times and the Brazilian "empire"; **Museu da República** (Palácio do Catete), Rua do Catete 153, tel. 285-6350. Subway to Catete station. Tue-Sun 12 to 5 pm, Sat-Sun 2 to 6 pm. Interesting neo-colonial building was the president's official residence until 1960; **Museu Nacional de Belas Artes**, Av. Rio Branco 190, tel. 240-0106. Subway to Cinelândia. Tue-Fri 10 am to 6 pm, Sat, Sun and holidays 2 to 6 pm; **Biblioteca Nacional,** Praça Floriana. Subway to Cinelândia. Guided tours daily 11 am, 3 and 5 pm, sometimes in English; **Museu de Arte Moderna**, Av. Infante D. Henrique 85 (Flamengo Park), subway to Cinelândia. Tue-Fri 12 to 5:30 pm; **Museu do Indio**, Rua das Palmeiras 55, tel. 286-8799. Subway to Botafogo. Tue-Fri 11 am to 5:30 pm, Sat, Sun and holidays 1 to 5 pm; **Museu do Bonde**, Rua Lélio Gama 75 A, tel. 240-5709. Mon-Fri 8 am to 4 pm, Sat 9 am to 1 pm, Rio's streetcar museum is located right at the terminus; **Museu Chácara do Céu**, Rua Murtinho Nobre 93, Santa Teresa. Can be reached by streetcar. Tue-Sun 2 to 5 pm. Country seat with lovely panoramas, and an art collection including several Picassos; **Museu do Carnaval**, Sambódromo, Rua Frei Caneca, tel. 293-7122, Tue-Fri 10 am to 5 pm.

Transportation

METRÔ (subway): Only two lines, but clean and safe. Runs Mon-Sat from 6 am to 11 pm; discount fare from 12 to 4 pm. The blue line (most used by tourists) begins in Botafogo. Info tel. 255-9292.

CITY BUSES: Estacão Rodoviária Mariano Procópio, Praça Mauá (downtown). Rio's city bus lines are so complicated that even Cariocas know only "their" bus. Unfortunately, there are frequent muggings and robberies on these buses as well. You're better off taking the subway or a taxi.

AIRPORT BUS: **Real Auto Ônibus**, from downtown to the Santos Dumont Airport; in the southern suburbs to and from Alvorada along the coastal road.

INTERCITY BUSES: Rodoviário Novo Rio, Av. Francisco Bicalho. All buses leave from here, except those to Petropolis and Teresópolis, which leave from the Meneses Cortes terminal on Av. Erasmo Braga.

TRAINS: **Trem de Prata**. The "silver train" leaves daily at 8:30 pm from Barão de Mau Èstation, Av. Francisco Bicalho in São Cristovão, and arrives in São Paulo at 5:30 the following morning. Costs US $120 including meals, tel. 293-4071.

TAXIS: Regular taxis are yellow with blue stripes and all have meters, which must be running. If this is not the case, negotiate the fare beforehand. Fares are higher at night and on Sundays. Air-conditioned limos that charge a flat (and higher) rate wait for customers outside airport terminals and large hotels. This safe means of transportation is an especially good option for the trip to the airport. **Transcootour**, tel. 590-2220. Regular taxis available around the clock.

CAR RENTALS: **Avis**, tel. 259-2121; **Hertz**, tel. 398-3162; **Unidas**, tel. 398-3844.

BOAT AND YACHT RENTALS: **Captains Yacht Charters**, tel. 224-0313.

BICYCLE RENTALS: **Rio Bikers**, tel. 259-6860, 274-5872.

Post Office / Telephones

Main Post Office, Av. Pres. Vargas 3077, tel. 293-0159. For stamps: Rua Visconde de Itaboraí, downtown.

Telephones: Downtown, Praça Tiradentes 41, open 24 hours. Copacabana, Av. Ns. Senhora da Copacabana 542, open 24 hours. Ipanema, Rua Visconde de Pirajá 111, Store No. 5, 6 am to 11 pm.

Tourist Information

Embratur: For information about the whole country, Rua Mariz e Barros 13, 6th Floor, near Praça da Bandeira, tel. 273-2212; **Flumitur**: For information about the state of Rio, Rua da Assembléia 10, tel. 252-4512; **Riotur**: For information about

Rio (city). In the same building as Flumitur, tel. 297-7117. There are also tourist offices at Pão de Azúcar and Corcovado.

Police
Rio Tourist Police, Leblon, Av. Afrânio de Melo Franco, tel. 511-5112.

Medical Assistance
Serviço Médico International Cruz Vermelha (International Red Cross), Praça Cruz Vermelha 10/12, tel. 217-4110.

ANGRA DOS REIS
Area Code 0243

Accommodation
EXPENSIVE: **Angra Inn**, Praia Grande, Estrada do Contorno 2629, tel. 65-1299. Wonderful beach, pool, anchorage, sports facilities and tennis courts. *MODERATE:* **Chalet de Angra**, BR 101, km 93, tel. 65-0176. Bungalows, pool.

Restaurants
Peixe Galo, Hotel Porto Galo, Itapinhoacanga, tel. 65-1022, seafood; **Taberna 33**, Av. Raul Pompéia 110, tel. 65-2404. Italian cuisine, open evenings only.

PARATÍ
Area Code 0243

Accommodation
EXPENSIVE: **Pousada do Ouro**, Rua Dr. Pereira 145, tel. 71-2033, fax 71-1311. Pool, sauna and a good restaurant. Boat excursions available. *MODERATE:* **Pousada Frade**, Rua do Comércio, tel. 71-1205, fax 71-2111. Room safes, pool. *BUDGET:* **Pousada das Canoas**, Av. Roberto Silveira 279, tel. 71-1133. Has a small restaurant and a pool.

Restaurants
Pousada do Ouro, Rua Dr. Pereira 145, tel. 71-2033; **Pousada do Sandi**, Largo do Rosario, tel. 71-2100. These are both good hotel restaurants.

PETRÓPOLIS
Area Code 0242

Accommodation
EXPENSIVE: **Pousada da Alcobaça**, Correas, Rua Agostinho Goulão 298, tel. 21-1240. Excellent atmosphere, 11 rooms, pool, sauna, tennis. *MODERATE:* **Albergo del Leone**, Rua Com. Marcolino A. de Souza 435, tel. 22-2350, fax 22-3587. 19 km north of Rio. Hotel in a park with pool, sauna; **El Siramat**, Camino de Céu 3000, tel. 3335. 19 km outside of Rio, lovely location, pool, sauna.

Restaurants
La Belle Meunière, Estrada União Indústria 2189, tel. 21-1573. French cuisine. House specialty is trout; **Trigo**, Estrada Bernardo Coutinho 1721. Good Brazilian cooking.

Museums
Palácio Imperial, Rua da Imperatriz 220, tel. 42-7012. Tue-Sun 12 to 5 pm; **Casa de Santos Dumont**, Rua do Encanto 22, tel. 31-2121. Tue-Sun 10 am to 5 pm.

Transportation
BUS STATION: Rua Dr. Porcúncula 75

Tourist Information
Petrotur, Praça da Confluência 3, tel. 43-3390.

TERESÓPOLIS
Area Code 021

Accommodation
EXPENSIVE: **Rosa dos Ventos**, Estrada RJ 130, km 226, 26 km north of Rio, tel. 742-8833, fax 742-8174. Exclusive hotel, room safes, pool, sauna, many sports activities, good restaurant. Guests must be 16 years or older! *MODERATE:* **Fazenda das Pedras**, Estrada RJ 130, 12 km north of Rio, tel. 742-5115. Pool, sauna, lake, horseback riding.

Restaurants
Zermatt, in Hotel Rosa dos Ventos (see above), tel. 742-8833. Swiss chef, reservations a must; **Margô**, Rua Heitor de Moura Estevão 259, German cuisine, downtown.

Transportation
BUS STATION: Rua 1° de Maio 100

Tourist information
Secretaria de Turismo, Praça Olímpica, tel. 742-9149.

ARMAÇÃO DOS BÚZIOS
Area Code 0246

Accommodation
EXPENSIVE: **Vila Boa Vida**, Rua Q, Lote 12, Praia da Ferradura, tel. 23-6767, fax 23-6727. 2 km from the village and 500 meters from the beach. Roomy bungalows with ocean view, two swimming pools; **Pousada Byblos**, Morro Humaitá 8, tel. 23-1162, small pool. *MODERATE:* **Auberge L'Ermitage**, Praia de Baía Formosa, Estrada Baía Formosa, tel. 23-1103. Room safes, tennis court, good restaurant. *BUDGET:* **Pousadinha em Búzios**, Rua Manoel Turíbio de Farias 202, tel. 23-1448, 8 rooms, in town center.

Restaurants
Satyricon, Rua José Bento Ribeiro Dantas 500, tel. 23-1595. Well-known Italian-style seafood eatery; **Le Streghe**, Rua dos Pedras 201, tel. 23-6137. Top-notch fish, shellfish and pasta.

Transportation
BUS STATION: Praça Santos Dumont.

Tourist Information
Situr, Av. Jos Bento Ribeiro Dantas 3711.

SÃO PAULO
A Multicultural Economic Wonder

São Paulo is sometimes called the "locomotive that pulls the rest of Brazil." The pulse of business and the stock market throb here as nowhere else in the country. Incomes are double the national average, and the 16 million inhabitants of metropolitan São Paulo account for about 12 percent of the nation's total population. Though it is 400 years old, this megacity is in fact a typical outgrowth of rapid socioeconomic change.

In 1530, wishing to keep up with the Spanish and at long last derive greater gain from his sprawling colony than only wood and tropical fruit could generate, King João III of Portugal sent Martim Alfonso de Sousa on an exploratory expedition to southwestern Brazil. Sousa first founded the colony of São Vicente on the island of the same name in 1532, and 11 years later he established the city of Santos, which has since become Brazil's busiest shipping center for exports.

Catholic (for the most part Jesuit) missionaries, wishing to save souls for the Church and acquire manpower for the greater glory of the crown, penetrated further into the interior of the colony. On January 25, the date on which the Church celebrates the conversion of St. Paul, Manuel da Nóbrega and Josê de Anchieta founded the Jesuit settlement of São Paulo. The year was 1554, and a museum, Casa Anchieta, now occupies and commemorates this historic site.

Lying 750 meters above sea-level and some 50 kilometers from the coast, São Paulo lies directly on the Tropic of Capricorn. The coastal mountain range, the Serra do Mar, rising to 1,000-1,400 meters between Santos and São Paulo, separates the city from the sea.

Left: The cylindrical São Paulo Hilton Hotel is a landmark of the largest metropolis in South America.

São Paulo is the most important urban industrial center in Latin America. The first stimulus to development came from the general economic expansion that followed the end of World War I. The rapid growth experienced by the automobile industry during the 1950s and 1960s transformed São Paulo into the "Detroit of South America." Today, nearly every automobile manufacturer in Brazil has its operations in this city. An astonishing 42 percent of Brazil's industrial output and 21 percent of its gross domestic product are accounted for by São Paulo. The area around São Paulo is blessed with fertile soil and a plentiful water supply, and in the 19th century conditions were already found to be ideal for coffee growing.

The multicultural city of São Paulo could be described, from an economic point of view, as the "largest German industrial center," since 800 companies here, employing 350,000 workers, are financed by German capital. The city's Japanese community is the largest outside of Japan itself. Every two minutes a baby is born in São Paulo, and 250,000 people from throughout Brazil move here each year, making the state of São Paulo far and away the most populous in the country.

Thus, São Paulo is a "boomtown" of vivid contrasts: while the very rich reside in 1,500-square-meter luxury apartments, over half the population inhabits squalid *favelas* (slums).

A vast expanse of buildings spread over an 8,000-square-kilometer area contains 1,250 restaurants of virtually every ethnic and culinary description, as well as 134 cinemas, 43 theaters, 48 museums and 49 libraries. Nine thousand city buses fight their way through the congested traffic. Thirty percent of all cars in Brazil are in this city – as are one-third of all helicopters; a great help to business people with appointments. Helicopter sightseeing flights are also available for tourists, this being one of the best ways to

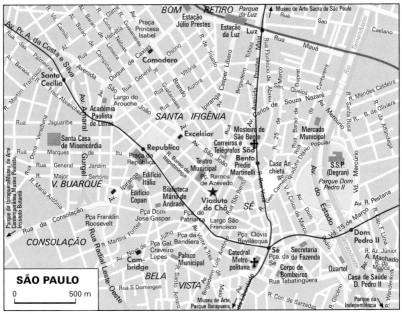

appreciate the scope of this bustling megalopolis.

The dearth of easily recognizable landmarks in São Paulo can sometimes create difficulties for visitors trying to find their way around this formidable urban behemoth. Or is it due to the "indifference towards memory and everything that lasts that is so typical of *Paulistas*?" as one Paulista author, Ignácio de Loyola Brandão wrote. It is in fact difficult to pinpoint a "downtown," although the area between **Praça da Sê** and **Praça de República** is generally so designated. For commuters, the cathedral square (Metropolitana) is a central location, because a number of subway lines (Sê station) intersect there. The Palace of Justice is also located on this perennially lively square, along with many works by Brazilian sculptors. The cathedral itself is a Neo-Gothic structure crowned by a cu-

Right: The large Japanese community in São Paulo celebrates its traditional holidays with Brazilian abandon.

pola – an architectural anomaly disturbing to no one that was consecrated in 1954 on the occasion of the 400th anniversary of the founding of the city.

Rua Boa Vista leads to the site of a former Jesuit school, **Casa Anchieta**, located just north of Praça da Sê on **Patio do Collegio**. Only a few doors and adobe walls of this historic building remain, and what was originally a monastery now houses a history museum. North of this is **São Bento**, a Benedictine cloister founded in 1650 that in 1912 was replaced by a Neo-Romanesque construction, thereby arousing the ire of many an art lover.

For a more interesting walk, proceed west from the northwest corner of Praça de Sê down Praça de Patriarca to Rua São Bento, where you can admire the **Viaduto do Chá**, the "Tea Viaduct," built in 1899. Formerly a railroad line into the Old City, it is now a pedestrian bridge that spans the Vale do Anhangabaú. Just to the north, at the intersection of São Bento and São Jão streets, stands South

America's first skyscraper, the **Predio Martinelli**. Completed in 1929, it is now São Paulo's municipal museum, and occasionally has exhibits devoted to the city's history.

Just south of the viaduct lies Largo São Francisco, where, in addition to a Franciscan monastery, there is also **São Francisco da Penitência**, a lay Franciscan church and the most aesthetically noteworthy ecclesiastical structure in São Paulo. The unusual manner in which the dome is set off from the nave makes the gilded high altar appear as though it were in the transept. The new main altar is decorated with sculptures by Manuel de Oliveira (18th century) that feature rather original iconography, such as Christ appearing to St. Francis as a seraph.

From the church it is only a short walk to Praça Ramos de Azevedo, site of the **Teatro Municipal**, a near replica of the Paris Opera House that is typical of the eclectic mix of architectural styles prevalent in São Paulo between 1903 and 1911. South of the theater, on Praça Dom

Josê de Gaspar, stands the **Biblioteca Mário de Andrade**, the largest library in São Paulo.

Praça da República

Now proceed north through the pedestrian zone and then down Avenida Ipiranga to **Praça de República**, São Paulo's most interesting plaza, especially on weekends. At the *Praça Dolce* (sweets market) that is held on Saturdays, visitors can purchase every conceivable type of homemade culinary delight (not only sweet ones), sometimes to the strains of live music. Sundays there is a crafts market, at which stamps and coins are also bartered. The pond and the generous number of trees in the plaza evoke the time in the 19th century when this was a shady resting place for thirsty livestock.

By contrast, **Aveida Ipiranga** is a harbinger of the 21st century, with its futuristic skyscrapers. One of them, the 164-meter-tall **Edificío Itália**, was commissioned by São Paulo's Italian com-

75

munity. Its rooftop restaurant and bar offer a compelling urban panorama. Just next door, two additional modernist edifices vie for attention: **Edificio Copan**, Oscar Niemeyer's sinuously curved combination apartment and office building; and the circular tower of the **São Paulo Hilton**.

Parque do Ibirapuera

For visitors with time to spare, this huge park in the southwestern part of the city (designed by Oscar Niemeyer and landscape architect R. Burle Marx) containing a lake, planetarium, open-air theater, and the **Museu de Arte Contemporânea** is a worthwhile outing. The **Assembleia Legislativa**, home to the São Paulo state legislature, sits at the northern end of the park. Meanwhile, the **Mon-**

Above: The architectural undulations of the Copan Building stand out in the São Paulo skyline. Right: Extracting snake venom at Instituto Butantã.

umento das Bandeiras, Victor Brecheret's affecting monument to the *bandeirantes* – flag-bearing pioneers who colonized Brazil's hinterland – stands watch at the top of Avenida Pedro Alvares Cabral.

Parque da Independência

This park was originally named Parque do Ipiranga, after the neighborhood it serves. Its main points of interest include the **Museu Paulista** (see following page) and the 1,600-square-meter **Monumento da Independência**, which contains 131 admirable bronze figures. It was designed in 1922 by Ettore Ximenez to commemorate the centennial of Brazilian independence, and was built on the site where the future Emperor Pedro I announced Brazil's secession from Portugal. Visitors can enter the **Capela Imperial** located inside the monument to view the tombs of Pedro I and his wife, Leopoldine. Next to the chapel stands the **Casa do Grito**, the "House of the Cry,"

where the Prince Regent held a nocturnal vigil before proclaiming Brazil's independence with the cry "Independence or death!"

Museums in São Paulo

Of São Paulo's 48 museums, the ones with fine art collections are most worth visiting. The **Museu de Arte Sacra de São Paulo** houses devotional objects from churches in São Paulo that are no longer active, as well as domestic altars and religious statues called *paulistinhas*.

The **Museu de Arte de São Paulo**, called **MASP** for short, is Latin America's preeminent art museum. Founded by the newspaper publisher Chateaubriand in 1947, the museum moved into new quarters on Avenida Paulista in 1968. The collection includes works by Titian, Goya, Rubens, Velázquez, Monet, Cézanne, Gauguin and Renoir.

Modern art devotees can visit Ibirapuera Park and its **Museu de Arte Contemporânea**, which displays works by both Brazilian painters and sculptors, as well as such masters as Henry Moore, Max Ernst, Wassily Kandinsky and Pablo Picasso.

The **Museu Paulista** (Museu do Ipiranga) is situated on a historic site on Ipiranga Hill. Both its history and natural science collections are of interest, although foreign visitors will probably be more taken with the museum's ethnology wing, where finds from pre-Columbian cultures as well as everyday objects from extant indigenous peoples are on view.

Located in a former plantation manor house where it was founded in 1899, the world famous university-affiliated **Instituto Butantã** does research on serums. The institute is proprietor of the world's largest snake farm, thousands of poisonous specimens of which – not to mention spiders, scorpions and other loveable creatures – are kept so that their venom can be extracted to make life-saving serums. Although the public is not invited to witness this procedure, visitors can, if they wish, commune with the animals in

the terrariums and burrows that constitute their habitat at the Institute.

Trains from São Paulo

A comfortable way to travel to Rio overnight from São Paulo is on the *Trem de Prata* (see *Guidepost* p. 70). The **Trem da Serra** began carrying bags of coffee from the São Paulo highlands to the port in Santos (see p. 79) in 1867. Today, the train is a weekend and holiday tourist attraction, and a leisurely five-hour, 130-kilometer trip. In the 16th century, the writer José de Anchieta described the marshy floodplain that Santos occupies as the "mouth of hell."

The trip is an interesting one from the very outset: the steel framework of the **Estação da Luz** train station in the **Bom Retiro** quarter was brought to São Paulo

Above: If you catch sight of this graceful ocelot in the rainforest, you'll never wear a fur coat again! Right: Tapirs are both aquatic and terrestrial.

from Glasgow at the turn of the century, and is one of the oldest structures in the city. On Sundays, a special train makes the 50-minute trip to the engaging railroad museum in **Paranapiacaba**.

Around São Paulo: Salve Floresta

Salve Floresta, the "Rain Forest Academy," founded in 1994, is situated 140 kilometers south of São Paulo and 14 kilometers from Tapirai in a 5,000 hectare private park in the coastal rainforest of **Mata Atlântica**, which contains 650 species of trees and 300 types of hummingbirds. Although agriculture and other activities have reduced Mata Atlâtica to four percent of its original size, this primeval forest teeming with birds is still well worth visiting, especially for nature and hiking enthusiasts. There are still wildcats – such as ocelots, for example – to be seen, and monkeys and snakes as well. The best time to visit is from March to October.

Santos

Santos (population 500,000) is Brazil's busiest port. Its wide and deep bay allows the largest vessels to dock at its six-kilometer-long piers. Situated on the island of **São Vicente**, with whose principal city of the same name (population 300,000) it has merged, Santos can be reached from São Paulo (72 kilometers away) either on the *Rodovia Anchieta* (SP 150) or via the more interesting *Estrada Velha do Mar*. Its beaches extend for seven kilometers parallel to Avenidas Presidente Wilson and Bartolomeu de Gusmão. The latter ends in the Ponta da Praia quarter, from which you can connect with a boat excursion through the **Baía de Santos**; it departs from **Ponte dos Práticos**. Coffee lovers should follow their noses down Rua XV de Novembro to **Rampa do Mercado**, where different varieties of coffee can be compared and bought at **Casa do Café**.

Guarujá, the constellation of swimming beaches favored by *Paulistas*, is on Ilha Santo Amaro, accessible by ferry from Santos. The area entices visitors with a total of 19 beaches, including those on the islands of **Pombeva** and **Cabras**. Water sports enthusiasts especially like **Enseada** and **Tombo**; calmer waters are found at **Guaiúba**.

Embu

Embu, known for its crafts, antique dealers and colonial furniture manufacturers, lies 27 kilometers west of São Paulo, and is best approached from the Régis Bittencourt highway. Many middle- and upper-class Paulistas converge on the art market held here on weekends and holidays at **Praça 21 de Abril**. The restored church of **Nossa Senhora do Rosário do Embu** on Largos dos Jesuãtas testifies to the founding of Embu in the 17th century as an *Aldeia Jesuitica*. The church's Baroque altar and wooden pulpit, the coffered ceiling in the sacristy, and the adjoining museum of religious art are worth seeing.

SÃO PAULO
Area Code 011

Accommodation

EXPENSIVE: **Caesar Park**, Cerqueira César, R. Augusta 1508, tel. 253-6622, fax 288-6146. Pool, sauna, room safes, non-smokers' rooms; **Maksoud Plaza**, Bela Vista, Alameda Campinas 150, tel. 253-4411, fax 253-4544. Best hotel on the square. Sauna, thermal pool, nightclub, excellent restaurant, non-smokers' rooms; **São Paulo Hilton**, downtown. Round building near Praça Republica. Av. Ipiranga 165, tel. 256-0033, 0800-11-8044 (toll-free), fax 257-3033. Pool, sauna, non-smokers' rooms; **Sheraton Mofarrej**, Cerqueira César, Alameda Santos 1437, tel. 253-5544, 0800-11-6000 (toll-free), fax 289-8670. Room safes, sauna, thermal pool, fitness center, restaurant on the 23rd floor with live music, non-smokers' rooms; **Transamérica São Paolo**, Santo Amaro, Av. das Nações Unidas 18591, tel. 523-4511, fax 523-8700. Has its own theater.

MODERATE: **Cambridge**, downtown, Av. 9 de Julho 216, tel. 239-0399, fax 239-0121; **Excelsior**, downtown, Av. Ipiranga 770, tel. 220-0377, fax 221-6653. Sauna, safes; **Palace Comodoro**, downtown, Av. Duque de Caxias 525, tel. 220-1211, fax 220-1283.

BUDGET: **Columbia Palace**, downtown, Av. São João 578, tel./fax 220-1033; **Flórida**, downtown, Largo General Osório 147, tel. 220-2811, fax 223-7991; **Términus**, downtown, Av. Ipiranga 741, tel. 222-2266, fax 220-6126.

Restaurants

São Paulo has an unusually large number of ethnic eateries to choose from. The Liberdade district is well known for its excellent Japanese restaurants.

CHURRASCARIAS: **Estrela do Sul**, Shopping Center Norte, tel. 290-6811; **Dinho's Place**, Paraíso, Alameda Santos 45, tel. 284-5333; **Rodeio**, Cerqueira César, R. Haddock Lobo 1498, tel. 883-2322; **Bassi**, Bela Vista, R. 13 de Maio 334, tel. 604-2375, serves choice beef and lamb.

JAPANESE: **Semba, Bela Vista**, Rua 13 de Maio 1050, tel. 283-1833. Closed Sundays. Superb quality, some ingredients imported from Japan.

ITALIAN: **Fasano**, Cerqueira César, Rua Haddock Lobo 1644, tel. 852-4000. One of the best restaurants in town; **Tartari's**, Cerqueira César, Alameda Tietê 360, tel. 853-0590. Northern Italian cuisine, shellfish, excellent wine list; **Roma Jardins**, Itaim, Av. Cidade Jardim 411, tel. 881-9445. Closed Mondays; **Dolce Villa**, R. Pedroso Alvarenga 554, tel. 3061-9882. Open evenings only, closed Sundays.

FRENCH: **La Casserole**, downtown, Largo do Arouche 346, tel. 220-6283. Superb atmosphere,

wood-paneled, closed Mondays; **La Cocagne**, Itaim, R. Campos Bicudo 129, tel. 881-5177, closed Sundays; **La Cuisine du Soleil**, Bela Vista, in the Maksoud Plaza Hotel. One of the best restaurants in the city, but of course expensive. Closed Sundays.

PORTUGUESE: **Adega Lisboa Antiga**, downtown, R. Brigadeiro Tobias 280. Open for dinner only, features fado music; **Portucale**, Vila Olímpia, R. Nova Cidade 418, tel. 828-0930. Sunday 12 to 5 pm, closed Mondays.

SPANISH: **Don Curro**, Pinheiros, R. Alves Guimarães 230, tel. 852-4712, shellfish specialities closed Mondays; **Valência**, Moema, Av. Lavandisca 365, tel. 5561-3917. Closed Mondays. Paella and the best quality seafood.

INTERNATIONAL: **Bistro**, downtown, Av. São Luis 258. Closed Sundays; **Porta do Carmo**, downtown, Rua Sete de Abril 425. Also serves Bahian dishes, closed Sundays; **Terraço Itália**, on the 41st floor of Edifício Itália. Marvellous view. Av. Ipiranga 344, tel. 257-6566.

SEAFOOD: **Amadeus**, Cerqueira César, R. Haddock Lobo 807, tel. 306-2859. Known for using the freshest oysters, crab, etc.; **Truta Rosa**, Alto da Boa Vista, Av. Ver. José Tuniz 318, tel. 247-8629, closed Mondays, superb quality trout specialities.

VEGETARIAN: **Cheiro Verde**, Cerqueira César, R. Peixoto Gomide 1413, tel. 289-6853.

Sights

Casa de Anchieta, Patio do Colégio 2, tel. 239-5722, Tue-Sun 1-6 pm; **Museu de Arte Sacra**, in Igreja da Luz, Av. Tiradentes 676, tel. 227-7694, Tue-Sun 1 to 6 pm; **Igreja da Ordem Terceira de São Francisco**, Largo de São Francisco 173, tel. 606-5297, Mon-Sat 8 am to 7pm, Sun 8 to 11 am and 4 to 7 pm; **Basílica de São Bento**, Largo de São Bento, tel. 228-3633. Gregorian chants Mon-Fri 7 am, Sun 10 am; **Edifício Martinelli**, Av. São João 35, tel. 35-1664; **Casa do Grito** and **Capela Imperial**, Parque da Independência, Tue-Sat 10 am to 5 pm, Sun 9 am to 5 pm; **Museu de Arte de São Paulo, MASP**, Av. Paulista 1758, tel. 251-5644, Tue-Sun 11 am to 6 pm; **Museu de Arte Contemporanea**, Parque do Ibirapuera, Pavilhao da Bienal, tel. 573-5255, Tue-Sun 12 to 6 pm; **Museu Paulista**, Parque da Independência, tel. 215-4588, daily 9:30 am to 5 pm; **Casa do Bandeirante**, Praça Monteiro Lobato, Butantã, tel. 211-0920, Tue-Fri 10:30 am to 5 pm, Sat-Sun 12 to 5 pm; **Instituto Butantã**, Av. Vital Brasil 1500, tel. 813-7222. Tue-Sun 9 am to 5 pm.

Rain Forest Academy

Salve Floresta: Contact address in Brazil: C.P.04, 18180-000 Tapirai, São Paulo, tel./fax 152-771393.

Buses leave from São Paulo; the trip takes two and a half hours. Stays can be booked in any good travel agency.

Transportation

TRAINS: **Trem da Serra** to **Santos** departs Sat, Sun and holidays at 8 am from Estação da Luz; return trip from Santos at 5 pm. Book at Dominus, Av. Dr. Vieira de Carvalho 115, tel. 220-2533; **Trem Tourístico** to **Paranapiacaba**, departs Sun only at 9:30 am from Estação da Luz; **Trem da Prata** to **Rio**, departs daily at 8:30 pm from Estação da Luz, tel. 825-7022. Suite for 2, R$360, double compartment R$120, meals included.

INTERCITY BUSES: For Santos and the seaside go to *Estação Rodoviária do Jabaquara*, Rua dos Jequitibás, subway Jabaquara. For all major cities inland (in Brazil) and in neighboring states: *Terminal Rodoviária do Tietê*, Av. Cruzeiro do Sul, subway stop *Tietê*, tel. 235-0322.

SUBWAY: **Metrô**, Central de Informações open 7 am to 7 pm, tel. 284-8877. Lines: Blue/*Azul*, North-South, Santana-Jabaquara; Red/*Vermelha*, East-West, Itaquera-Barra Funda; Green/*Verde*, Paraíso-Clínicas.

TAXIS: **Teletaxi**, tel. 223-1977; **Use Taxi**, tel. 578-0633.

CAR RENTALS: **Budget**, tel. 256-4355; **Localiza**, tel. 945-2133, 0800-31-200.

WALKING TOURS: Sun 9 am and 3 pm. Three hours long, begins at Praça da República.

HELICOPTER: **Helijet**, tel. 542-3905; **Líder**, tel. 5561-6511.

Post Office

Main Post Office: Praça do Correio (corner of Av. São João).

Medical Services

Clínica Albert Einstein, Morumbi, Av. Albert Einstein 627, tel. 845-1233.

Tourist Information

Informações Turísticas: Rua 15 de Novembro 347, tel. 607-5642; Praça da República 154, Posto (kiosk); *Delegacia Especializada de Atendimiento ao Turista:* Av. São Luís 115, tel. 254-3561.

SANTOS
Area Code 013

Accommodation

EXPENSIVE: **Mendes Plaza,** Gonzaga, Av. Floriano Peixoto 42, tel. 289-4243, fax 284-8253. Best hotel, room safes, pool, sauna, tennis and playing field; **Parque Balneário**, Praia do Gonzaga, Av.

Ana Costa 555, tel. 289-5700, fax 284-0475. Beach hotel, pool, room safes, good restaurant.

MODERATE: **Avenida Palace**, Praia do Gonzaga, Av. Pres. Wilson 10, tel. 289-3555, fax 289-5961; **Praiano**, Praia do Jos Menino, Av. Br. de Penedo 39, tel. 237-4033, fax 237-7478.

BUDGET: **Maracanã Santos**, José Menino, Av. Pres. Wilson 172, tel. 237-4030. A small hotel on the coastal road somewhat outside of town.

Restaurants

Cantina Liliana, Gonzaga, Av. Ana Costa 404, tel. 284-5999, Italian cuisine; **Mar del Plata**, Praia Ponta da Praia, Av. Alameda Saldanha da Gama 137, tel. 238-4253, seafood, closed Mondays; **Old Harbour**, in Hotel Parque Balneario, Av. Ana Costa 555, international cuisine; **Tertúlia**, Praia Ponta da Praia, Av. Bartolomeu de Gusmão 187, tel. 236-1641, churrascaria.

In Santos, try the *frutos do mar* in one of the seafood restaurants along the Presidente Wilson coastal road.

Transportation

TRAIN STATION: Largo Marquês de Monte Alegre. *INTERCITY BUSES:* Praça dos Andradas 45, tel. 234-2194. *FERRIES:* To **Guarujá**, from Praça da República, 6 am to 11:50 pm; *Dersa*, Praia Ponta da Praia, tel. 236-3399, 24 hours.

Tourist Information

Bondinho, Praia do Gonzaga, tel. 284-2377.

EMBU
Area Code 011

Accommodation

EXPENSIVE: **Rancho Silvestre**, Estrada Votorantim 700, tel. 7961-1911, fax 7961-1500. In a park with a lake, pool, tennis courts and a sauna. *MODERATE:* **Embu Park**, BR 116 Sul, km 283, tel. 494-5123, fax 494-3586. Bungalows on a lake, pool, sauna.

Restaurants

Orixás, R. N.S. do Rosário 60, tel. 494-3977. Brazilian cuisine. Closed Mon and Fri; **Patacão**, R. Joaquim Santana 95, tel. 494-2051. International cuisine. Closed Mon, on Sun only open for lunch.

Museums

Museu de Arté Sacra dos Jesuítas, Largo dos Jesuítas 67, tel. 494-5333, Sat-Sun 12 to 5 pm.

Bus Station

Estação Rodoviária, Rua SulanoTrindade.

MINAS GERAIS
Mineral Resources and the Baroque

Minas Gerais, Brazil's fifth-largest state, is larger than France, and with almost 18 million inhabitants is relatively densely populated. Gold and diamond prospecting during the colonial era had a profound effect on this mountainous region, not the least significant of which was that many Baroque art treasures were financed by profits from the mines.

Apart from precious stones, the state also has large deposits of iron ore, manganese, bauxite, zinc and other minerals; it also has numerous sites of historical interest to offer. The meat-processing and dairy industries, as well as food products such as coffee, sugar cane and fruit, make significant contributions to the economic well-being of Minas, as the state is usually called.

The *Mineiros*, the inhabitants of this prosperous corner of Brazil, are different from *Cariocas*, *Paulistas*, or *Bahianos*. They have a reputation for being reserved, distrustful, tight-lipped and thrifty, but at the same time hard-working and mindful of their traditions. Minas Gerais has given Brazil many of its famous citizens, among them presidents, artists, and the renowned architect Oscar Niemeyer.

BELO HORIZONTE

The city is named after the 1320-meter-high hilly ridge forming the "beautiful horizon" on its outskirts. With the exception of visitors who pass through on their way to the Baroque villages further inland, most foreigners come to Belo Horizonte on business. However, if you happen to be passing through, you should consider setting aside some time for a

Left: Soapstone vendors wait for customers in front of Aleijadinho's masterpiece, São Francisco, in Ouro Preto.

brief visit. Belo Horizonte, 800 meters above sea level, was inaugurated as the capital of Minas Gerais in 1897, replacing Ouro Preto because of its superior accessiblity to vital transport routes. Originally designed for a projected 200,000 *Mineiros*, the town quickly grew into a modern metropolis, and now has over three million inhabitants.

The interesting sights in the center of town can easily be reached on foot, beginning with **Praça da Liberdade** (Independence Square), site of the state government's main administrative building, Palácio do Governo, and the municipal library, Biblioteca Pública. The square is a meeting place for young and old, and is especially animated on market days. Fridays are for flowers, Saturdays are given over to antiques, and on Sundays craftspeople sell their work. Various regional delicacies are also available from food vendors in the marketplace.

Following Av. João Pinheiro north from the square takes you to **Museu Mineiro**, the art museum of Minas Gerais, which is located in the former senate building and features the works of Manuel da Costa Athayde, the preeminent painter of the Brazilian Baroque. This brief tour ends a short distance away from here at the **Parque Municipal**, which is situated at the intersection of Avenidas Álvares Cabral and Afonso Pena. To be found here as well are the main post office; Othon Palace, the city's largest hotel; and in the park itself, the Palácio das Artes, which houses a crafts center, theater and art gallery.

Pampulha, a neighborhood designed in 1940 by Oscar Niemeyer when JuscelinoKubitschek was mayor, is 10 kilometers north of Belo Horizonte. The **Estádio Mineirão**, Brazil's third largest soccer stadium (capacity 120,000) is located here, as are the city's small airport and an artificial lake with an 18-kilometer-long shoreline. Niemeyer designed two buildings for the lake shore,

one a casino now used as an art museum and called **Museu de Arte**; and the other a church, **São Francisco de Assis** (1943).

This revolutionary structure was hailed as a work of art when it was first built, although the conservative ecclesiastical officials of the time initially refused to let it be consecrated. The parabolic curve of the walls and roof, the free-standing bell tower, and above all the *azulejos* (tiled murals) on the choir by Candido Portinari depicting the life of St. Francis, combine to form a jewel of modern ecclesiastical architecture that the church hierarchy has also learned to treasure.

Sabará

Situated 720 meters above sea level and 25 kilometers east of Belo Horizonte, Sabará (population 100,000) is a perfect portal through which to enter the world

Above: The Fransiscan church in Pampulha, Belo Horizonte is one of Oscar Niemeyer's most successful works.

of the Minas Gerais Baroque – a venerable and glorious representative of which is to be found on Praça Getúlio Vargas: **Nossa Senhora da Conceição** dates from 1701, making it one of the oldest Baroque churches in the entire Minas area. The three-naved church features a coffered ceiling, and contains several of the Asian motifs that constitute an important contribution of Portugal's former colonies in the Far East to the many-faceted Brazilian Baroque.

Unusual from several standpoints is the chapel in Largo do Ó known as **Nossa Senhora do Ó**, the name being an allusion to the pregnancy of the Virgin Mary, to which Catholics are not allowed to make explicit reference. The decoration of the interior of this chapel (whose exterior is relatively unornamented) is typical of the early Baroque in Minas: impressive wood carvings on the choir, and exotic red, blue and gold Chinese motifs on the front wall. Aleijadinho, generally acknowledged to be the master of the Minas Baroque, was active in Sabará in the 1860's, and contributed to the facade of the Carmelite church **Nossa Senhora do Carmo** (see p. 91).

Visitors to Sabará shouldn't miss the **Museo do Ouro** (Gold Museum) in Asa da Intendência, which originally was the government office that regulated every aspect of gold mining. The museum has a scale model of a mine on display, complete with scales, panniers and gold jewelry, as well as a minting press dating from 1670.

Parque Nacional da Serra do Cipó

The first place of touristic interest visitors will encounter along highway MG 010 (which is the most scenic northbound route) is **Lagoa Santa**, a city known for its collection of prehistoric objects on display at the **Centro de Arqueologia Annette Laming Emperaire**. Even more intriguing are the dripstone formations 13 kilometers north of Lagoa Santa at **Gruta da Lapinha**, where visitors descend 40 meters to a 511-meter-long underground pathway that snakes past stalactites and stalagmites. These limestone formations came into existence roughly 600 million years ago when this region, the Rio das Velhas-Bassain, formed part of the ocean floor.

A hundred kilometers north of Belo Horizonte in the Serra do Espinhaço lies the 33,800-hectare **Serra do Cipó** national park, whose vegetation is composed predominantly of tall grasses and scrub, forming a kind of prairie called *campos de altitude* (highlands). The park abounds in wildlife, including the capuchin hummingbird, which is found nowhere else in the world but in this national park. In addition to avian species such as the field woodpecker, rare mammals like ocelots, anteaters and marsh deer also make their homes here. There is also plentiful plant life, including cacti, bromelia and orchids, as well as canyons

MINAS GERAIS

0   25   50 km

and cascades. The park can be reached from the MG 010. After turning right onto a dirt road at the Hotel Veraneio, continue for three kilometers until you reach the entrance to the park. As some of the park is on private property and is used for pastureland, visitors should be sure to close gates behind them.

Continuing north on the MG 010 through Conceição do Mato Dentro takes you to **Serro**, which is situated 255 kilometers from Belo Horizonte. This town of 20,000 is famous as the birthplace of Chica da Silva (see p. 86). The town center has preserved several of its original colonial buildings, making it a suitable locale in which to take a rest from driving and look around a bit.

DIAMANTINA

Diamantina (population 50,000) lies 280 kilometers northeast of Belo Horizonte at 1,113 meters above sea level. Throughout its history, its evocative name has given rise to fabulous legends.

Some illustrious Brazilians have their roots here as well: it is the birthplace of Juscelino Kubitschek, a former president of Brazil; and Chica da Silva, the nation's most celebrated slave, was active here. The first treasure seekers arrived in 1713 in search of gold. They found none, but the discovery of precious stones did not exactly come as a bitter disappointment, especially to the King of Portugal. When word that prospectors had stumbled upon diamonds reached the royal palace, he placed Diamantina under his direct control and forbade anyone to enter the town without royal authorization. Diamantina remained isolated for nearly a century, developing into a moderate-sized, enchanting and unique Baroque city that lies well off the beaten track.

By living dissipated lives, two administrators of the King's wealth assured themselves a place in history: Felisberto Caldeira Brant, who managed to lose his riches faster than he acquired them; and João Ferandes de Oliveira, who crowned a female mulatto slave from Serro named Chica da Silva "Queen of Diamantina." He also commissioned a castle and a church for her, and to satisfy her longing for the far-off sea, he created a lake by damming the Rio Rijuco and gave her a sailing ship, which was the scene of festive celebrations.

A walking tour around Diamantina begins at **Mercado dos Tropeiros**, the open market hall on Praça Barão Guaicui, which was originally an assembly point for expeditions into the interior. Continuing north takes you past an unremarkable cathedral, and then to **Casa do Intendente Câmara**, an extremely well-preserved 18th-century colonial structure at the corner of Ruas das Mercês and Direita. Followed eastward, the latter street leads to a house that Pater Rolim, one of the rebels in the uprising led by Tiradentes, once lived in and which is now the **Museu do Diamante.** The museum contains an unusual assemblage of

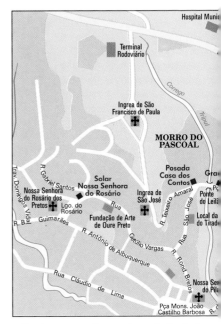

collections: secular and ecclesiastical works of art from the 17th and 18th centuries; English and Chinese furniture; and documents pertaining to the work of diamond prospectors, and the types of punishment and torture to which slaves were subjected. Further east on Praça Juscelino Kubitschek stands the august former Palace of Justice, **Casa do Antigo Forum**, which dates from the 18th century. Diagonally across the plaza rises the Franciscan church of **São Francisco de Assis** (1766), whose main altar is entirely gilded. Just north of the church on Rua São Francisco (and open to the public) is the **villa** in which President Juscelino Kubitschek once lived.

Just to the west of the cathedral and only a short walk down Rua do Carmo stands the loveliest church in the entire area, **Nossa Senhora do Carmo**, which was commissioned by João Ferandes de Oliveira for his mistress Chica da Silva. Some disagreement arose over the site at the time it was built, because church officials objected to a plan that called for

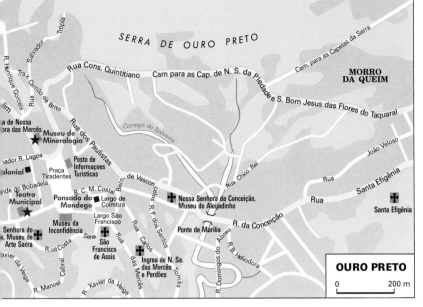

SERRA DE OURO PRETO

Rua Cons. Quintitiano   Cam para as Cap. de N. S. da Piedade e S. Bom Jesus das Flores do Taquaral

Cam. para as Capelas da Serra

MORRO
DA QUEIM

R. Henrique Gorceix

Salvador   Trópia

Trav. Camilo de Brito

Rua dos Paulistas

Corrego do Sobreira

a de Nossa
ora das Mercês
★ Museu de
Mineralogia

Posto de
Informações
Turisticas

olonial ■   Praça
Tiradentes

nde do Bobadela

Teatro
Municipal ★

Ponsado do ■ Largo de
Mondego   Coimbra

B. C. M. Costa

de Vascon Celos

R. F. dos Santos

Rua Chico Rei

João Veloso

Rua

Rua

Santa Efigênia

✠
Santa Efigênia

✠ Nossa Senhora da Conceição,
Museu do Aleijadinho

Largo São
Francisco

Senhora do ✠
a, Museu de
Arte Sacra

Museu da
Inconfidência

✠

R.ua Costa

Sena

São
Francisco
de Assis

Ponte de Marília

R. da Conceição

R. Domingos do Abreu

R.B. Heliodora

Rua Carlos

Rua

das Mercês

Tomás

xavier

da Veiga

R. Manoel

Cabral

R. Xavier da Veiga

✠ Ingrea de N. Sa.
das Mercês
e Perdões

OURO PRETO

0   200 m

situating the bell tower in a small valley. This was at the express wish of Chica da Silva herself, however, who, it is said, feared that the ringing of bells would impinge upon her early morning sleep. The most striking works of art in the church are ceiling frescos (adjacent to the gilded organ) by José Soares de Araújo, depicting in masterfully muted tints Elijah's ascent to heaven. A short distance further north on Praça Lobo Mesquita stands the **villa** Chica da Silva lived in. This striking 18th-century edifice, which is open to the public, features a *trelicas*; a terrace with a trellis-like enclosure made of wood.

OURO PRETO – Black Gold

Although there are numerous colonial gems in Minas Gerais, **Ouro Preto** without doubt constitutes the architectonic crown jewel of the entire region. Located 96 kilometers southeast of Belo Horizonte at nearly 1,200 meters above sea level, it is accessed over a winding road in approximately two hours of driving time. Viewed from the bus station above the city, the visitor marvels at the many splendors it presents to the eye. Anyone wishing to become acquainted with all it has to offer should plan to devote at least three days to doing so, as a one-day excursion from Belo Horizonte simply does not allow enough time to absorb the unique atmosphere of this small Baroque city, which has been declared a UNESCO World Cultural Heritage Site.

Founded in 1711 as Vila Rica (City of Riches), the city supplanted Mariana as state capital 10 years later. By the mid-19th century, 300,000 people were already living in the 15 towns scattered around the mining region of "Vila Rica," whose mineral riches contributed significantly to the flourishing of architecture and culture in the Minas region. A plan for the city's growth, a new phenomenon in colonial Brazil, was instituted in 1720. The city's name was changed to Ouro Preto (Black Gold) in 1823 owing to the discovery of gold deposits in black iron-oxide-rich rocks.

One man in particular left his mark on Ouro Preto, as well as other communities in this region, with his incomparable works: Antônio Francisco Lisboa, popularly known as **O Aleijadinho**, or the "Little Cripple," who was born in 1730 in Lisbon. At the age of 47, he contracted a mysterious disease similar to leprosy and consequently lost all his fingers and toes. He learned architecture from his father, Manuel Francisco de Costa Lisboa, who was also an architect, and in 1750 entered an academy of arts and crafts where he studied sculpture, carpentry, drawing and wood carving. One of his most important masters in the art of sculpture was the Lisbon-trained João Gomez Bautista.

Aleijadinho contributed two side chapels to Nossa Senhora do Carmo, which was built by his father (see p. 91), and in 1766 began work on his masterpiece, the

Above: A sculpture of Christ by Aleijadinho.
Right: The colonial city of Ouro Preto, which blends harmoniously into the narrow valley that encloses it.

façade of the Franciscan church of São Francisco. After he fell ill in 1777, it became necessary to carry him to work. Later, he had his hammer and chisel tied to the stumps of his arms and concealed his disfigured face behind a shawl. In 1805, he completed his incomparable statues of the Twelve Prophets, as well as the 64 superb sculptures at Congonhas do Campo (see p. 94). These were his last great works, and he never again accepted any large commissions. In 1812, the artist went blind. Aleijadinho died in poverty two years later.

Praça Tiradentes

Just south of the bus station, visitors meet up with **São Francisco de Paula**, the first of the city's 13 Baroque churches, from which they are treated to a wonderful panoramic view of Ouro Preto – still looking much as it did in the 19th century – and of the green hills on which it is situated. A ten-minute walk along the main street leads past Nossa Senhora das Mercês and to the main square, **Praça Tiradentes**.

A favorite meeting place for the city's youth as well as for tour groups is the **statue of José Joaquim da Silva Xavier**, who was called Tiradentes (Tooth Puller) owing to the fact that he earned his living as a dentist. It was in this square that he assembled his followers, the *Inconfidentes* (Wary Ones), and called for a rebellion against Portugal's attempt to levy a retroactive tax on the fifth part, or *quinto*, of all gold discovered. If the crown failed to collect a predetermined sum, the *derrama* was levied, which required each citizen to pay a share of the missing amount. In 1792, Tiradentes, the leader of the uprising, was hung in Rio, and his head was brought to Ouro Preto and displayed in the square that now bears his name. His statue stands opposite the former **Municipal Palace**, built by forced labor in

1800 and now the site of the **Museu da Inconfidência**, which displays documents pertaining to the unsuccessful rebellion, as well as colonial furniture, and sculptures by Aleijadinho.

Behind the monument and above the square rises the grandiose former **Governor-General's Palace**, which now houses both the university's Department of Mining and the small but fascinating **Museu de Mineralogía**. Visitors can inspect samples of the region's wealth of precious stones, as well as spectacular finds from elsewhere in Brazil. The balcony of the palace has a flower garden bursting with color, a good vantage point from which to observe the hustle and bustle of the main square of this vibrant city – which fortunately has not been turned into a museum.

São Francisco: Aleijadinho's Masterpiece

The two steep uphill streets east of the Tiradentes monument lead to **Largo São Francisco**, where large numbers of soapstone vendors eager to sell their wares await tourists on a visit to one of the most glorious Baroque churches in Latin America. Built by the Third (lay) Franciscan Order in 1765 and consecrated in 1810, the structure was completely restored in 1820. The **Igreja da Ordem Terceira de São Francisco de Assis da Penitência** is famous as Aleijadinhos's masterpiece of flawlessly harmonious design, in every respect the equal of later Baroque works by the Asam Brothers and Balthasar Neumann. The visitor's eye is initially struck by the arched façade, as well as the towers set back from it that are incorporated into the main structure; and then by the two extraordinary tympana above the portal. The upper composition depicts Francis of Assisi receiving the five stigmata from Christ, while the lower one consists of a portrait of the Virgin Mary wearing a crown, lavishly bedecked with jewels.

The inside of the church contains other works by Aleijadinho. The main altar,

made of mahogany, is a magisterial inter-pretation of one of the most frequently employed iconographies of the colonial period in Minas Gerais, the Apostles and the Virgin Mary. In the center of this altar stands St. Francis of Assisi, in whose name the church was consecrated. Also well worth seeing are the chanceries, of which there are almost always two in Portuguese churches, and the *lavabo* (basin) in the sacristy. The ceiling fresco depicting Mary as a cinannamon-skinned mulatto surrounded by angels is a work by Manuel da Costa Thayde, who often assisted Aleijadinho.

East of Praça Tiradentes

Proceeding uphill to the northeast through narrow, picturesque streets leads

Above: Brazilians often buy their vegetables from street vendors. Right: Art afficionados wishing to view the art treasures of Ouro Preto should count on some challenging uphill walks!

you to the parish church of Ouro Preto, **Nossa Senhora da Conceição**, which was designed by Aleijadinhos' father, Manuel Francisco de Costa Lisboa, and built by Antônio Dias between 1727 and 1760. Both Aleijadinho and his father are buried here, and the **Museu do Alei-jadinho**, which is also housed in this structure, contains religious art, colonial furniture and works by Aleijadinho.

An interesting stop on the way back down the hill is the 18th-century **Ponte de Marilia**, a stone bridge with benches and marvelous fountains. The pilgrimage up the long steep hill to the church of **Santa Efigênia** begins here and is worth undertaking, not only for the church it-self, but also for the chance to peer into the kitchens, living rooms, and tiny bars and shops encountered on the arduous way up. As you huff and puff, take com-fort in the fact that the locals have to struggle up this steep incline year-round. Visitors who make it to the top of the hill and to the plaza in front of the church will find the panoramic view breathtaking –

probably in the most literal sense. Built by and for slaves, this church is thought to have been financed by Chico Rei, an enslaved African prince whose discovery of a gold mine allowed him to buy his freedom, and who was subsequently revered like a king. For a brief period, from 1733 to 1745, the church was under the overall control of Francisco Xavier de Brito, who was the teacher of Aleijadinho's father. Both the vestment cupboard in the sacristy and the balustrade are made of Brazilian rosewood. The paintings on the choir reflect Chinese influence from the Portuguese colony of Macao.

Just behind the Museu da Inconfidência (on Rua do Carmo) stands the magnificent Carmelite church of **Nossa Senhora do Carmo**, which was begun by Manuel Francisco de Costa Lisboa at the same time as the Franciscan church and was completed by Lisboa's son, Aleijadinho. Next door to the church is the **Museu de Arte Sacra**, whose collection consists primarily of sculptures by Francisco Xavier de Brito, as well as sacred objects in silver.

A sight not to be missed is the **Teatro Municipal**, which dates from 1769, making it the oldest theater in Latin America. Originally called the Casa da Ópera, it constituted conspicuous proof of the burgeoning wealth of "Vila Rica." It lies northwest of the Carmelite church, and in addition to being the site of frequent concerts and theatrical performances, it can also be toured by day. A stairway leads to **Rua Conde de Bobadela**, whose shops and restaurants make it the liveliest and most frequented in all of Ouro Preto. Walk straight down this street and turn right, and you will come upon picturesque **Praça Reinaldo Alves de Brito**, with its magnificent and still-functioning fountain, Chafariz dos Contos, designed by Aleijadinho and dating from 1760. A small vegetable market is held in this square every morning. On the corner stands Casa dos Contos, a typical colonial construction that was originally used to weigh and melt down gold. It has undergone thorough restoration and is now open to the public.

Madonna of the Pillar

Proceeding to the west and, again, up-hill (via Rua São José and Rua Rondolfo Bretos) leads you to one last splendid church, **Nossa Senhora do Pilar** (1733). Although unremarkable from the outside, the single-naved decagonal structure features lavish Baroque decoration, including dragons' heads and pudgy-cheeked cherubs.

The church derives the *do pilar* part of its name from the Madonna that stands on a pillar in the main altar. The interior was designed by Aleijadinho's uncle, and the choir (1747) by Francisco Xavier de Brito. The galleries over the side altars and the vaulted coffered ceiling lend the church a serene, seamless harmony, and the Chinese influences on its decoration are reminders of the heyday of Portugese colonial power. The extravagance of the interior of the church clearly demonstrates that the gold that was donated to the Church was not included in the *quinto*, the compulsory payment made to the Crown: the colonists preferred to use the gold to beautify their churches rather than send it to the universally disliked royal family in far-off Lisbon.

A short walk down Rua Antônio de Albuquerque back towards Tiradentes Square leads to **Largo do Rosário** and **Nossa Senhora do Rosário dos Pretos** (1785), the double-ellipse Rosicrucian church that dominates the plaza. On its northern end is the city's best hotel, the completely refurbished **Hotel Solar Nossa Senhora do Rosário**. This still largely intact 18th-century structure (complete with defunct gold mine) features 37 exquisitely appointed and luxurious guest rooms, as well as an ex-

Right: The Baroque high altar of the church of São Francisco in Mariana.

clusive French restaurant, Le Coq d'Or, whose chef studied with Paul Bocuse.

MARIANA

Although only 12 kilometers east of Ouro Preto, **Mariana**, the first capital of Minas Gerais, is not often included on tourists' itineraries despite the fact that gold financed artistic wonders here as well. This quiet provincial city of 40,000 inhabitants, named in honor of Maria Anna of Austria (wife of Dom João V), is well worth a half-day's tour.

From the bus station at Praça J. Kubitschek, follow the signs marked *Centro da Cidade* all the way to the main square, **Praça Cláudio Manoel**, where you will find the **Basílica da Sé** a good spot to begin your tour of the city.

Built by Manuel Francisco de Costa Lisboa between 1711 and 1760, the magnificence of this structure – whose façade is by Aleijadinho – testifies to the city's former importance as the first bishopric of the state of Minas Gerais. The wooden cupola spanning the choir is by an anonymous artist, and the painting of *The Baptism of Christ* is by Athayde. On Fridays at 11 a.m. and Sundays at noon, concerts are given on the German organ, which dates from 1701 and is overlaid with Chinese ornamentation.

Just to the left of the church is a structure with a richly-decorated façade, copestone windows and capitals: the **Casa Capitular**. Built in 1771, it now serves as the **Museu Arquidiocesano** (Archdiocese Museum) and contains 18th- and 19th-century religious art. Works by Aleijadinho and Athayde are also on display here.

After proceeding down Rua São Francisco past the **Casa do Conde de Assumar**, the former Governor-General's palace built in 1715, you arrive at a superb group of buildings on the **Praça João Pinheiro**. The **Casa de Câmara e Cadeia**, today the prefectorial seat, was

built in 1768 and originally had a dual function – it served as the administrative center for the colonial government and as a prison. One of the most interesting of its kind in Brazil, the building (especially its front staircase) reflects influences from northern Portuguese architecture. On this square, too, the architectural identical twins of **São Francisco de Assis** and **Nossa Senhora do Carmo**, the former Franciscan and the latter Carmelite, stand opposite each other. The Franciscan church was begun in 1763; work on the Carmelite structure was initiated 20 years later. The tympanum above the portal depicting São Francisco is by Aleijadinho. Both of these single-naved structures have Doric pilasters on their towers, but only above the highest ledge, and it is this element that differentiates them: the Franciscan church's towers are broad and angular, while the Carmelite's are round.

Four kilometers from Mariana in the direction of Ouro Preto lies **Mina da Passagem**, a gold mine that was aban-

doned in 1985 and which is now the property of the Mineralogical Society of Passagem, itself founded in 1819 by the German geologist Ludwig Wilhelm Baron von Eschwege. A tour guide shows visitors around the natural lakes and tunnels that comprise the 15-square-kilometer area of the mine, which is 120 meters underground. Nowadays, women are allowed to visit the mine, although this was not the case when it was active, owing to a prospectors' superstition that women bring bad luck by day.

CONGONHAS DO CAMPO

Congonhas do Campo, 83 kilometers south of Belo Horizonte, is justifiably proud of its Baroque basilica, which has been declared a UNESCO World Heritage Site. No art lover should miss the opportunity to savor this masterpiece by the incomparable Aleijadinho!

It is inadvisable to try to pack Congonhas and Ouro Preto into a one-day outing, as there are simply too many

places to see that ought not to be missed. Visitors traveling by car from Rio (350 kilometers away) can reach the city from the BR 040. The city's name is derived from *Luxemburgia polyandra*, a common plant known in Portuguese as *congonhas do campo*. The pilgrimage church of Senhor Bom Jesus de Matosinhos is visible from quite a distance away, and the Via Sacra, which leads up to it, was designed as a Way of the Cross by Aleijadinho.

Aleijadinho's Way of the Cross

Beginning in 1797, Aleijadinho, seriously ill and badly disfigured (but aided by his assistants), worked furiously on the 64 mahogany figures that adorn the six chapels on the **Via Sacra**. Although the statues can now only be viewed through wooden grillwork, the artistic perfection of the faces of Jesus and the

Above: Aleijadinho's Twelve Prophets greet arriving pilgrims. Right: The basilica of Bom Jesus de Matosinhos in Congonhas.

Apostles can still be appreciated, as can the larger-than-life cruelty of the soldiers. The figures were painted in vivid hues by Francisco Xavier Carneiro and other artists. Manuel da Costa Athayde brought Aleijadinho's long creative pilgrimage to completion with his sensitive use of colors on the figures representing the Last Supper, the Passion and the Crucifixion. Beginning at the bottom of Maranhão, the steep hill that leads up to the basilica, the visitor encounters the Last Supper, the Mount of Olives, the Capture, Derision, the Crown of Thorns, the Bearing of the Cross, and in the sixth chapel, the Crucifixion.

Moved to silence and wonder on the staircase of **Basílica Senhor Bom Jesus de Matosinhos**, one is completely captivated by the figures of Josea and Jeremiah. These soapstone sculptures are two of the **Twelve Prophets**, Aleijadinho's last masterpieces, which he and his workers created between 1800 and 1805. One helper, Maurício, was crushed to death by a statue, but Aleijadinho continued to work like one possessed, strapped to a wooden scaffolding, with hammer and chisel attached to the stumps of his arms. The figures, which vary in size, look as though they have stepped directly from the pages of the Old Testament, their very souls visible in their faces. After Hosea and Jeremiah come Baruch and Ezekiel; at the bottom of the steps, Daniel and Hosea; on the terrace to the left Jonah, Obadiah and Amos; and to the right Joel, Habakkuk and Nahum. The spirit of the Baroque is fully in evidence here, in the harmony of the church, the forecourt with the prophets, and the Stations of the Cross.

The basilica owes its existence to Feliciano Mendes, a descendant of the royal House of Bragança who believed that Jesus of Matosinho had cured him of a serious disease, and who consequently took a solemn vow that he would commission a church in his honor. After

spending years amassing the necessary funds, work began on the church in 1758, and it was completed in only three years. Ever since, pilgrims, most of them hoping to be cured of a disease, have come from every corner of Brazil on September 14, the anniversary of the miracle cure. Many visitors also come to the church throughout the year to marvel at the last great work of the "little cripple."

SÃO JOÃO DEL REI

Two hundred kilometers south of Belo Horizonte, São João del Rei (population 75,000) is the southernmost Baroque city in Minas Gerais. *Bandeirantes* from São Paulo (cf. p. 22) discovered gold and founded the first settlement here in the early 18th century. The town's most famous native son is Tancredo Neves, who in 1984 became the first democratically elected president of Brazil following 18 years of military rule. A **memorial** was built in his honor near the historic **Ponte do Rosário**, one of three stone bridges

that spans the Corrego do Lenheiro, the brook that babbles through the town. Unlike Ouro Preto, São João has been extensively industrialized, which has greatly changed its character.

Among the most interesting sights are the church of **São Francisco de Assis** at Praça Frei Orlando. Built in 1774 according to a plan by Aleijadinho, the convex form of the single-naved church and the round towers that are incorporated into the façade make a singular and striking impression. Aleijadinho's exuberantly decorated portal featuring the Virgin Mary wearing a crown, as well as volutes and cherubs (all in soapstone), bear witness to the virtuosity of this great artist.

Several of São João's secular structures are also worth visiting, in particular the colonial mansions that originally belonged to prosperous families. In close proximity to the Franciscan church, at number 174 Ruá José Maria Xavier, stands the baronial manor **Solar do Barão de São João del Rei**. Also worth a visit is the manor house called **Solar da**

Baronesa de Itaverava, as well as the monumental fountain dating from the 19th century. Both of these structures are on Largo do Carmo, near the Carmelite church.

TIRADENTES

The town of **Tiradentes** (population 10,000), which was originally called Arraial Santo Antônio, is only 14 kilometers from São João del Rei. After Brazil became independent, the town was renamed in honor of its illustrious native son, the "tooth puller" (*tiradentes*) and martyr to the cause of independence, José Joaquim da Silva Xavier. The history of the rebellion he led is documented in the **Museu Padre Toledo**, located in the former home of Father Toledo, one of the co-conspirators in the revolt. Next door stands an 18th-century colonial building in mint condition that now houses the **Casa da Cultura**.

A little farther down Rua Toledo is the parish church of **Santo Antônio**. Begun in 1710, the gilding on its seven altars is among the most elaborate in Brazil. It also contains an over 200-year-old (and, thanks to German financial assistance, recently restored) organ from Porto, Portugal.

Three blocks north of the church an intriguing 18th-century fountain, **Chafariz de São José**, delivers water from three spouts that are differentiated by function: one is for people to drink from, a second is for washing, and a third for thirsty beasts of burden.

Visitors wishing to devote more than one day to an excursion from Belo Horizonte to São João and Tiradentes should consider spending the night in more tranquil Tiradentes. Highly recommended for this purpose is the punctiliously restored colonial-style guest house **Solar da Ponte**, whose 14 rooms offer visitors an unbeatable combination of comfort and style.

BELO HORIZONTE
Area Code 031
Accommodation

MODERATE: **Merit Plaza**, R. dos Tamoios 341, tel. 201-9000, fax 271-5700. Good location, room safes; **Othon Palace**, Av. Afonso Pena 1050, tel. 273-3844, fax 212-2318, centrally located at the Parque Municipal, large rooms, pool, sauna; **Palmeiras da Liberdade**, R. Sergipe 893, tel./fax 261-7422; **Serrana Palace**, R. dos Goitacazes 450, tel. 201-9955, fax 273-8085, pool, sauna.

BUDGET: **Ambassy**, R. dos Caetés 633, tel. 201-0222, fax 201-3108; **Comodoro Tourist**, R. dos Carijós 508, tel. 201-5522, fax 201-5843.

Restaurants

CHURRASCARIAS: **Cervejaria Brasil**, Funcionários, R. dos Aimorés 78, tel. 225-1099; **Cia do Boi**, R. Paraíba 1041, tel. 261-6949, evenings only.

ITALIAN: **Splendido**, R. Levindo Lopes 251, tel. 281-3367, good atmosphere, excellent cooking.

PORTUGESE: **Portugália**, Savassi, R. Tom de Souza 981, tel. 261-4273, Mon-Fri 8 pm to midnight, Sat noon to 1 am, on Sundays only open for lunch, family-owned.

SEAFOOD: **Marlin**, Savassi, R. Sta. Rita Durão 420, tel. 225-2128, closed Mondays.

Museums

Museu Mineiro, Av. João Pinheiro 342, tel. 269-1168, Tue-Fri 11:30 am to 5 pm, Sat/Sun 10 am to 4 pm. **Palácio das Artes**, Av. Afonso Pena 1537, tel. 237-7333, daily 9 am to 9 pm.

Bus Station

Praça Rio Branco, tel. 201-8111.

Post Office

Correios, Praça Afonso Arinos.

Tourist Information

Belotur, Rua Tupis 149, tel. 220-1310.

DIAMANTINA
Area Code 038
Accommodation

MODERATE: **Pousada do Garimpo**, Av. da Saudade 265, tel. 531-2523, fax 531-2316. The only reasonably good hotel in town.

BUDGET: **Diamante Palace**, Av. Sílvio Felício dos Santos 1050, tel./fax 531-1561; **Tijuco**, R. Macau do Meio 211, tel./fax 531-1022.

Restaurants

Grupiara, R. Campos Carvalho 12 A, tel. 531-3887, regional cuisine; **Vista da Serra**, Av. Sílvio Felício dos Santos 1050, tel. 531-1392, int'l cuisine.

Sights

Museu do Diamante, R. Direita, tel. 531-1382, Tue-Fri 12 to 5:30 pm, Sun 9 am to noon; **Casa de Juscelino Kubitschek**, R. São Francisco, tel. 031-531-3607, Tue-Sat 9 am to 5 pm, Sun 9 am to 1 pm;

Casa de Chica da Silva, Praça Lobo Mesquita, Mon-Fri 12 to 6 pm.

Bus Station

Estação Rodoviária, Largo Dom João, tel. 531-1471.

Tourist Information

Casa da Cultura, Praça Antônio Eulálio 53, tel. 531-1636.

OURO PRETO
Area Code 031

Accommodation

EXPENSIVE: **Pousada do Monndego**, Largo de Coimbra 38, tel. 551-2040, fax 551-3094. Centrally located next to the Fransiscan church. Pleasant rooms, friendly atmosphere, somewhat noisy; **Solar Nossa Senhora do Rosário**, R. Getúlio Vargas 270, tel. 551-5200, fax 551-4288. Colonial atmosphere with modern comforts. Tastefully appointed rooms, sauna, room safes, non-smokers' rooms. *MODERATE:* **Grande Hotel**, R. Sen. Rocha Lagoa 164, tel. 551-1488, fax 551-1612, nice view; **Pousada Casa Grande**, R. Cons. Quintiliano 96, tel./fax 551-4314. *BUDGET:* **Colonial**, Travessia Pe. Camilo Veloso 26, tel. 551-3133, fax 551-3361; **Pousada Casa dos Contos**, R. Camilo de Brito 21, tel. 551-1148, fax 551-2160.

Restaurants

Casa do Ouvidor, R. Conde de Bobadela 42, tel. 551-2141. Near the main square in a colonial building, excellent regional cooking, often patronized by tour groups at lunch time. Open daily 11 am to 3 pm and 7 to 10 pm; **Casa Grande**, Praça Tiradentes 84, tel. 551-5067; **Le Coq d'or**, French restaurant in Hotel Solar Nossa Senhora do Rosário. French chef with innovative ideas who combines local traditions and French refinement. Daily 12 to 3 and 7 to 11 pm.

Sights

Museu da Inconfidência, Praça Tiradentes, tel. 551-1121, Tue-Sun 12 to 5:30 pm; **Museu de Mineralogia**, R. Padre Rolim/Praça Tiradentes, tel. 551-1666, Mon-Fri 12 to 4:45 pm, Sat/Sun 9 am to 1 pm; **Museu do Aleijadinho**, R. Bernardo de Vasconcelos, tel. 551-3282, Tue-Sat 8:20 to 11:30 am and 1:30 to 4:45 pm, Sun 12 to 5 pm; **Museu de Arte Sacra**, Igreja N.S. do Carmo. tel. 551-1383, Tue-Sun 8 to 11 am and 1 to 5 pm; **Teatro Municipal**, R. Brig. Monsqueira, Tue-Sun 1 to 5:30 pm; **Casa dos Contos**, Praça Reinaldo Alves de Brito, tel. 551-1444, Tue-Sat 12:30 to 5 pm, Sun 8:30 am to 1 pm. *CHURCHES:* **São Francisco**, Tue-Sun 8:20 to 11:45 am and 1 to 4:45 pm; **N.S. da Conceição**, Tue-Sun 8 to 11:30 am and 1 to 5 pm; **Santa Efigênia**, Tue-Sun 8 to 11:30 am and 1 to 5 pm; **N.S. do Carmo**, Tue-Sun 8 to 11:30 am and 1 to 5 pm; **N.S. do Pilar**, Tue-Sun 12 to 5 pm.

Bus Station

Rua Pres. Rolim 661, tel. 551-1081.

Tourist Information

Ass. de Guias, Pr. Tiradentes 41, tel. 551-2655.

SÃO JOÃO DEL REI
Area Code 032

Accommodations

MODERATE: **Porto Real**, Av. Eduardo Magalhães 254, tel./fax 371-7000, pool, room safes; **Vereda Park**, R. Presidente Machado 313, tel./fax 371-4420, pool. *BUDGET:* **Chafariz Palace**, Av. 31 de Março 553, tel. 371-4295.

Restaurants

Quinto do Ouro, Praça Severiano de Rezende 4, tel. 371-7577, daily 11 am to 11 pm, regional specialties; **Cantina do Ítalo**, R. Min. Gabriel Passos 317, tel. 371-8044, daily 11 am to midnight. Italian.

Sights

Igreja São Francisco de Assis, Praça Frei Orlando, daily 8:30 am to noon. Mass Sundays at 9 am.

Bus Station

Rua Cristóvão Colombo 599, tel. 371-5617.

Tourist Information

Pr. Dr. Antônio Viegas, tel. 371-3522, 6 am to 6 pm.

TIRADENTES
Area Code 032

Accommodation

EXPENSIVE: **Solar da Ponte**, Praça das Mercês, tel. 355-1255, fax 355-1201. Hotel in a park with spacious rooms, pool, sauna. *BUDGET:* **Pousada Serra Vista**, Av. Israel Pinheiro, tel. 355-1404, fax 355-1290, pool; **Pousada das Artes**, R. São Francisco de Paula 86, tel. 355-1109, 10 spartan rooms.

Sights

Museu Padre Toledo, R. Toledo, daily 9 am to 5 pm.

Bus Station

Praça do Terminal.

Tourist Information

Secretaria de Turismo, Rua Resende Costa 71, tel. 355-1212.

MINAS GERAIS
Sights and Museums

SABARÁ: **Museu do Ouro**, R. da Intendência, tel. 031-671-1848. Tue-Sun 12 to 5:30 pm.
LAGOA SANTA: **Centro de Arqueologia**, R. Acadêmico Nilo Figueiredo 62, tel. 031-681-1958, Mon-Fri 12:30 to 5:30 pm; **Gruta da Lapinha**, km 13 on the road to *Conceição do Mato Dentro*, open daily 9 am to 4:30 pm.
PARQUE NACIONAL DA SERRA DO CIPÓ: Information: Ibama, tel. 031-291-6588. Guided tours on horseback, Pousada Canto Verde, MG 010, km 94, tel. 031-296-5298.
MARIANA: **Museu Arquidiocesano,** R. Frei Durão, Tue-Sun 9 am to noon, 1 to 5 pm; **Mina de Passagem**, tel 031-557-1255, daily 9 am to 5:30 pm.

THE SOUTH
Oktoberfest for the Gaúchos

RIO GRANDE DO SUL
SANTA CATARINA
PARANÁ
CATARATAS DO IGUAÇU

THE SOUTHERN REGION

The Southern Region of Brazil comprises the states of **Rio Grande do Sul**, **Santa Catarina** and **Paraná**. Here, between the 23rd and 33rd southern parallels, there are four distinct seasons – and sometimes even snow in winter. It is thus understandable that European immigrants, especially those of German, Austrian or Italian origin, feel at home here. They have also worked long and hard to transform this part of Brazil into both the country's breadbasket and its most productive wine-growing region.

The first German settlers, who were recruited in Hamburg, were greeted by the Emperor and his wife upon their arrival in Rio. On July 24, 1824, the new arrivals founded São Leopoldo (north of Porto Alegre), the first German settlement in southern Brazil. The Emperor's recruitment of Europeans was motivated by two related circumstances: southern Brazil was sparsely populated, and its southern borders were in need of protection. Moreover, there were ongoing boundary disputes with Argentina and Paraguay –

Previous pages: Cataratas do Iguaçu, a UNESCO World Cultural Heritage site. Left: The inhabitants of Rio Grande do Sul call themselves Gaúchos.

although not with Uruguay, which only gained its independence in 1828. Because the European settlers worked as farmers and in traditional trades, a societal structure developed that was oriented towards small farms and away from large plantations, thereby obviating the need for slave labor. In present-day Rio Grande do Sul, approximately one-third of the population is of German descent, and in Santa Catarina the figure is about 15 percent.

RIO GRANDE DO SUL

Rio Grande do Sul is the largest state in southern Brazil, and with 10 million inhabitants it is also the nation's most populous. Proud of their tradition of cattle ranching, the people of this, the wealthiest state in Brazil, call themselves *Gaúchos*, and are reputed to be Brazil's authentic "machos." The region has given the country five of its presidents, although three of them were rather unpopular military dictators.

Rio Grande do Sul has made itself indispensable to the northern states through the cultivation of rice, soybeans, corn and wheat. Manioc, tobacco and wine grapes also grow extremely well here. In addition, 80 percent of Brazil's coal reserves are found in this, the southernmost state in the region, which also accounts for close to 10 percent of the country's gross domestic product.

Porto Alegre

The "cheerful harbor" is the place where most tourists begin their visit to southern Brazil. There are also good air and bus connections from here to Rio and São Paulo, as well as to the capital cities of neighboring countries. Porto Alegre is the country's largest interior harbor, although it is not as busy as it was in the past. The city was founded in 1732 on the eastern bank of the Rio Guaíba by Portuguese immigrants. Ships leaving the harbor find their way to the Atlantic through the nearly 10,000-square-kilometer "Duck Lagoon," **Lagoa dos Patos**. Porto Alegre is more than twice as far from the Brazilian capital city of Brasília (2,100 kilometers) as it is from the neighboring Spanish-speaking capitals of Montevideo (880 kilometers) and Buenos Aires (1,060 kilometers). The city has 1.5 million inhabitants, many of whom are descendants of Italian, German or Polish immigrants. Its buildings reflect the influences of modern architecture.

The entire historic center of Porto Alegre is concentrated on a small hill called **Praça Marechal Deodoro**. The enormous Neo-Renaissance dome surmounting the **cathedral** (which was not completed until 1986) dominates the pleasant church square. Next door to the cathedral stands **Palácio Piratini**, a neo-rococo palace containing outstanding wall murals by the Italian painter Aldo Locatelli that was built in 1921 to house the offices of the regional government. At the lower end of the square is the city's most interesting edifice from an art-historical standpoint, **Teatro São Pedro**, a Portuguese Baroque structure dating from 1858. This theater, which is a national monument, was lovingly restored and modernized in 1984 at the urg-

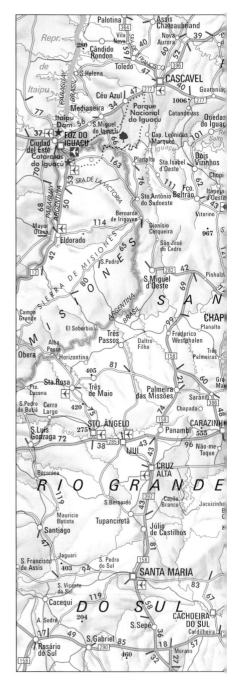

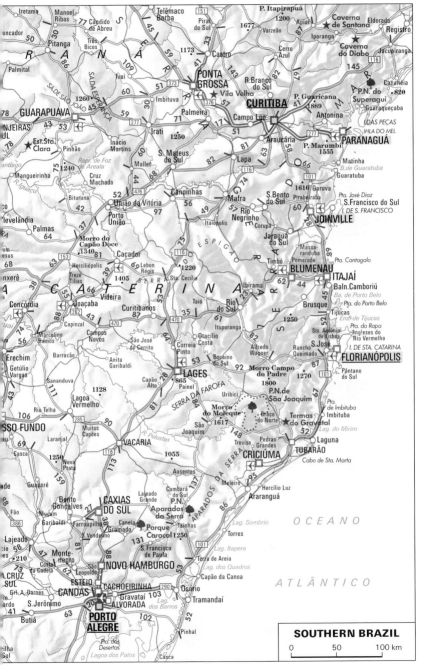

ing of Eva Sopher, a theater enthusiast of German origin.

The **Mercado Público** at Praça XV de Novembro is a busy and colorful market that is open Monday through Saturday. The structure in which it is held is a copy of the renowned Mercado da Figueira in Lisbon.

São Leopoldo

Thirty-four kilometers north of Porto Alegre lies the city of **São Leopoldo**, founded in 1824 by a group of German immigrants consisting of farmers and craftsmen, two doctors, a pharmacist, and a Lutheran pastor and his family. Early settlers were welcomed to São Leopoldo at the **Casa do Imigrante**, which is now a museum. The city's early history is also documented at the **Visconde de São Leo-**

Above: Gaúchos demonstrate their skills at the Rodeio Crioulo. Right: Itaimbezinho Canyon, in Aparados da Serra National Park.

poldo museum. A must for railroad buffs, the **Museu do Trem**, is located in the former railway station, which was built by Englishmen in 1875.

Serra Gaúcha

In contrast to the *pampa* (grassy plains) located in the southern part of the state, the **Serra Gaúcha**, which lies to the north of Porto Alegre, consists largely of a high forested plateau. It is part of the southern Brazilian shield, which is made up of two layers. The lower one, comprised of sedimentary stone, is about 250 million years old, while the upper level is basalt, which formed from cooling lava streams some 150 million years ago.

Canela, 140 kilometers northeast of Porto Alegre, is 830 meters above sea level. Winter temperatures sometimes go below freezing, and about every 20 years there is snow, which is a great novelty for Brazilians. Three kilometers to the northwest stands the 42-meter-tall and 2.7-meter-diameter **Pinheiro multisecular**,

an araucaria tree that is estimated to be at least 500 years old. This type of conifer was Brazil's most important source of wood until extensive logging of the Amazon's forests began in the 1960's. Other impressive specimens of this tree are at **Parque Caracol**, a recreational area nine kilometers away and a good place for a day's outing. It features paths that crisscross an araucaria forest, picnic sites, and **Cachoeira do Caracol**, a 131-meter-high cascade.

Eight kilometers to the west, and at the same altitude as Canela, is the town of **Gramado**, which is famous for its annual film festival in August. A regional (and tasty) attraction you can sample throughout the year is *café colonial* – brunch consisting of home-made sausage, jam, hot chocolate, cake and cheese.

Aparados da Serra National Park

Located 117 kilometers northeast of Porto Alegre at 907 meters above sea level, **São Francisco de Paula** is the best place to begin a visit to Aparados da Serra National Park, which is Rio Grande do Sul's largest natural wonder, although no buses go there and the only access is over an unpaved road. Perhaps its very remoteness has helped preserve the pristine condition of this 12,000 hectare park (founded in 1959), with its unspoiled araucaria forests and plentiful fauna, including tapirs, ocelots and red deer. The park's name is derived from its sheer cliffs, which are at their most spectacular when viewed from **Canyon Itaimbezinho** and some of which form fissures in the basalt plateau of up to seven kilometers wide and 700 meters deep.

SANTA CATARINA

Santa Catarina (population 5,000,000) is one of the smallest states in Brazil, although it is larger than Portugal. It is well known for its traditional European half-timbered houses and Oktoberfest celebration, as well as for its textile factories and splendid beaches.

Florianópolis

In 1748, immigrants from the Azores arrived on the lovely island of Santa Catarina, where they founded Nossa Senhora do Desterro. In 1823 the settlement became the provincial capital, and in 1895 the seat of the state government, at which time it was renamed **Florianópolis**, in honor of Marshall Floriano Peixoto, a hero in the war with Paraguay.

A quarter of a million people live in and around the bay, both on islands and on the mainland. The town's more than 40 beaches draw flocks of visitors from neighboring countries, especially Argentina. The beaches facing the mainland on the bays of Bahía Sul and Bahía Norte should be avoided, however, due to extremely polluted conditions. The historic center of Florianópolis is concentrated

Above: Santa Catarina's beaches appeal to younger surfers, too. Right: Blumenau is famous for its half-timbered houses, as well as for its Oktoberfest.

around **Praça 15 de Novembro**. The 18th-century cathedral is especially worth visiting, as is **Palácio Cruz e Sousa**, which still contains its original furnishings and is now a history museum. Two blocks north on Rua Deodoro is **São Francisco da Ordem Terceira** – one of the town's most interesting sights, owing to its collection of paintings by Victor Mereilles. The history of the indigenous inhabitants of this region is documented in the **Museu de Antropologia**, located on the university campus.

Ilha de Santa Catarina

This 70-kilometer-long island is best explored by car. In the north lies **Santo Antônio de Lisboa**, a historic village featuring a church, **Nossa Senhora das Necessidades**, built in 1750, as well as a sweeping view of the northern bay and the mainland that lies across from it. At the beach in **Jurerê** a little farther to the north can be found one of the island's many ruined forts, Fortaleza São José,

from which two small islands are visible. The one to the left is **Ilha de Anhatomirim**, on which there is another fort, Forte Santa Cruz, which is open to the public. The ferry leaves from **Canasvieiras**, only one beach farther up the road.

The island's Atlantic beaches are favored for their brisk surf and clear water. One of the most frequented of these lies to the northeast and is called **Praia dos Ingleses** or "Beach of the Englishmen." From here it is only 20 kilometers to **Barra da Lagoa**, located on the eastern tip of the island. Its blue houses and 18th-century Portuguese-style church, **Nossa Senhora da Conceição** (which boasts a silver church bell), make for an Azores-like atmosphere. In addition to tourism, the island's inhabitants earn their livelihood from fishing. The women of the island are also expert lace makers.

From here you have the option of taking a side trip inland to a fresh-water lake, **Lagoa da Conceição**, a nature reserve situated between the mountains that stretch across the island and its coastline, 15 kilometers from Florianópolis. Visitors can hike around the dunes and lake, rent a boat, or simply luxuriate in the beauty of the natural surroundings.

Joaquina Beach, further to the south, is a surfer's nirvana. The other beaches nearby, **Campeche**, **Morro das Pedras**, and **Armação** are also favored by surfers, and from the latter beach there are boats to the island resort of **Ilha Campeche**. West of Armação, visitors can go fishing at Lagoa do Peri, a nature reserve.

Blumenau

Blumenau has two distinguishing features, both suggested by its Germanic name: it is host to the largest **Oktoberfest** south of Munich, which attracts over one million beer enthusiasts each year (begins on the first Friday in October and lasts two full weeks). And it is also the quintessence of a Brazilian German community, complete with half-timbered houses and cafés serving Black Forest

107

cake. In 1850, a pharmacist named Hermann Blumenau from Lower Saxony crossed the Rio Itajaí on a raft with a group of German immigrants. He then proceeded to found – in the name of the "Society for the Protection of German Emigrants" – the city which now bears his name. Approximately 30 percent of Blumenau's 200,000 inhabitants are of German descent.

German traditions can also be (re)experienced in early September in Brazil during **Semana de Blumenau**, or year-round at the Gasthaus Frohsinn, the "Cheerful Inn," which serves traditional German specialties. The town also has a colonial history museum, the **Museu da Familia Colonial**, appropriately housed in the former residence of the city's founder, who died in 1899.

Above: Village blacksmith with his wife – originally from Pomerania they now live in Pomerode. Right: The woodcarvers of "Thirteen Linden Trees" are master craftsmen.

Pomerode

The majority of Blumenau's inhabitants speak only Portuguese, but in Pomerode nearly everyone is bilingual. In addition to Portuguese, various German dialects are also spoken, among them Pomeranian German. Pomerode, which is 30 kilometers northwest of Blumenau, was founded by immigrants from Pomerania. With its many well-preserved half-timbered houses and relatively affluent population of 20,000, Pomerode is, for many Brazilians, "typically" German, a label that is to some extent borne out by an overnight stay in the excellent Pension Schroeder or by a visit to the *Torten-paradies* (Cake Paradise). The **Museu Pomerano** contains numerous reminders of the harsh life led by the first European settlers.

Joinville

Despite the many well-preserved 19th-century half-timbered houses located in

its historic town center, the industrial city of **Joinville** in northern Santa Catarina is not often visited by tourists. The city (population 400,000) was founded in 1851 by Baron von Joinville after he married the sister of Emperor Dom Pedro II. The first settlers were German, Swiss and Norwegian immigrants. The city has an interesting **Museu Nacional da Imigração** located in the **Palácio dos Príncipes de Joinville**, which dates from the time of the Emperor. Well worth a visit is the **Cemitério do Imigrante**, a national monument, where visitors can see the graves of the first settlers.

The pre-history of Brazil is exceptionally well documented in the **Museu Arqueológico del Sambaqui**, which has on display the most significant archeological finds from the state of Santa Catarina. The coast can be tranquilly explored by taking a day-excursion boat to **Ilha do Mel** and **Ilha de São Francisco**, both of which have some splendid beaches. The boat leaves from Bairro Espinheiros, but only with a minimum of 15 passengers.

The tourist office has information about departure times.

Treze Tílias

"Thirteen Linden Trees" was founded in 1933 by Andreas Thaler, a former Austrian cabinet minister, and was settled primarily by Austrian farmers from the Tyrol. Located inland at an elevation of 800 meters, Treze Tílias, with its population of 4,000 and typical Tyrolian farmhouses, is reminiscent of a rambling Alpine village. Here, deep in the highlands of the **Serra do Espigão**, it even snows now and then in winter, and the wood carvings of religious icons, a specialty of the town's inhabitants, are prized throughout Brazil. The homemade chocolate, *chocolate caseiro*, as well as the wines and cheeses produced by the local Italian community, are also in great demand. The **Festa da Imigração Austríaca** commemorating Austrian immigration is held annualy in early October, and fine Austrian cuisine is served in an

atmosphere of old world charm at the Hotel Tirol, as well as at the Kandlerhof.

PARANÁ

In the state of Parana, in an area that occupies nearly two million square kilometers, live approximately nine million people, for the most part descendants of European immigrants. Most of the state lies at an elevation of 600-800 meters, ensuring a mild climate ideal for the cultivation of coffee, maté and soybeans. Paraná's shoreline is only 100 kilometers long, but some superb beaches lie just offshore on the islands in the Bay of Paranaguá.

Curitiba

It's a pity that for most tourists the Paranian capital city of Curitiba (popula-

Above: Curitiba, the "Capital of Ecology," has excellent bus service. Right: Curitba's historic town center.

tion 1.5 million) is merely a stopover on their way to the Iguaçu waterfalls, for this city, situated 900 meters above sea level and nicknamed the "Capital of Ecology," certainly merits a two- or three-day visit.

Germans, Italians, Poles and Ukranians have all left their mark on Curitiba, which has prospered since being named the capital of Paraná in 1853. The city became an ecological paragon during Jaime Lerner's tenure as mayor. A much-admired figure throughout Brazil and especially in his own region, he saved Curitiba from drowning in its waste-disposal and traffic problems. He is also responsible for the community having more parks and lakes per inhabitant than any other Brazilian city. The city's crime rate is also well below the national average, and the numerous and varied events on its lively cultural calendar are eminently affordable.

Torre Mercês, the 110-meter-high television broadcast tower, provides an excellent bird's-eye view of the city's many parks and modern buildings. Since

buses go right into the center of town (which is closed to automobile traffic), the best way to begin a visit to Curitiba is by strolling through its large pedestrian zone, which begins at **Rua das Flores** (Flower Street) and links two large squares, Praça Santos Andrade and Praça Osório. The usual stores, cafés, banks, as well as the post office, are located here, as is Curitiba's most important museum, **Museu Paranaense**, founded in 1916 in a 19th-century Art Nouveau palace, which was originally a government building. One of the most prestigious history museums in Brazil, it is particularly worth visiting for its extensive collections of artifacts of the indigenous Indian groups who originally lived in the region.

The inviting **Museu de Arte Comtemporânea** is located south of Praça Zacarias. The **cathedral** on Praça Tiradentes was rebuilt in the 19th-century in Neo-Gothic style and is not of great interest; but the magnificent 18th-century buildings of **Largo da Ordem** lie only a short distance away. Particularly note-worthy are **Casa Romário Martins** (No. 30), **São Francisco de Chagas** and **Nossa Senhora do Rosário**, the latter two being churches of the Franciscan and Rosicrucian orders respectively, as well as the town's most important ecclesiastical structures.

Two blocks northeast of this plaza is a restored mansion, **Solar do Barão**, which is now a cultural center and meeting place for art buffs of all persuasions. A few meters east lies the **Passeio Público**, a seven-hectare park with a zoo, lake and walking paths.

Two of Curitiba's attractions will be of particular interest to railroad enthusiasts: the nostalgic steam locomotive ride to Lapa on the **Maria Fumaça**, and the trip on a modern train to the coastal city of Paranaguá. This venerable locomotive makes the 60-kilometer, three-hour trip to the popular excursion destination of **Lapa** only two Sundays per month. If at all possible, visitors should try not to miss the breathtakingly scenic trip to the port city of the state of Paraná. Trains de-

part relatively early in the morning from the Curitiba train station.

Vilha Velha

The strange, at times animal-like rock formations at **Vilha Velha**, (95 kilometers northwest of Curitiba) make an appealing day trip. This state park also has **Caldeirães do Inferno**, three up to 100-meter-deep sinkholes filled with water, one of which can be explored by elevator.

Paranaguá

The 110-kilometer railroad that was built in 1885 from the capital of Paraná to the then-important port of Paranaguá once constituted an indispensable lifeline. Today, because it passes through the spectacular Atlantic rain forest, the **train trip** from Curitiba to Paranaguá is mainly a tourist attraction. The train snakes its

Above: The intriguing rock formations at Vila Velha in the state of Paraná.

breathtakingly scenic way across more than 40 bridges and alongside numerous cascades. It's only a 56 kilometer drive from Curitiba to Paranagua on the BR 277, along which there are also generous numbers of scenic glories. A more thrilling way to get there, though, especially for devotees of winding roads, is via the coast highway, **Via Graciosa**, a registered national monument that was built in 1873 and part of which follows a 17th-century bridle path. To get there, drive out of Curitiba on the BR 116 towards São Paulo, continue for 36 kilometers, and then proceed south on PR 410.

Paranaguá was founded in 1648, 50 years before Curitiba; yet today it has a population of "only" 100,000. Jesuits began construction of a theological seminary here in the 18th century, but they were driven out of Brazil before they could complete it. The structure is now home to the intriguing **Museu de Arqueologia e Etnologia**, which contains artifacts from local sites, as well as folk art. The colonial buildings of interest are on

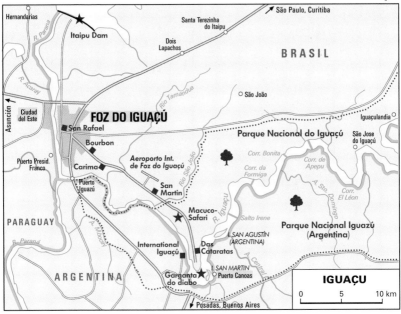

Rua da Praia, among them the **Palácio Visconde de Nácar**, now City Hall, built in 1856. Also worth seeing is the Baroque **Nossa Senhora do Rosário** cathedral, which bears witness to this port city's former prominence. It's in the center of town on Largo Mons. Celso

Offshore, and either a two-hour boat ride from Paranaguá or a 30-minute drive from Pontal do Sul (48 kilometers east of Paranaguá), is the idyllic nature park **Ilha do Mel** (Honey Island). The attractions here include not only the 18th-century **Forte Barra** (a national historical monument), but also a 60-meter-high 19th-century lighthouse. The main attractions, however, are the island's pristine beaches. Overnight stays should be planned well ahead of time, as accommodations are in short supply.

CATARATAS DO IGUAÇU
Waterfalls and National Park

Once upon a time, while watching over the Caingangue tribe, the snake god M'Boi fell in love with Naipi, the daughter of the tribal chief. But the enchanting Naipi was in love with the brave warrior Tarobá, and since the chief did not dare to deny the snake god his daughter, the lovers fled in a canoe. Seeing this, M'Boi angrily struck the riverbed with his enormous tail, creating a gigantic chasm in which the lovers died. Thus does legend explain the existence of the waterfalls of Iguaçu.

Geology's more scientific explanation is that the falls date back to the Cretaceous period, some 120 million years ago, when repeated lava flows over the older stone surface formed a basalt covering that in places is up to 1,600 meters thick. The terraces of the falls were then formed by the varying susceptibilities to water seepage – and thereby erosion – of the various rock layers.

Iguaçu – The Big Water

In Tupi-Guarani, **Iguaçu** means "the big water," an apt name for this natural

113

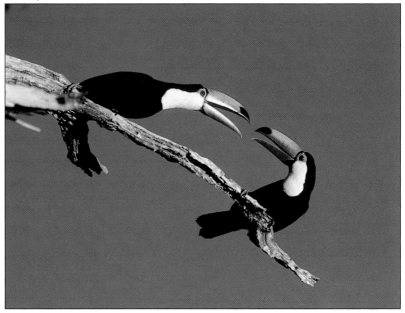

wonder, inasmuch as the falls comprise 275 cascades of varying dimensions that are 2,700 meters at their widest point and 72 meters at their highest. Up to 6,500 cubic meters per second of mostly rust-brown water come crashing over the rock, although this varies seasonally. Compared to Iguaçu, even Niagara is small, measuring "only" 47 meters in height and 1,300 meters across.

The rainy season in January and February, when the water level in the falls reaches it peak, is also high tourist season, as Argentinian and Brazilian schools are on summer vacation. Thus, during this period, it can be both very crowded and oppressively hot and humid (up to 45°C) at the falls, and there is frequent rain: total annual precipitation in this region averages 2,000 mm.

Above: A pair of toucans having an argument on a branch at Parque Nacional do Iguaçu. Right: The visitors' walkway at "Devil's Gorge," where a natural outdoor shower is gratis.

The almost surreal quantities of water rushing over the falls, the spray, and the sheer power of the river – which frequently carries away bridges and walkways in its flow – are fascinating to watch. However, visitors intent on taking photographs or videos of the falls during the high season will point and shoot mostly in vain, as the intense spray almost completely hides the falls themselves! This makes months like October and November, when there is little rain, a more inviting time to visit, as the individual cascades can be seen, along with the lush green vegetation surrounding them. And – good news for photographers – there are almost always rainbows when the sun is shining.

In addition to the many kinds of waterfowl that frequent the falls, visitors might also catch sight of a sea turtle sunning itself on the rocks. A visit during the Easter holiday period is best avoided due to the numerous jumbo jets that arrive daily at Puerto Iguazu's tiny airport on the Argentinian side of the falls, carrying

hordes of tourists who are shepherded *en masse* to the cascading waters.

The waterfalls are within the Brazilian-Argentinian **Parque Nacional do Iguaçu**, which was opened in 1939, and in 1986 was designated a UNESCO World Cultural Heritage Site. The Brazilian side of the park extends over an area of 170,000 hectares, making it the largest national park in southern Brazil. The Argentinian side on the south bank of the Rio Iguaçu encompasses an area of 55,000 hectares.

Although rarely glimpsed by tourists, many kinds of animals live in the park, such as tapirs, ocelots, capuchin and howler monkeys, as well as the agouti and paca, both of which are large tropical rodents. Less shy are the colorful toucans, various species of parrot and the caciques, a species of starling, which meticulously hang their pouch-shaped nests from palm trees. Always to be seen are dozens of black vultures in search of carrion. There are also coatis, which are increasingly losing their natural timidity and nosing around in garbage bags and even tourists' tote bags – a result of having been fed by visitors, despite the fact that it is forbidden to do so. Park regulations that require visitors to stay on marked paths unless they have a permit to do otherwise make good ecological sense and should be complied with.

Those who have the good fortune to stay at the **Hotel das Cataratas** will find the falls right outside their front door. This four-star hotel built in neocolonial style in 1958 is surrounded by the park's fauna and flora. Visitors should at least have a look at this idylically situated hotel, take a stroll in the lovingly landscaped park, or perhaps stop for a drink at the hotel bar. The best place from which to watch the sunset is the lookout tower, which can be reached via the staircase in the reception area.

The Macuco Safari

Visitors interested in the local flora and fauna should consider signing up for a **Macuco Safari**, which is a small-group guided tour through the forest: first comes a Jeep ride, then a short hike, and finally a brief boat trip on the Iguaçu River that ends under the falls. During the forest walk, the guide points out assai palms, which yield delicious palm hearts; gigantic philodendra; blooming orchids (depending on the season); and on a lucky day perhaps even monkeys and agoutis. The expert boatsmen sometimes catch sight of and point out a droll capybara (sometimes known as a "water pig"), the largest known rodent and cousin to the guinea pig.

Once all passengers have put on the mandatory lifejackets, and cameras have been stowed out of harm's way (of the spray), the wild ride begins, with all on board putting their trust in the craft's two powerful outboard motors. First there is a stop at the Isla San Martin to photograph the Argentine falls. Then the boat heads towards the huge main cascade, Garganta do Diabo, where the water plunges down with a deafening roar, and the spray furnishes what for many is a welcome shower. The boat cannot safely go right up to the main falls, but at passengers' request, the boatsman will maneuver the craft so close to one of the smaller falls that plunges over San Martin Island that no one will remain dry. This is without a doubt the most exciting way to experience the falls!

Garganta do Diabo

A 900-meter-long path from the observation platform directly below the Cataratas Hotel leads to the mighty 72-meter-high **Garganta do Diabo** (Devil's Gorge). Here, visitors can enjoy a refreshing shower on one of the footbridges, although the strength of the

Right: The man-made waterfall at Itaipu Dam is the world's largest hydroelectric facility.

spray varies with the direction of the wind (the tropical temperatures make it hardly worthwhile to rent rain gear).

An additional lookout point facing Garganta do Diabo is provided for the obligatory photo. From here, visitors can also observe the dips and loops of the sooty swift, a species of swallow that builds its nest behind the sheets of water. An elevator takes you to the road above for a small fee, but you can also take the stairs (free of charge). A short path leads upstream along the Iguaçu to a snack bar, which is located right next to the stop from which the bus to Foz do Iguaçu departs.

For photographers, the **helicopter flight** is not to be missed, although it is a bit expensive. However, the thrill of making three passes over the falls in eight minutes is well worth the price, and it is only from the air that the visitor begins to appreciate the huge and intricate scale of this natural wonder, and the lush vegetation surrounding it.

The Argentine Side of the Falls

The best close-up view of many of the smaller cascades can be obtained from the Argentine side of the falls, which is best approached from the 55-hectare Argentine national park, located 30 kilometers from Foz do Iguaçu. Visitors short on time should contact a travel agency to reserve a seat on a tour bus, whereas those short on cash can opt for the regular bus. There are two worthwhile hiking options at the falls, **El Camino Superior** and **El Camino Inferior** (respectively, the upper and lower paths). In order to appreciate the many different views of the individual falls in a leisurely way, visitors should allow 45 minutes for each of these two walks. A stairway leading down to the landing stage for the ferry to **Isla San Martin** forks off from the lower path just before the Salto Ramirez. This island features a

beach (but at low tide only), as well as an observation platform with an incomparably breathtaking view of the falls.

The side-trip to Puerto Canoas, which used to have a footbridge to the main cascade, "Devil's Gorge," is not recommended, as the bridge was destroyed a number of years ago by high water and there are currently no plans to replace it. Guided tours that go as far as the remains of the bridge are not worthwhile: in addition to being expensive they are dangerous as well, since the boat takes passengers to just above the falls, where the current can be extremely swift.

Itaipu Dam

Rio Paraná, which the Iguaçu empties into, used to plunge over Sete Quedas, a waterfall as spectacular as Iguaçu that was swallowed up some years ago by Itaipu's huge man-made lake. *Itaipu* means "singing stone," which in this case is literally true: 18 turbines have been humming away since the dam was built in 1991. The facility produces 12,600 megawatts of power that mainly supply industries in São Paulo, 1,000 kilometers distant. During the 15 years it took to build the dam, the population of Foz do Iguaçu increased tenfold. Construction of the plant was a cooperative project with neighboring Paraguay, which, being much smaller than Brazil, only uses 50 percent of the energy produced by a single turbine. Visitors can take a tour of the dam (free of charge), which is located 20 kilometers northwest of the city; there is also a film (in English) about the technology that was used to build the wall of the dam, which is as tall as a 65-story building.

Local travel agencies offer package tours that combine a trip to Itaipu with a visit to the nearby Paraguayan city of Ciudad del Este (formerly called Puerto Stroessner). However, this tour is most emphatically not recommended, as the border area is a hotbed of smuggling activities and, depending on conditions, it can take hours to cross it.

PORTO ALEGRE
Area Code 051
Accommodation
MODERATE: **Master Palace**, centrally located, Rua Sr. dos Passos 221, tel./fax 221-2212. Exclusive downtown location. Pool, sauna, heating, room safes; **Plaza Porto Alegre**, centrally located, Rua Sr. dos Passos 154, tel. 226-1700, fax 221-9706. Well-run, popular restaurant, heating; **Plaza São Rafael**, centrally located, Avenida Alberto Bins 514, tel. 221-6100, fax 221-6883. Largest hotel, well situated, excellent restaurants. Heating, pool, sauna, non-smokers' rooms; **Alfred Executivo**, centrally located near the marketplace, Avenida Otávio Rocha 270, tel. 221-8966, fax 226-2221. Small hotel, heating; **Lido**, near center of town, Rua General Andrade Neves 150, tel. 226-8233, fax 226-8009, heating; **Ritter**, Largo Vespasiano Júlio Veppo 55, tel. 221-8155, fax 228-1610, old-fashioned hotel, centrally located near the bus station.
BUDGET: **Real Palace**, Farroupilha, Rua Cel. Vicente 421, tel./fax 224-0555, somewhat noisy, heating; **Santa Catarina**, Farroupilha, Rua General Vitorino 240, tel. 224-9044, fax 224-9101.
Restaurants
CHURRASCARIAS: **Chef's Grill**, Rio Branco, R. Miguel Torres 424, tel. 330-8749, small place, good service, huge helpings; **Nova Bréscia**, Navegantes, R. 18 de Novembro 81, tel. 342-3285. House specialty *rodízio* with unusual meat dishes, such as quail, lamb, etc.
ITALIAN: **Al Dente**, Auxiliadora, R. Mata Bacelar 210, tel. 343-1841, evenings only, closed Sundays, best Italian place in town, northern Italian cooking, trout, truffle and mushroom dishes; **Copacabana**, Cidade Baixa, Praça Garibaldi 2, tel. 221-4616, closed Mondays.
FRENCH: **L'Assiette**, Moinhos de Vento, Rua Dr. Florêncio Ygartua 106, tel. 222-4978, closed Sundays. Award-winning cuisine, classic and innovative dishes.
GERMAN: **Wunderbar**, Moinhos de Vento, Rua Mq. do Herval 598, tel. 222-4967, evenings only. German cuisine with a Brazilian touch.
SEAFOOD: **Cândido's**, São Geraldo, Av. São Pedro 940, tel. 343-5079. Large menu, pleasant atmosphere; **República dos Camarões**, Floresta, Rua Cel. Bordini 156, tel. 343-5020, closed Sundays, crab, mussels, etc.
REGIONAL: **Baumbach**, São Geraldo, Av. Viena 254, tel. 346-4322, closed Mondays. Very popular place, inviting atmosphere, excellent cooking with a German touch, good service.
Sights
Mercado Público, Praça 15 de Novembro, Mon-Fri 7:30 am to 7:30 pm, Sat 7:30 am to 6:30 pm; **Palácio Piratini**, Praça Marechal Deodoro, tel. 210-4170, Mon-Fri 9 to 11:30 am and 2 to 5:30 pm; **Theatro São Pedro**, Praça Mal. Deodoro, tel. 227-5100. Guided tours may be booked in advance for Tue-Fri 12 to 6 pm or Sat-Sun 4 to 6 pm.
Transportation
RIVER OUTINGS on the Rio Guaíba leave from the gasometer in front of *Usina do Gasômetro*, Barco Noiva do Caí, tel. 11227-1529, Mon-Fri 3 pm, Sat 3 and 4:30 pm, Sun 11 am, 3 and 4:30 pm.
BUS STATION: Estação Rodoviária, Largo Vespasiano Júlio Veppo, tel. 225-8173.
Post Office
Av. Siqueira Campos, Mon-Fri 8 am to 6 pm, Sat 8 am to noon.
Tourist Information
Epatur, Cidade Baixa, Travessa do Campo 84, tel. 225-4744, Mon-Fri 8:30 am to 6:30 pm.

SÃO LEOPOLDO
Area Code 051
Accommodation
Hotel Suarez, R. São Caetano 273, tel./fax 592-7822. Comfortable, restaurant, heating, room safes.
Restaurants
Tirolesa, Av. Getúlio Vargas 1802, tel. 592-1918, closed Mondays, international cuisine; **Schneider**, Av. Getúlio Vargas 3815, tel. 592-7342, churrascaria.
Museums
Casa do Imigrante, Av. Feitoria 3140; **Visconde de São Leopoldo**, Av. D. João Becker 491, tel. 592-4557, Tue-Sun 2 to 5:30 pm; **Museu do Trem**, Praça Mauá, tel. 592-1943, Tue-Fri 9am to noon and 2 to 5 pm, Sat-Sun 2 to 5 pm.

CANELA
Area Code 054
Accommodation
EXPENSIVE: **Continental Serra**, R. José Pedro Piva 220, tel. 282-4444, fax 282-4455. Park, heated pool, sauna, tennis, heating; **Laje de Pedra**, Av. Pres. Kennedy, tel. 282-4300, fax 282-4400, largest hotel, beautiful park, wonderful view, heated pool. Sauna, massage, tennis, heating, good restaurants.
MODERATE: **Vila Verde**, Rua Boaventura Garcia 292, tel./fax 282-1156. Park, bungalows, pool, heating, playground.
BUDGET: **Villa Vecchia**, Rua Melvin Jones 137, tel. 282-1051, rooms with heating and TV.
Sights
Parque Nacional dos Aparados da Serra, tel. 251-1305 (park administration).
Tourist Information
Informações Turísticas: Praça João Corrêa, tel. 282-1287.

FLORIANÓPOLIS
Area Code 048
Accommodation
MODERATE: **Cabanas da Praia Mole**, Praia Mole, Estr. Geral da Barra da Lagoa 2001, tel. 232-0231, fax 232-0482. Wonderfully situated on a lagoon, rooms and chalets, heated pool, beauty farm, minigolf, room safes; **Diplomata**, near the bus station, Av. Paulo Fontes 1210, tel. 224-4455, fax 222-7082. Nice view of the Hercílio Luz bridge; **Florianópolis Palace**, centrally located, R. Artista Bittencourt 14, tel. 222-9633, fax 223-0300, pool, sauna; **Ponta das Canas Praia**, Praia de Ponta das Canas, Av. Dep. Fernando Viegas 560, tel./fax 284-1311. Beach hotel, boat rentals, windsurfing, fishing, room safes; **São Sebastião da Praia**, Campeche, Av. Campeche 1373, tel. 237-4066. Beach service, pool, tennis, room safes.
BUGGET: **Pousada Edelweiss**, José Mendes, Rua Luís Pedro Ferreira 86, tel./fax 223-4591. Nice view, pool; **Pousada Mar de Dentro**, Sto. Antônio de Lisboa, Estrada Caminho dos Açores 1929, tel. 235-1521. Only eight rooms, pool, convenient location.

Restaurants
With the sea at your doorstep, the natural choice at dinner time is one of the seafood restaurants in or around Florianópolis. Since the various ethnic restaurants serve primarily seafood, they have not been categorized separately.
Martim-Pescador, Beco do Surfista, 17.5 km outside of town, tel. 232-0660. Highest quality, impeccable cooking, superb grilled fish, shrimp, squid. Closed Mondays; **Toca da Garoupa**, Jurerê, R. Accacio Melo 78, tel. 282-1188, always the freshest catch, huge portions; **Mar Massas**, Morro do Badejo/Lagoa da Conceição, Estrada Geral do Canto da Lagoa 3843, tel. 232-0890. Italian pasta and seafood specialties, lovingly prepared; **Cantábria**, Lagoa da Conceição, Estrada Geral da Joaquina 755, tel. 232-0325. Spanish dishes in a rustic Brazilian atmosphere.

Sights
Palácio Cruz e Sousa, Praça 15 de Novembro 227, tel. 221-3501, historical museum. Tue-Fri 10 am to 7 pm, Sat 1 to 7 pm, Sun 3 to 7 pm; **Museu de Antropologia**, Trindade, Campus Universitário, tel. 231-9325, Mon-Fri 9 am to noon and 1 to 5 pm.

Transportation
BUS STATION: Estação Rodoviária, Av. Paulo Fontes, tel. 224-2777.
CAR RENTALS: **Avis**, tel. 236-1426; **Unidas**, tel. 236-1424.

Tourist Information
Informações Turísticas: Praça 15 de Novembro, tel. 224-0024.

BLUMENAU
Area Code 047
Accommodation
MODERATE: **Plaza Hering**, Rua Sete de Setembro 818, tel. 326-1277, fax 322-9409. Centrally located, good restaurant, pool; **Viena Park**, Vila Formosa, Rua Hermano Huscher 670, tel. 326-8888. Pool, sauna, sports complex with tennis courts, room safes; **Blumenhof**, Ponta Aguda, Rua das Missões 103, tel./fax 326-4868, pool; **Glória**, Rua Sete de Setembro 954, tel. 326-1988, fax 326-5370. Centrally located, restaurant/café, heating.
BUDGET: **Cristina Blumenau**, central, Rua Paraíba 380, tel. 322-1198; **Steinhausen**, Bairro da Velha, Rua Minas Gerais 53, tel./fax 329-2437.

Restaurants
Frohsinn, Morro do Aipim, access via Rua Itajaí 598, tel. 322-2137. Beautiful view, German cuisine, closed Sundays.
Moinho do Vale, Ponta Aguda, Rua Paraguai 66, tel. 326-3337, on the river, international cuisine.
Tiefensee, Garcia, Rua Amazonas 2322, tel. 324-0807, churrascaria. Only open for lunch on Sundays.
Cafehaus Glória, in the Hotel Glória (see above). *Café colonial* is served here (see page 105).

Museums
Museu Histórico da Família Colonial, Alameda Dq. de Caxias 78, tel. 326-6977. Also botanical garden. Daily 8 to 11:30 am and 1:30 to 5:30 pm; **Museu de Ecologia Fritz Müller**, Rua Itajaí 2195, tel. 326-6830, Mon-Fri 8 to 11:30 am and 2 to 5:30 pm.

Bus Station
Estação Rodoviária, Itoupava Norte, Rua 2 de Setembro 1222, tel. 323-2155.

Tourist Information
Informações Turísticas, Rua 15 de Novembro 420, tel. 1516.

POMERODE
Area Code 047
Accommodation
MODERATE: **Bergblick**, Rua George Zepelin 120, tel./fax 387-0952, eight rooms, lovely view, fine restaurant; **Schroeder**, Rua 15 de Novembro 514, tel./fax 387-0933, traditional establishment, pool.

Restaurants
Recanto do Salto, Rua Frederico Weege 960, tel. 387-0234. Excellent international cuisine, closed Mondays; **Prima Pasta**, Rua Hermann Weege 2500, tel. 387-0532, Italian specialties.

Bus Station
Estação Rodoviária, Rua Luiz Abry 719, tel. 387-0387.

Tourist Information
Informações Turísticas, Portal, Rua 15 de Novembro, tel. 387-0213.

JOINVILLE
Area Code 047

Accommodation
MODERATE: **Tannenhof**, R. Visc. de Taunay 340, tel./fax 433-8011, best hotel on the square, good restaurant, pool; **Germânia**, R. Min. Calógeras 612, tel./fax 433-9886. Tastefully decorated rooms, pool. *BUDGET:* **Alpinus**, Rua 15 de Novembro 3281, tel./fax 433-7770. Only 14 rooms; **Avenida Palace**, Av. Getúlio Vargas 75, tel./fax 433-8070.

Restaurants
Bierkeller, R. 15 de Novembro 497, tel. 422-1360, German cuisine, closed Sun-Mon; **Casa do Bacalhau** R. Mário Lobo 93, tel. 422-9635. Portuguese cuisine, closed Mondays; **Ataliba**, 15 de Novembro/BR 101, Expoville. tel. 422-1870, churrascaria.

Museums / Sights
Museu Arqueológico do Sambaqui, Rua Da. Francisca 600, tel. 433-0114, Tue-Sun 9 am to noon and 2 to 6 pm; **Museu de Arte**, R. 15 de Novembro 1400, tel. 422-5626, daily 9 am to 9 pm; **Museu Nacional da Imigração e Colonizasão**, Palácio dos Príncipes, R. Rio Branco 229, tel. 433-3736, Tue-Sun 9 am to 5:30 pm; **Cemitério do Imigrante**, R. 15 de Novembro 978, Mon-Fri 2 to 5:30 pm. **Estação Ferroviária**, R. Leite Ribeiro 11, tel. 422-2550. Historic train station from 1910, daily 8 am to 6 pm.

Bus Station
Estação Rodoviária, Rua Cuiabé tel. 433-2991.

Tourist Information
Informações Turísticas, Pórtico, Rua 15 de Novembro/BR 101, tel. 422-8177.

TREZE TÍLIAS
Area Code 0495

Accommodation
MODERATE: **Treze Tílias Park**, Rua Videira 585, tel./fax 37-0277. Wonderful location, heated pool, sauna. *BUDGET:* **Tirol**, Rua São Vicente de Paula 111, tel. 37-0125, fax 37-0239. 26 clean and pleasant rooms, heated pool, sauna; **Alpenrose**, Rua Min. João Cleophas 340, tel./fax 37-0273.

Restaurants
Kandlerhof, R. Videira 80, tel. 37-0276. Austrian cuisine, lunch only on Sundays; **Felder**, Av. Min. Andreas Thaler 16, tel. 37-0258, Austrian cuisine.

Tourist Information
Associação do Turismo, Rua Min. Antonio Carlos Reis 18, tel. 37-0141.

CURITIBA
Area Code 041

Accommodation
LUXURY: **Bourbon**, Rua Cândido Lopes 102, tel. 322-4001, fax 322-2282. Near the cathedral, largest hotel, pool, sauna, heating, non-smokers' rooms; **Grand Hotel Rayon**, Rua Visconde de Nacar 1424, tel. 322-6006, fax 322-4004. Centrally located, heated pool, sauna, heating, non-smokers' rooms; **Best Western Mabu**, Praça Santos Andrade 830, tel. 322-1122, fax 233-7963. Central, pool, sauna, heating, room safes, non-smokers' rooms. *MODERATE:* **Elo**, Rua Amintas de Barros 383, tel./fax 262-7131, pool, sauna; **Promenade**, Rua Mariano Torres 976, tel. 322-4341, fax 323-1593, pool, heating. *BUDGET:* **Inter Palace**, R. 15 de Novembro 950, tel./fax 223-5282; **San Diego**, Rua Ébano Pereira 405, tel. 222-2524, fax 222-8270.

Restaurants
CHURRASCARIAS: **Badida**, Batel, Av. Batel 1486, tel. 243-0473; **Devon's**, Centro Cívico, Rua Prof. Lysimaco Ferreira da Costa 436, tel. 254-7073, choice meats, *rodízio*.
FRENCH: **Boulevard**, centrally located, Rua Volontarios da Pátria 539, tel. 224-8244. Considered the best in town, Brazilian ingredients with French refinement, closed Sundays; **Île de France**, Praça 19 de Dezembro 538, tel. 223-9962. Has had the same owner for 40 years, elegant ambiance, evenings only, closed Sundays.
BRAZILIAN: **Escola Senac**, Rua André de Barros 750, second floor, tel. 322-4334. Cooking school, an excellent value for the money; **Estrela da Terra**, Mercês, Rua Lycio Grein de Castro Velloso 180, tel. 335-3492. Country cooking, closed Mondays.

Museums
Museu Paranaense, Praça Generoso Marques, tel. 222-5345, historical museum, Mon-Fri 9:30 am to 5:30 pm; **Museu de Arte Contemporânea**, Rua Des. Westphalen 16, tel. 222-5172, Mon-Fri 10 am to 7 pm; **Museu de Arte Sacra**, Setor Histórico, Igreja da Ordem, Largo da Ordem, tel. 322-1525, Tue-Fri 9 am to noon and 1:30 to 6:30 pm, Sat-Sun 9 am to 1 pm.

Sights
Torre Mercês, Rua Prof. Lycio de Castro Velloso 191, tel. 322-8080, Tue-Fri 12:30 to 8:30 pm, Sat-Sun 10:30 am to 8:30 pm; **Solar do Barão**, Rua Pres. Carlos Cavalcanti 533, tel. 322-1525. A cultural center open Mon-Fri 9 am to noon and 2 to 6:30 pm.

Transportation
TRAIN STATION: Estação Rodoferroviária, Portão 8, tel. 322-9585. For the train to Paranaguá, buy tickets five days in advance! *BUS STATION: Estação Rodoviária*, Av. Pres. Affonso Camargo 330, tel. 322-4344. *RENTAL CARS:* **Avis**, tel. 222-4777, **Localiza**, tel. 253-0330.

Post Office
Rua XV de Novembro/Rua João Negrão.

Tourist Information
Departamento de Turismo, Tel. 200-1511.

PARANAGUÁ
Area Code 041

Accommodation
MODERATE: **Araucária Mar**, Rua João Estevão, tel./fax 422-2121. Heated pool, sauna, tennis, good restaurant; **Dantas Palace**, Rua Visconde de Nacar 740, tel. 423-1555, fax 422-7075. Good restaurant.
BUDGET: **Morada de Leste**, Praia de Leste, Rua Afonso Camargo 281, tel./fax 428-2251.

Restaurants
Danúbio Azul, Rua 15 de Novembro 95, tel. 423-3255, seafood; **Le Bistro**, in the Dantas Palace (see above), nice view, international cuisine.

Museums
Museu de Arqueologia e Etnologia, Rua Gen. Carneiro, tel. 422-0228, Tue-Sun 12 to 5 pm.

Transportation
BUS STATION: Estação Rodoviária, Rua João Estevam, tel. 423-1215, in Pontal do Sul tel. 455-1341.
TRAIN STATION: Estação Ferroviária, tel. 422-8211.
BOAT OUTINGS: Embark next to the *Danúbio Azul* restaurant, Rua 15 de Novembro 95, tel. 422-0992. In Pontal do Sul, the boat is the "Nova Brasília." 30 min sailing time, daily 7 am to 7 pm.

Tourist Information
Informações Turísticas: Estação Ferroviária, tel. 423-1122.

FOZ DO IGUAÇU
Area Code 045

Accommodation
LUXURY: **Bourbon**, Rodovia das Cataratas 2.5 km, tel. 523-1313, fax 574-1110. Best hotel outside the park. Pool, tennis, cosmetics salon, four restaurants, two bars, sauna; **Das Cataratas**, Parque Nacional do Iguaçu, tel. 523-2266, fax 574-1688. Although rated only four-star owing to its lack of a sauna, this is the best address in the area. It is right next to the falls, extremely well managed, has a large pool, two restaurants, a bar, tennis, and room safes.
MODERATE: **Carimã**, Rodovia das Cataratas km 5. tel. 523-1818, fax 574-3531. Spacious grounds, pool, sauna, tennis, restaurant; **San Martin**, Rodovia das Cataratas km 13, tel. 523-2323, fax 574-3207. Conveniently situated halfway between the airport and the park. Under Argentine management, pool, restaurant, bar; **San Rafael**, Rua Almirante Barroso 1660, tel. 523-1611. In the center of town and somewhat noisy, ideal for night owls. Small pool, good restaurant; **Torrance**, Rua Manêncio Martins 108, tel. 523-2124, fax 523-2149. Well situated, pleasant rooms, pool. *BUDGET:* **Pousada Verde Vale**, Rua Engenheiro Rebouças 335, tel.

574-2975. 20-bed villa with a friendly atmosphere, for guests with modest expectations; **Bella Itália**, Av. República Argentina 1732, tel. 523-5300, fax 574-4737; **Del Rey**, Rua Tarobá 1020, tel. 523-2027, relatively quiet, near Rio Paraná.

Restaurants
Antônio Maria, Rua Alm. Barroso 1466, tel. 574-3388, excellent Portuguese cuisine; **Cabeza de Boi**, Av. Brasil 1325, tel. 523-2100. A popular churrasceria right in the center of town; **Du Cheff**, in the San Raffael Hotel (see above), good seafood restaurant; **Rafain**, Rodovia das Cataratas km 6.5, tel. 523-1177, very large steak house with live music, on the road to the falls; **Santino Pezzi**, Rua Alm. Barroso 1713, tel. 574-5969. Popular Italian place, large choice of seafood dishes.

Transportation
AIRPORT: The three large Brazilian airlines offer several flights daily from Rio, São Paulo and Curitiba. **Varig**, Av. Brasil 821, tel. 574-3889, 574-1433; **VASP**, Av. Brasil 845, tel. 523-2212, 574-2799; **Transbrasil**, Av. Brasil 1225, tel. 523-1734, 574-2029.
BUS STATION – INTERNATIONAL: Km 5 on Av. Costa e Silva, tel. 522-2680, 522-3633. Buses leave for such destinations as Argentina, Paraguay, Curitiba and São Paulo. Companies include **Sulamericana**, tel. 522-2050 and **Pluma,** tel. 522-2515.
BUS STATION – REGIONAL: Av. Juscelino Kubitschek/Av. Rep. Argentina, tel. 522-2590. Connections to the Parque Nacional. Buses leave every 30 minutes, but only go to the entrance of the park. To get all the way to the falls, take the "Cataratas" bus which leaves (and makes the return trip) every hour on the hour. The last bus back departs at 7 pm.
CAR RENTAL: **Hertz**, 523-2097; **Localiza**, 522-1608.

Post Office
Rua Rio Branco

Tourist Information
Foztur, R. Almirante Barroso 1300, tel. 574-2196.

Excursions
Parque Nacional do Iguaçu, Rodovia das Cataratas km 18, tel. 574-1687. Daily 7 am to 6 pm. A fee is charged for each day you spend in the park.
Macuco Safari, Rodovia das Cataratas km 25, tel. 574-4244, 574-3748, fax 574-4717. The trip takes about 90 minutes.
Helisul Helicopter Flights, Rodovia das Cataratas km 16.5, tel. 523-1190, fax 574-4114. Flights over the falls only (7-8 min); flights over the falls and Itaipu (35 min). Prices vary according to the number of passengers (minimum two).
Itaipu-Binacional, Av. Tancredo Neves, 10 km from Foz do Iguaçu, tel. 520-6999. Mon-Sat 8 am to 4 pm; guided tours at 9 and 10 am, and 2, 3 and 4 pm.

THE MIDWEST
Utopia and
Untamed Waters

BRASÍLIA
PANTANAL

THE MIDWEST

The **Centro Oest**, or Midwest, is comprised of the states of **Mato Grosso**, **Mato Grosso do Sul** and **Goiás**, and within Goiás, the **Distrito Federal**, the federal district which includes Brasília. With an area of 1.6 million square kilometers, the Midwest is the second largest region in Brazil, but with only six inhabitants per square kilometer is the least populous after the Amazon region.

The conurbations of Brasília and Goiânia (the capital of the state of Goiás) are quite different from each other, however, since Brasiliá is the most densely populated inland area in South America. Settlement was slow and gradual in the 17th and 18th centuries, but picked up speed during the 19th century, especially in Mato Grosso do Sul (which only became a separate state in 1979 after breaking off from Mato Grosso). The population of the region increased 600 percent between 1920 and 1980.

The first prospectors for gold arrived in Goiás as early as the 16th century, although gold fever didn't reach its peak

Previous pages: The Pantanal – a threatened animal paradise. Left: The glass roof of Brasília's cathedral creates a space flooded with natural light.

until the 1800's. Today, the mining of precious stones is as important in Goiás as iron and manganese mining are in Mato Grosso do Sul. Timber, rubber, fruit, soybeans and cotton are also significant contributors to the region's economic well-being, although livestock breeding outdistances them all: about 40 million cattle, chiefly zebus, graze the pastures of Brazil's midwestern region.

BRASÍLIA –
Futuristic Vision or Nightmare?

The surprise is visible on the face of virtually every newcomer: What happened to the fabled rain forest and the hot and humid climate? Instead, a flat savanna landscape extends as far as the eye can see. Although most visitors are duly impressed by **Brasília**, few could ever imagine actually living here: the relentlessly rectangular grid layout is too sterile and unapproachable. Brasília is located at 1,200 meters above sea level on the Planalto Central (the Brazilian central highlands) in an area surrounded by *campos cerrados* – flat sub-tropical evergreen grasslands on which 50,000 workers erected the city in only four years' time.

In 1883, the Salesian priest Don Bosco had a vision of a promised land on a wide

plain located between the 15th and 20th parallels, and indeed, Brasília's location between the 15th and 16th parallels appears to bear out this prophecy. Over the years, the confluence of the mystical and the real in Brasília has attracted to this metropolis a multi-cultural cross section of UFO researchers, clairvoyants, and sects comprising over 800 groups, leading one former minister of culture to call Brasília the "capital of the Aquarian age." There are also 1,500 temples associated with Afro-Brazilian cults, in addition to the Catholic Church, to which 90 percent of all Brazilians belong.

In 1891, a constitutional amendment calling for the nation's capital to be moved from Rio de Janeiro was passed by the legislature. But it was the high-powered and visionary Juscelino Kubitschek, the Minas Gerais-born grandson of Czech immigrants, who ultimately realized this pharaonic project. Kub-

Above: Brasília has become a center for diverse religious and esoteric groups.

itschek had already made a name for himself as governor of his home state with innovative road construction and energy projects; but the new federal capital became his life's work. In 1955, he was elected president of Brazil, the same year in which Parliament decided to build a new center of goverment. Kubitschek took office on January 31, 1956, and began laying the groundwork for construction of Brasília at the end of that year. A little over two years later, in June 1958, the dedication ceremony was held for the Presidential Palace, the first structure to be completed, and on April 21, 1960, the 168th anniversary of the death of the national hero Tiradentes, a festive inaugural ceremony for the new federal capital took place.

Situated in what was once to all intents and purposes the middle of nowhere, 1,100 kilometers from Rio, 1,500 kilometers from Salvador, and 2,300 kilometers from Recife, the **Federal District** (*Distrito Federal*) was carved out of the eastern part of the state of Goiá, so as to

126

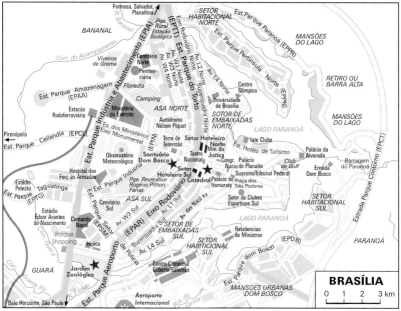

BRASÍLIA

0 1 2 3 km

prevent local politics from interfering with the business of the federal government. However, the financial outlays required to build the city set the stage for an inflationary spiral that has transformed Brazil into the world's largest debtor nation.

Most visitors to Brasília arrive at its international airport, which has become a hub for inland air traffic. Whether you are on a flight from the coast to Manaus or changing planes on the way to the Pantanal, you can tour the city's main sights in three hours. There is also a bus from Rio to Brasília that takes 18 hours. Making the trip between the two cities by car is not recommended, as the highway is extremely monotonous.

Brasília, a city built for the automobile, is not the best place in the world to be a pedestrian, as distances between the interesting sights are too long to be covered on foot. The alternatives to walking include bus tours, seats for which can be reserved in a travel agency or hotel; or simply taking a taxi from the airport or bus station to one's sightseeing destination – in which case the precise time of travel and price should be agreed upon with the driver in advance. Inasmuch as traffic jams are non-existent in Brasília, the itinerary that follows can easily be fit into a single afternoon (all sights are described in detail below).

For purposes of orientation and convenience, the best place to begin a visit to Brasília is at the television broadcast tower Torre de Televisão. From there, follow the Eixo Monumental east to the cathedral, Palácio do Itamaraty, and Praça dos Três Poderes, where the Congresso Nacional, Palácio do Planalto, Palácio da Justiça, Maquete da Cidade and the huge Brazilian flag can be viewed in a single sweeping panorama. The way back leads through the Esplanada dos Ministérios, facing which are the Teatro Nacional and the cathedral. Proceeding past the bus station and shopping centers, you come first to the residential area of Asa Sul, and then to the Santuário Dom Bosco.

127

A City in the Form of an Airplane

In March 1957, two students of Le Corbusier's, Oscar Niemeyer and Lucio Costa, won a competition for the master plan of the new city (the landscape architect Roberto Burle Marx also worked on the project). Using the cross as a basic form, they devised a stylized airplane that is easily recognizable from the air. In the plane's "cockpit" are located the executive, legislative and judicial branches of government. The ministries are in "first class," the banks, theaters and cathedral in "business class," and the hotels and shopping areas, aptly, in "tourist class." The 10-kilometer-long fuselage is bisected by the 14-kilometer-wide "wings," residential areas known as *superquadras*. The main bus station sits at the intersection of the wings and fuselage.

Above: Like a huge chalice – Brasília's cathedral with the Four Evangelists. Right: The Parliament Building and next to it the "bureaucrats' tower."

The 218-meter-high **Torre de Televisão**, visible from virtually everywhere in the city, has a 75-meter-high observation platform that offers a magnificent view of Brasília. On weekends and holidays, locally-made handcrafts are sold at the foot of the tower. The **Eixo Monumental** (Monumental Axis), at 250 meters across the widest street in the world, begins here, and leads to the city's most significant buildings.

The **cathedral**, which seats approximately 4,000 people and was designed by Oscar Niemeymer and Joaquim Cardozo, is regarded as a masterpiece of ecclesiastical architecture. In front of the ramp leading down to the church stand Ceschiatti's striking sculptures of the Four Evangelists, as well as a huge concrete disk symbolizing the Eucharist, and a towering chalice. The boldly conceived glass roof, which is supported by 16 concrete ribs, symbolizes Christ's crown of thorns. The structure's light-flooded interior projects an uplifting atmosphere of spatial freedom, and the two angels sus-

pended from the ceiling look as though they were truly floating in the air. This circular space, which contains little in the way of appurtenances, is also renowned for its superb acoustics.

The 16 government office towers devoid of embellishment that Niemeyer built on either side of the Monumental Axis spare the people who work there the hot midday sun through their east-west orientation. More distinctive buildings were designed for the Foreign Ministry and Ministry of Justice. The **Palácio do Itamaraty** (Foreign Ministry), with its fountains, artificial lake and sculpture of the five continents by Bruno Giorgi, is restful to the eye amidst the concrete and glass urban landcape. Facing the *Palácio* stands the **Ministério da Justiçia**, its entrance flanked by towering columns of water. The eastern end of the Eixo Monumental leads to the "cockpit" and the **Praça dos Três Poderes** (Plaza of the Three Powers). Legislative power is exercised in the **Congresso Nacional**, whose two branches (Chamber of Dep-

uties and Senate) meet under separate domes. The lawmakers' offices are located in the twin 28-story office towers next door. The executive branch, including the president's office, is housed in the austere **Palácio Planalto**, and just across the way the statue of Justitia stands watch over the edifice where the **Supremo Tribunal Federal** (Supreme Court) meets. This building's black glass façade framed by white platforms makes a rather stark impression.

A curious sight here is the strange, oversized **Pombal** – dubbed the "clothespin" owing to its shape – which serves as a dovecote. Next to it, atop what is probably the tallest flagpole in the world, the 286-square-meter national flag flutters in the wind. Monthly replacement of this national symbol is financed by each of the 26 federal states on a rotating basis. Urban planning enthusiasts who would like to get a feel for the overall design of Brasília can inspect the large model of the city, the **Maquete da Cidade**, located below the plaza.

To the northeast of the "cockpit," on the banks of an artificial lake called **Lago Paranoá**, stands the **Palácio da Alvorada** (Palace of Dawn), the official residence of the Brazilian president. The complex, with its large swimming pool, lovely formal gardens, and small chapel, can only be viewed from a distance and is not open to the public. By contrast, when the more populist president Itamar Franco was in office, visitors who wished to could tour the premises. Within easy walking distance of the bus station, the **Teatro Nacional**, which is shaped like a pre-Columbian pyramid, towers over the intersection of the north-south and east-west axes, symbolizing the Indian origins of Latin American culture. The **Santuário Dom Bosco**, located in Brasília's southernmost residential area, is a site that no visitor should miss, if at all possible. The entirety of this cubical space is set off by mosaic-style windows

Above: 16 shades of blue create a hushed atmosphere in the Santuário Dom Bosco.

comprised of 16 different shades of blue glass whose seemingly infinite numbers of hues, varying as they do with the direction and intensity of the light, make this the most impressive edifice in this one-of-a-kind city.

From the Santuário, a side trip to the **Jardim Zoológico** can easily be made by taxi (but be sure to agree with the driver on the time of the return trip). The zoo, famous for its large cats (leopards, pumas, panthers, ocelots), is located about nine kilometers outside the city center on an airport access road.

Outside of Brasília

About 10 kilometers northwest of the city lies the 28,000-hectare **Parque Nacional de Brasília**, with its *cerrado* vegetation that is typical of this region, as well as a stunning range of tropical flora and fauna. Visitors energetic enough to explore the park on foot will encounter such exotic trees as the *buriti* palm, or may even meet up with an army of termites industriously constructing their conical nest. Since most mammals that inhabit the savanna are nocturnal, a daytime visit will be mainly appreciated by bird lovers. Visitors sometimes have the good fortune to spot a *seviema*, a large bird of the savanna, or *nandu*, a relative of the ostrich.

History buffs should consider taking a side-trip to **Planaltina**, 40 kilometers from the park. In 1922, the cornerstone of what was to become the Distrito Federal was laid in this city, which is still administratively part of the district. Planaltina also has an interesting history museum that contains documents pertaining to the founding of Brasília.

Pirenópolis

This charming, modest-sized city, nestled at the foot of the red-hued "Pyrenees" at an altitude of 770 meters, can be reached by driving west from Brasília on highway BR 070 for 130 kilometers. Spanish immigrants named the range (some of whose peaks rise to 1,385 meters) **Pirineus**, and the village **Pirenópolis**, as a nostalgic evocation of the mountains they had left behind. The city was officially founded by gold prospectors in the early 18th century. An annual festival, the **Festa do Divino Espíritu Santo** (first held in 1819), takes place here 50 days after Easter. This event, which draws visitors from throughout Brazil, features a pageant portraying Charlemagne in the Orient, as well as an equestrian game known as the *cavalhada*. Ever since the days of the Emperor, a master of ceremonies has been chosen for each year's festivities, but this is a costly honor, as he traditionally pays for the bands and fireworks.

Pirenópolis was classified as a national monument in 1989. It has three appealing 18th-century churches, the most interesting of which, **Nossa Senhora do Rosário**, has one-meter-thick adobe walls and dates from 1728.

BRASÍLIA (Area Code 061)
Accommodation
EXPENSIVE: **Kubitschek Plaza**, Setor Hoteleiro Norte, Qd. 2, bl. E, tel. 316-3333, fax 321-9365. Well-managed hotel, spacious rooms, pool, sauna, room safes, good restaurant.
MODERATE: **Manhattan**, Setor Hoteleiro Norte, Qd. 2, bl. A, tel. 319-3060, fax 321-5683. Modern and favored by VIP's, pool, sauna; **Nacional**, Setor Hoteleiro Sul, lt. 1, tel. 321-7575, fax 223-9213. The city's largest hotel, pool, sauna; **Bristol**, Setor Hoteleiro Sul, Qd. 4, bl. F, tel. 321-6162, fax 321-2690, pool; **Bittar Plaza**, Setor Hoteleiro Norte, Qd. 2, bl. M, tel. 225-7077, fax 225-7109.
BUDGET: **Planalto**, S. Hoteleiro Sul, Qd. 3, bl. A, tel. 322-1828, fax 225-8050; **Mirage**, S. Hoteleiro Norte, Qd. 2, bl. N, tel. 225-7150, fax 322-1462.
Restaurants
CHURRASCARIAS: **Spettus**, Setor Hoteleiro Sul, Qd. 5, bl. E, tel. 223-9635, *rodízio*, very popular. *BRAZILIAN:* **Bargaço**, Setor Habitações Individual Sul, Qd. I 10/12, tel. 248-1824. Located on Lake Parano; **Papaguth**, Academia de Tênis, tel. 316-6162. *ITALIAN:* **Trovata**, Comércio Local Sul, Qd. 405, bl. C, lj. 28, tel. 244-0538; **Villa Borghese**, Comércio Local Sul, Qd. 201, bl. A, lj. 33, tel. 226-5650, closed Mondays.
Sights
Congresso Nacional, Mon-Fri 2 to 5 pm; **Palácio do Planalto**, Fri 9 to 11 am and 3 to 5 pm; **Palácio do Itamarati**, guided tours at 10 am and 4 pm Mon-Fri; **Parque Nacional**, tel. 233-4055; **Supremo Tribunal Federal**, Mon-Fri noon to 7 pm; **Teatro Nacional**, tel. 242-1447.
Transportation
BUS STATION: **Rodoferroviária**, Setor Noroeste, tel. 233-7200. *TAXIS:* **Brasília**, tel. 344-1000; **Cidade**, tel. 321-8181. *AIRLINES:* **Varig/Rio Sul**, tel. 244-3455; **Vasp**, tel. 365-1425; **Transbrasil**, tel. 365-1188; **TAM**, tel. 365-1000; **Pantanal**, tel. 365-1534. *AIRPORT:* Tel. 365-1224.
Post Office
Correios at the airport.
Tourist Information
Setur, Praça Três Poderes, tel. 223-6266.
PIRENÓPOLIS (Area Code 062)
Accommodation
MODERATE: **Pousada d. Pirenus**, Chácara Mata do Sobrado, tel./fax 331-1345. Park, pool, sauna.
Museums
Histórico Regional, Rua Nova 33, Tue-Sat 1 to 5 pm, Sun 9 am to noon; **Museu das Cavalhadas**, Rua Direita 39, Fri-Sun 9 am to 6 pm, regional culture.
Transportation
BUS STATION: Av. Neco Mendonça.

PANTANAL

Pântano means "swamp," which is what this 230,000-square-kilometer area literally is, but only from November to April, when it is flooded and becomes one large expanse of nutrient-rich mud. The **Pantanal** basin, which is only 100 meters above sea level, extends across parts of the states of Mato Grosso do Sul and Mato Grosso. However, in Mato Grosso (which means "large forest") relatively few trees now remain due to the fact that the state's livestock breeders practice slash-and-burn clearing in order to create pastureland for their livestock. Nonetheless, the Pantanal is still the area in South America with the highest concentration of wildlife. In the dry season, because animals tend to converge on the last remaining pools of water, visitors can expect to catch sight of more wildlife than during a week-long stay in the Amazon region.

Pantanal is bordered by the table mountains Chapada dos Parecis to the north, the Planalto Central highlands to the east, the Rio Paraguai to the west, and by the arid Chaco Boreal lowlands to the south. The smaller northern zone, **Pantanal Norte**, is part of Mato Grosso and can be reached from the capital city of **Cuiabá**. The best jumping-off point for the southern-lying **Pantanal Sul** is **Campo Grande**, capital of neighboring Mato Grosso do Sul.

The optimal time to visit is during the dry season, which lasts from May to September, when both the temperatures and the insect population decrease to tolerable levels. There are non-stop flights to Cuiabá from Brasília and São Paulo, and from the latter to Campo Grande; there are also flights from other cities to Cuiabá and Campo Grande, but with stopovers. The bus from Rio to Campo Grande takes about 20 hours, and to Cuiabá 30 hours. Most hotels, guest houses and farms offer minimum three-to four-day stays, nearly all including full board and transportation. Accommodations in the Pantanal range from basic to comfortable, and are well suited to the prevailing landscape and climate. The types of lodgings available include private bungalows (*cabanas*), guest houses (*pousadas*) and farms (*fazendas*). Travel agencies offer three- to four-day or week-long stays that include room and board, transportation, shuttle service and excursions. Many of these accommodations can only be reached by boat or aircraft.

In 1988, an entrepreneur from São Paulo named Robert Klabin decided to expand his horizons beyond raising livestock into the realm of environmental protection, and in particular ecotourism. In his **Refúgio Ecológico Caiman**, visitors can learn about the Pantanal's unique ecosystem. There are accommodations for up to 72 guests in the four lodges that make up the *fazenda*, which is a 236-kilometer, four-hour drive from Campo Grande. Boat trips on the **Rio Aquiduana**, rides on easygoing horses, sightseeing excursions on a flatbed truck, and walks through the forest are among the activities available at the Refúgio.

Another way to visit the Pantanal is to take a day trip from either of the regional capitals. This is not recommended, though, as the distances are long and the roads poor, especially in the rainy season, when the few available roads often become impassable. Originally, the *Transpantaneira* (Pantanal's main highway) was to extend from Poconé all the way to Corumbá. But the project was abandoned at the border with the two states at Puerto Jofre after completion of only 143 kilometers, as 126 bridges were required for this stretch alone!

Corumbá lies 400 kilometers northwest of Campo Grande at the Paraguay River on the Bolivian border, and is an excellent jumping-off point for visits to the **Parque Nacional do Pantanal**. However, as the 135,000-hectare park is

in a remote area at the Bolivian border, it is only accessible by boat, and is therefore difficult for authorities to patrol, making it a favorite haunt of poachers. Corumbá itself has a notorious reputation for being a smugglers' paradise. The town also has a Wild West atmosphere harking back to the last century, complete with gun-toting men. The Brazilian airlines Vasp, Tam and Pantaneira all have regularly scheduled flights to Corumbá.

A Wildlife Paradise in the Watery Wilderness

In the rainy season from November to April, the 175 rivers here deposit a layer of fertile mud over a 62,000-square-kilometer area. Because the region has a gentle gradient, its principal river, the **Rio Paraguai**, has a drop of only two to

Above: The rainy season transforms much of the Pantanal into swampland. Right: The spectacled cayman is a source of mineral nutrients for butterflies.

three centimeters per kilometer, taking a meditative 100 days to wend its way through the region. Thus, the flooding, far from being wild or threatening, is slow, thereby allowing people, animals and plant life ample time to prepare. Over the years, even farm animals have adapted: the Pantanal's domestic bovine, *Gado pantaneira*, a descendant of the zebu that was brought from India in 1880, has developed shorter hair because of the heat, and thicker skin as protection against insects. Even the hooves of horses bred in the Pantanal have adapted: when in water for long periods they don't rot, as do other horses'.

The great diversity of animal species in this region arises from vast differences in habitat. Savanna flood plains, dry forests and Amazon-like zones co-exist with *caatinga* (grassy plains with scrub vegetation), and with areas in which farmers are forced to dig deep wells to provide water for their livestock. A total of 80 mammal, 50 reptile, 650 bird and 240 fish species have been found here, none

of them indigenous. There are also 13 endangered species, among them the jaguar, great otter and giant anteater. The swamp deer was also on the endangered list after its numbers declined to about 7,000 in the 1970's. However, improved protective measures have increased its numbers to about 40,000. The capybara, the largest rodent in the world, is ubiquitous, and is even found amongst herds of livestock. Three north-south migratory bird routes traverse this region as well, and because it is so richly endowed with fish, the Pantanal is a veritable avian feeding paradise.

Caimans and Piranhas

The Pantanal is world-famous for its *jacaré* (spectacled) caimans, which are crocodiles that grow to a length of up to three meters. In the past, their numbers were depleted by poachers, but since the sale of crocodile leather was prohibited in Paraguay in 1993, the caiman population has risen to an estimated 10 million.

Now visitors can glimpse them from their cars, sunning themselves by the hundreds on river banks. The black howler and capuchin monkeys are indigenous to this region, as are the *nandu*, or South American ostrich, the *jabirú* (the largest known variety of stork), and the rare hyacinthine macaw (the largest known parrot). Of the many types of heron found here, the *colhereiror*, or roseate spoonbill, is most conspicuous owing to its pink plumage. The scarlet ibis makes its presence known with a loud screeching, and the cry of the turkey-like crested screamer resounds like a trumpet. Five species of brightly hued kingfisher hunt for their daily intake of fish in the rivers, and some visitors might be fortunate enough to catch a glimpse of an anaconda, a large nonpoisonous snake.

Various kinds of eagles hunt in the Pantanal as well, while the black vultures, or *urubus*, eat the carrion they leave behind. Less often caught sight of is the tapir (the largest South American mammal living in the wild), and the

various large felines including jaguars, pumas and ocelots, which also make their homes here. The rivers teem with great schools of the infamous piranha. The best-tasting freshwater fish are the *dourado* (*Salminus maxillosus*) and the huge *bacu* (*Piaractus mesopotamicus*). Birds are more numerous than anywhere else in Brazil, owing to the large schools of fish in the region's waters.

Stink Trees and Floral Splendor

The most striking tree in the Pantanal is the *ipê roxo* (*Bignoniaceae*), which displays its leafless but magnificent pink blossoms in August and September. The *buriti* palm grows on the river banks, while the water hyacinths grow in such wild profusion in the waterways that they almost choke them in places. The rivers also contain palm-covered islands called *capões* on which animals seek refuge

Above: The jabiru (a large stork) is the most spectacular bird in the Pantanal.

from riverine floods. Native to this region as well is the sandpaper tree, so called because its leaves are abrasive enough to be used for wood-smoothing purposes. The inhabitants of the Pantanal have aptly named another indigenous tree *fede-fede* (stink-stink) for the strong fecal smell it emits when its bark is scratched. Because insects find the odor of these trees irresistible, they are often planted in the farthest corner of the back yards of houses so that the bugs flock to the tree and leave the humans in peace.

Hidrovia: A Water Expressway

Fortunately still on the drawing board is **Hidrovia**, a 3,303-kilometer-long canal with a deep bed that would follow the course of the Paraná and Paraguai rivers, thereby posing a serious threat to this natural paradise. Its purpose is to provide a navigable year-round route for freighters carrying ore and grain; it would also shorten by half the time it takes ships to get from Cáceres to Nueva Palmira in Uruguay. During the dry season, vessels over 2,000 tons are now unable to navigate the river's relatively shallow channels, while smaller craft can safely do so only during daylight hours.

On January 1, 1995, much to the dismay of conservationists and ecologists, a consortium called Mercosur was founded to press ahead with Hidrovia. Opponents of the project hope that its enormous cost – US $55 billion – will sink it. Also, the question as to who actually needs this maritime superhighway has still not been answered. Mercosur's target markets are in the coastal cities, far from this underpopulated backland. And while the port at Cáceres can handle nearly one million tons of freight per year, it has never yet processed more than 27,000. Environmentalists are now pinning their hopes on tourism, which would provide the region's inhabitants with enough income to forestall this destructive project.

CAMPO GRANDE (Area Code 067)
Accommodation
MODERATE: **Exceler Plaza Amambaí**, Av. Afonso Pena 444, tel. 721-0102, fax 721-5666, pool, sauna; **Campo Grande**, Rua 13 de Maio 2825, tel. 761-6061, fax 724-8349; **Concord**, Av. Calógeras 1624, tel. 384-3081, fax 382-4987, pool; **Internacional**, Amambaí, Rua Alan Kardec 223, tel. 384-4677, fax 721-2729, pool.

BUDGET: **Iguaçu**, Amambaí, Rua D. Aquino 761, tel. 384-4621, fax 721-3215; **Palace**, Rua D. Aquino 1501, tel. 384-4741, fax 382-3604.

Restaurants
Centurion, Rua da Paz 530, tel. 721-1060. Best restaurant in the city, top-notch international cuisine with an Italian touch, open for dinner only Mon-Sat, Sun noon to 5 pm; **Casa Grande**, Rua 14 de Julho 757, tel. 383-3018, international cuisine; **Casa do Peixe**, Amambaí, Rua Dr. João Rosa Pires 1030, tel. 382-7121, seafood, only open for lunch on Sundays; **Khalil Karnes**, Rua Furnas 142, tel. 726-3715, churrasco, *rodízio*, closed Mondays.

Museums
Dom Bosco do Índio, Rua Barão do Rio Branco 1843, tel. 383-3761. Ethnological museum focusing on the Mato Grosso region, 7 to 11 am and 1 to 5 pm.

Transportation
BUS STATION: Amambaí, Rua Joaquim Nabuco 200, tel. 383-1678. *AIRPORT:* Tel. 763-2444. *AIRLINES:* **Varig/Rio-Sul**, tel. 763-1213, 383-4070; **Vasp**, tel. 763-2389, 382-4091; **TAM**, tel. 763-2438, 383-2933; **Pantanal**, tel. 763-1322, 383-3238. *CAR RENTALS:* **Le Mans**, tel. 724-7000; **Localiza**, tel. 0800-31-2000. *TAXIS:* **Coopertáxi**, tel. 761-1828.

Post Office
Av. Calogeiras/Rua Aquino.

Tourist Information
Semcetur, Rua Barão do Rio Branco, tel. 383-4112.

PANTANAL-SUL (Area Code 067)
Accommodation
Beira-Rio, 200 km west of Campo Grande on Rio Miranda, tel./fax 242-1476. 17 rooms for 3-4 persons each, restaurant, pool, boats; **Fazenda Natural Country**, 130 km north of C. Gr., tel. 625-0001. 12 rooms, pool, sauna; **Fazenda Salobra**, 211 km west of C. Gr., tel./fax 242-1162, 18 km from Miranda, 23 rooms, boats, horses; **Pousada do Pantanal, Fazenda Santa Clara**, Rio Abobral, 120 km southeast of Corumbá, transportation from C. Gr., tel. 725-5267, 231-5212. Ten four-person rooms, boats, horses; **Refúgio Ecológico Caiman**, 236 km west of C. Gr., transporation from C. Gr., tel. 242-1102, 011-883-6622, fax 011-883-6037. 5,000-hectare farm in existence since 1988, accommodates 72 guests, pool, horses, boats, photo safaris.

Boats with Cabins
Arara Pantaneira II, from Corumbá tel. 231-45888, fax 231-7103. 14 double cabins, fishing and photo safaris on the Paraguai; **Botel Pantanal Explorer II**, from Cáceres tel. 065-381-4959, three cabins, each for four persons, excursions and fishing trips on the Paraguai.

CUIABÁ (Area Code 065)
Accommodation
LUXURY: **Eldorado Cuiabá**, Av. Isaac Póvoas 1000, tel. 624-4000, fax 624-1480. Best hotel in town, good restaurant, pool, room safes; **Global Garden**, Bosque da Sáude, Av. Miguel Sutil 5555, tel. 624-1660, fax 624-9966, good restaurant, pool.

MODERATE: **Verona Park**, Várzea Grande, BR 364, 15 km out of town, tel. 684-2600, fax 684-1420, pool, sauna, reasonable; **Fazenda Mato Grosso**, Coxipó, Rua Antônio Dorileo 1100, tel. 361-2980, fax 661-1276, farm, pool, horses, boat trips.

BUDGET: **Mangabeiras**, Várzea Grande, Av. da F.E.B. 1275, tel./fax 685-3131.

Restaurants
Casa Suíça, Pico do Amor, Av. Miguel Sutil 4200, tel. 627-2077. Excellent Swiss cuisine, dinner only, closed Mondays; **Arlecchino**, Rua Cândido Mariano 874, tel. 322-4185. Italian cuisine, closed Mondays; **Cacalo Peixaria**, Sta. Rosa, Av. Lavaps 203, tel. 322-7778. Good selection of seafood dishes; **Getúlio Grill**, Av. Getúlio Vargas 1147, tel. 624-9992, churrasco; **Gaúcha**, Várzea Grande, Av. João Ponce de Arruda 877, tel. 381-2897, churrasco, *rodízio*.

Transportation
BUS STATION: Alvorada, Av. Mal. Deodoro, tel. 621-3512. *AIRPORT:* Tel. 682-2213. *AIRLINES:* **Varig**, tel. 682-1140; **Vasp**, tel. 682-3737; **Transbrasil**, tel. 682-3597; **TAM**, tel. 682-3650, 321-7947. *CAR RENTALS:* **Le Mans**, tel. 381-2821; **Localiza**, tel. 381-4827. *TAXIS:* **Alocar**, tel. 321-9777; **Colorado**, tel. 322-1121.

Tourist Information
Funcetur, Praça da República 131, tel. 624-9060.

PANTANAL NORTE (Area Code 065)
Accommodation
Cabanas do Pantanal, 42 km southeast of Pocon on Rio Piraim, tel. 623-4141. 18 rooms, pool, boats. Agency: Confiança Turismo, Cuiab, Rua C. Mariano 434, tel. 321-4142, fax 322-1353; **Porto Jofre Pantanal**, at the end of the Transpantaneira, tel. 321-0263, pool, boats; **Pousada das Araras**, Transpantaneira at km 32, tel. 682-2800, fax 682-1260, pool, boats, horses; **Pousada Porto Cercado**, on Rio Cuiab 42 km from Poconé, tel. 721-1726, 682-1300, pool, boats; **Pouso da Garça**, Barão de Melgaço, Rio São Lourenço, 35 minutes by air from Cuiabá, tel. 322-491, pool, boats.

THE NORTHEAST
Beaches and Sertão

BAHIA / SALVADOR
PERNAMBUCO
RECIFE / OLINDA
JOÃO PESSOA
NATAL / FORTALEZA
SÃO LUÍS

THE NORTHEAST REGION

The nine states that comprise this large region all have Atlantic beaches as well as capital cities that double as ports, the only riverine harbor among them being Teresina, which is the capital of the Brazilian state of Piauí. Because Salvador da Bahia, Recife and Fortaleza enjoy good reputations in the tourist industry, they are popular charter-flight destinations. But relatively small Sergipe and Alagoas are as little known as Maranhão, the northernmost of the nine states, which is nearly as large as Germany.

Of the 30 percent or so of Brazil's population that lives in this region (which occupies a fifth of the country's land mass), over half live in poverty; for this region bears the stamp of sugar-cane production and the slavery that accompanied it. Here the structures of colonial society are largely intact. The yearning of these impoverished *Nordestinos* to escape drought, hunger and misery has transformed vast numbers of them into cheap and willing workers in the metropolises of São Paulo, Rio and Belo Horizonte.

Previous pages: In Salvador's restored Old City – the Pelourinho district, with the blue slaves' church. Left: A novice of the Candomblé religion in a trance.

The region can be divided into four geographical zones. The 150-kilometer-wide strip that runs along the coast and which was once covered with lush tropical forests is known as Zona da Mata. Brazil's colonial masters cut down these forests, first to export the brazilwood they found there, and later to create arable land for sugar-cane production, which was followed by cocoa, cotton, tobacco and beans. The most populous cities are in this zone, making it the most densely populated in the region.

Agreste, gateway to the Sertão, is primarily given over to cattle raising, although with over 1,000 mm of precipitation per year, plantation-style farming still generates large profits.

The famed (and notorious) Sertão accounts for half of the land area in the northeast. Irregular precipitation and sometimes catastrophic droughts are an integral part of life in this region. Due to the fact that moisture is wrung from the eastern trade winds as they pass over the coastal mountains, and because both run-off and evaporation levels are high, the area has a semi-arid climate, with as little as 300 mm of precipitation in some years. The indigenous peoples call the native vegetation *caatinga* (white forest) since the bushes, cacti and small trees, brown during dry periods, transfor themselves into a blossoming white and green oasis after the heavy, albeit infrequent, downpours to which the Sertão is prone.

The Meio-Norte, which occupies over one-quarter of the land area in the northeast region, is blessed with abundant precipitation that provides relatively favorable conditions for farming and cattle raising. However, ever since the arrival of the first settlers, most of this land has been concentrated in the hands of a small group of landowners.

BAHIA

Bahia – with a land area of 561,000 square kilometers larger than France and with over 12,000,000 inhabitants the most densely populated state in northeastern Brazil – is famous for the splendid beaches that grace its 1,100-kilometer-long coastline. But the state's interior also has attractions that visitors might want to consider setting aside some time to see, among them the canyons and table mountains of Chapada Diamantina National Park, whose highest peak, Pico do Barbado, rises to 2,033 meters. Bahia also has **Rio São Francisco**, the third-longest river in South America, which was dammed in northern Bahia to create a 200-kilometer-long lake. The river traverses the state for 3,361 kilometers, finally meeting the Atlantic at the border with the two northern-lying neighboring states of Sergipe and Alagoas. Rio São Francisco was an inland shipping waterway for many years, and prior to construction of the Sobradinho Dam, the inhabitants of the Sertão had hoped that the river would provide some much-needed relief during periods of drought.

The region is not particularly rich in mammalian wildlife. However, owing to the fact that Bahia's coastal waters have not been overfished, the region abounds in marine life. For this reason restaurant menus along the Bahia coast offer a generous selection of superb seafood specialties, many of them inspired by the lively innovativeness of the various African cuisines that were brought to Brazil during the colonial period.

Cooking is not the only aspect of Bahian life on which black Africa has left its imprint: there is also a distinctive Afro-Brazilian culture, including the Candomblé cult, the capoeira "martial arts" dance, and infectious rhythms, all of which were already a strong presence in this region in the 16th century. The reason for this is pretty self-evident: The province's economy prospered during colonial times, in large measure owing to slaves, over four million of whom worked on Bahia's cocoa, tobacco and sugar plantations.

Until the mid-20th century, agriculture was the mainstay of the economy in northeastern Brazil. In 1960, 40 percent of the active labor force was working on plantations, but by the beginning of the 1990's the number had fallen to 15 percent, in great measure owing to recurring droughts in the latter decades of the 20th century. Spurred on by the discovery of petroleum in All Saints' Bay, Pólo Petroquímico, an industrial center comprised of 70 petrochemical companies, was built north of Salvador in Camaçari. Important sources of regional income include petroleum and copper, as well as the gold and gem mines in the interior: Bahia produces aquamarines of unusually high quality.

About 55 percent of Bahians work today in the service, tourism and administrative sectors. The palm beaches, much-loved by southern Brazilians, also attract Europeans and other foreigners.

SALVADOR DA BAHIA
Baroque and Capoeira

Cidade do Salvador da Bahia de Todos os Santos – "City of the Savior of All Saints' Bay" – is the full name of the metropolis known worldwide as Salvador,

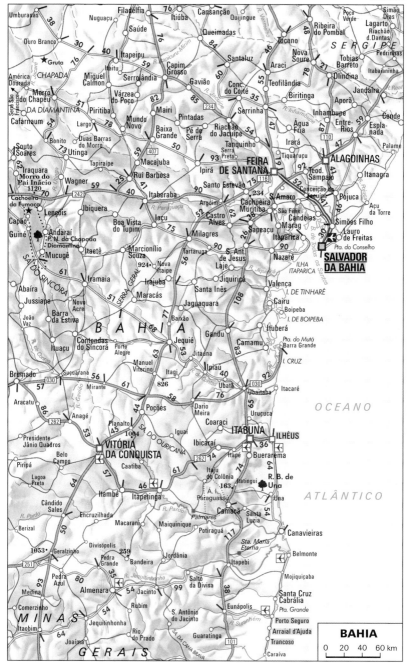

BAHIA

0   20   40   60 km

and simply as *Bahia* by the over two million *Baianos* who live here. Amerigo Vespucci named the place where the city now stands after the festival in the ecclesiastical calendar on which he discovered it: November 1, 1501 – All Saints' Day. In 1549, Bahia was officially founded by Governor-General Tomé de Souza in the name of the Portuguese Crown as the seat of the colonial government, and remained the colony's sole provincial capital until 1763.

When the Dutch took possession of part of northeastern Brazil in the 17th century, they also came (in 1624) to Salvador, where they constructed several forts that still figure prominently in Bahia's cityscape. The division of Salvador into an upper and a lower city is reminiscent of Lisbon, as are its elevators. Jorge Amado, Brazil's best-known writer and a

Above: The Lacerda Elevator is the quickest way to get from the lower to the upper city. Right: A Bahian fries acarajés (bean croquettes), a Salvadoran speciality.

resident of Bahia, describes his city as "planted on the hills, surrounded by the sea." Its unique setting makes it shine forth in radiant light, because "in Bahia, one's eyes are dazzled by the sea."

Cidade Alta – The Historic Upper City

If a visitor tells their taxi driver that they want to go to the upper city, they will be taken to **Praça Tomé de Souza**. A novel way of getting there, however, is to take the **Elevador Lacerda**, which for a nominal fee rapidly covers the 72 meters between Praça Cairu in the lower city (opposite the Mercado Modelo) and Praça Tomé de Souza in the upper city (runs 5 a.m. to midnight). However, while the elevator is inexpensive, crowded conditions on board also attract pickpockets, and visitors are therefore advised to be watchful when using it. Opposite the "mountain station" stands the 17th-century **Paço Municipal**, where Salvador's City Council now meets. To its right is the splendid **Palácio Rio**

Branco, which until 1979 was the Governor-General's mansion, but which since 1986 has been a museum with exhibits about the era of the Governor-General in Bahia.

To the left of the Palaçio stands an unsightly government building that offends the eye. Pompously named **Palácio Tomé de Souza**, this squat cement nightmare on pillars should be shunned, and the visitor should instead savor the satisfying view of the lower city, the harbor and All Saints' Bay, with the circular **Forte São Marcelo** in the foreground and **Ilha de Itaparica** in the background.

This panorama inspired contemporary author Antonio Riserio to write: "On a sunny day, Bahia is a cross between Africa and Latin America. In aesthetic terms this means: Salvador is a Baroque city that, despite its concrete monstrosities and frivolous postmodern façades, reaches out to the eye of the beholder; a city that is imaginatively giving birth – between the capricious play of the sea and its cloister-crowned hills – to the elements of a veritable cultural melting pot."

If you continue past the city council building and then turn left, and go past Igreja da Misericórdia, you will arrive at the cathedral square, **Praça da Sé**, which contains the Palácio Episcopal. One block further up the street, overlooking a gracious square known as Terreiro de Jesus, is the **Catedral Basílica**. This episcopal church was originally the house of worship for a Jesuit theological seminary that was planned to be much more extensive than the structure that was ultimately built. The cornerstone was laid in 1657, and the basic framework completed in 1672. Both the marble-like stones on the façade and the niche statues of Jesuit saints are of Portuguese origin. The interior is fairly spartan, but the whole edifice is crowned with a splendid vaulted coffered ceiling. Of interest as well are the 13 altars – each executed in a different Baroque style – and especially

the sacristy, which is open to the public (an admission fee is charged). Its ceiling frescos and 17th-century Portuguese tiles (*azulejos*) make it one of the most magnificent churches in Latin America. The sacristy also contains a very large vestment cupboard decorated with inlays of tortoise shell, ivory and various tropical woods.

Flame trees with scarlet blossoms and a fountain that allegorizes the four most important rivers in Bahia transform **Terreiro de Jesus**, the square before the cathedral, into an oasis of upper city calm. There are even hammocks available (but only for sale!) from street vendors, who also sell lace dresses and jewelry. The **Cantina da Lua** at the corner of Rua Alfredo Brito beckons invitingly to both locals and tourists, who can sit at an outdoor table sipping a glass of fruit juice or an excellent *cachaça* (sugar-cane spirits) cocktail as they look out over the endlessly fascinating pageant of plaza life. For the music-minded, concerts are held in the evenings upstairs at the Cantina.

145

Next door stands the church of **São Pedro dos Clérigos** and, facing it, the **Igreja de São Domingos**, decorated with a rococo façade. Both structures date from the 18th century and are only open on Sundays.

The southern end of Terreiro de Jesus adjoins **Praça Anchieta**, a plaza of lesser size on which, after going past several jewelry shops and art galleries, you reach the **Igreja de São Francisco**. If the amount of gilding were a measure of a church's wealth, this would have to be regarded as the wealthiest in all Brazil. Construction was begun in 1798, but the cloister next door dates from 1686. The church packs a large – and to the modern eye perhaps excessive – quantity of Baroque decorative exuberance into a relatively small space. But the gilded cherubs, dark rosewood sculptures and tiled murals in the atrium depicting the life of St. Francis of Assisi lend the church a soothing harmony.

During colonial times, a separate room adjoining the nave was provided for the exclusive use of slaves, who were encouraged to attend mass but were forbidden to cast their eyes upon their masters while worshiping. Well worth setting aside time for is a visit to the **Stations of the Cross**, which is open to the public after years of restoration work. The 37 painted wall tiles, executed in the 18th century by anonymous Portuguese artists, address some of the 103 quasi-religious philosophical themes contained in the **Teatro Moral de la Vida Humana**, the "Moral Drama of Human Life," published by Rubens' teacher Otto van Veen in 1608. Home truths such as "In unity there is strength," "Money rules the world" and "Money can buy anything" are elucidated with scenes from antiquity.

The façade of the Franciscan church just next door and to the left, **Igreja da Terceira Ordem de São Francisco**, is particularly noteworthy. Exuberantly decorated with stone sculptures, it recalls colonial churches in Mexico and Peru, and is the only Baroque ecclesiastical façade of its kind in Brazil.

The Pelourinho Quarter

Until a few years ago, this picturesque Baroque enclave of Salvador was deteriorating rapidly and appeared to be beyond hope. By the end of the 1980's, the artists of African descent living in the neighborhood were the only ones making any efforts to rescue it. Every Sunday evening local drummers and percussionists from the group Bloco Afro Olodum held a free open rehearsal on the sloping plaza, Largo do Pelourinho. They subsequently made a live recording in the U.S., on which the spice of Afro-Brazilian drum rolls was added to Paul Simon's *The Obvious Child*. The unusual driving rhythms made the title a worldwide hit in 1990, brought Simon once again into the limelight, and established the reputation of the now renowned drummers of Olodum. Young people in Brazil then began taking an interest in both Salvador's raw *Axé* music and in Bloco Afro Olodum's rehearsals. At the same time, heretofore undreamed of amounts of money suddenly began flowing into the crumbling Baroque city, and in 1992, in an unprecedented show of solidarity, the municipal government decided to support the musicians' initiative by completely renovating and restoring several hundred buildings in the historic town center.

Since the definitive resurrection of the historic Baroque quarter, once listless Pelourinho ("pillory" in Portuguese) has been transformed into a lively cosmopolitan quarter, with round-the-clock locales frequented not only by tourists from all over the world, but also by music-loving Brazilian youths. The neighborhood offers an abundance of live music set to irresistible rhythms, Afro-Brazilian and other ethnic restaurants, and whimsical boutiques.

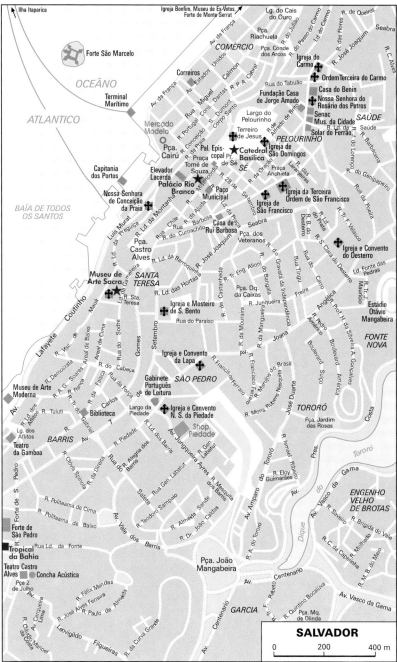

↑ Ilha Itaparica

Igreja Bonfim, Museu de Ex-Votos,
Forte de Monte Serrat →

Lg. do Cais
do Ouro

R. de Queiroz

Pça.
Riachuela

COMÉRCIO

Pça. Conde
dos Arcos

Seabra

Igreja do
Carmo

Forte São Marcelo

OCEÂNO

Correios

Ld. do Carmo

R. do Passo do Carmo

R. José Joaquim

R. das Flores

R. C. Alves

OrdemTerceira do Carmo

ATLANTICO

Terminal
Marítimo

Av. da França

Av. Estados Unidos

R.P.A. Cabral

Rua do Tabuão

Casa do Benin

Fundação Casa
de Jorge Amado

Nossa Senhora do
Rosário dos Petros

Largo do
Pelourinho

Senac

Mercado
Modelo

Rua Miguel Calmon

R. Portugal Cons. Dantas

S. Dumont

PELOURINHO

Mus. da Cidade

Solar do Ferrão

SAÚDE

R. Saúde

Capitania
dos Portos

Pça.
Cairú

R. Conceição da Praia

Corpo Santo

Terreiro
de Jesus

R. de Almeida de Brito

R. Ld. da Saúde

R. Barbacena

Pal. Epis-
copal

Praça
Tomé de
Souza

Igreja de
São Domingos

Catedral
Basílica

Elevador
Lacerda

Praça
de Sé

SÉ

Igreja de
São Francisco

R. do Lorenço do Genipapeiro

Palácio Rio
Branco

Paço
Municipal

Praça
Anchieta

R. das Laranjeiras

Nossa Senhora
de Conceição
da Praia

R. da Misericordia

R. 28 de Setembro

R. da Oração

Igreja da Terceira
Ordem de São Francisco

Rua da Poeira

BAÍA DE TODOS
OS SANTOS

R. da Ajuda

Rua Chile

R. da Barbosa

Casa de
Rui Barbosa

Seabra

R. Ld. do Prata

R. T. F. Velasco

Luís Murat

R. Ld. da Prégúica

R. do Currlachito

Pça. dos
Veteranos

R.B. do Destero

R. Clara da Destero

Igreja e Convento
do Desterro

Pça.
Castro
Alves

R. Ld. da Montanha

R. Ld. da Barroquinha

R. José Joaquim

R. Tr. Eng. Alioni

Rua Tingu

Ld. Fonte das
Pedras

Museu de
Arte Sacra

R. B. Garnelra

SANTA
TERESA

R. Ld. das Hortas

R. da Castanheda

Pça. Dq.
da Caixas

R. do Bangila

R. do Carro

Angélica

R.T.J. Mauricio

R. Sta.
Teresa

R. Junqueira

Freire

Estádio
Otávio
Mangabeira

Coutinho

Maúa

R. do Sodré

Igreja e Mosteiro
de S. Bento

R. da Mouraira

Joana

Av.

R. Pedro Américo

Prof. H. da Silveira A. Gonçalves

Boulevard Suíço

Boulevard América

FONTE
NOVA

Lafayette

Setembro

Gomes

Rua do Paraíso

R. Francisco Ferraro

R. Mangueira

R. Mendro do Brasil

José Duarte

Costa

Museu de Arte
Moderna

R.A.G. Soares

Areal de Cima

Areal de Baixo

Rua da Força

Gabinete
Português
de Leitura

Igreja e Convento
da Lapa

SÃO PEDRO

R. Mons. Ruben Nesquita

TORORÓ

Av.

R. Ld. dos Aflitos

R. Tuiuti

R. Pança

R. da Falica

Carlos
Gabriel

Biblioteca

Largo
da Piedade

Igreja e Convento
N. S. da Piedade

Pça. Jardim
das Rosas

Lg. dos
Aflitos

BARRIS

R. Clóvis Spinola

R. da Direita

Rua do Piedade

R. da Alegria dos
Barris

Av. Junqueira Ayres

R. Gen. Labatut

Shop.
Piedade

Tororó

Tororó

Teatro
da Gamboa

Pedro

R. Ld. da Fonte

Sálete

R. Gen. Labatut

R. Mesquita
dos Barris

ENGENHO
VELHO
DE BROTAS

Av. Amparo do

R. Ismael Ribeiro

R. Eloy
Guimarães

Av. Vasco da Gama

R. Siveiro

R. Brígida do Vale

Forte de S.

R. Politeama de Cima

R. Politeama de Baixo

Av. Vale dos Barris

R. Teodoro Sampaio

R. Almeida Sande

R. Dr. João Caldas

Pres.

Dique

R.C. da Capelinha

Av. Vasco da Gama

Forte de
São Pedro

Tropical
da Bahia

Pça. João
Mangabeira

R. Quintino Bocaiúva

Pça. Mq.
de Olinda

R.M. B.do Melo

Teatro Castro
Alves

Concha Acústica

Pça 2
de Julho

Av.

Centenário

GARCIA

R. Cerqueira Lima

R. Félix Mendes

R. José Alves Ferreira

R. Paulo de Almeida

R. Chico Manoel da Costa

Leovigildo

Filgueiras

R. da Curva Grande

R.T.F. Ribeiro

R. Amparo

SALVADOR

0   200   400 m

147

The Olodum drummers, who have since been catapulted to fame by a music video they made with Michael Jackson, perform on Tuesday nights at **Largo Tereza Batista**, one of the many new – and for tourists highly recommended – gathering places in the upper city. The free (and consequently full-to-overflowing) Sunday afternoon rehearsals are still held on Largo do Pelourinho, but in view of the large crowds no valuables should be either brought or worn to this event.

The large edifice at the front of the plaza houses two museums, the Museu da Cidade and **Fundação Casa de Jorge Amado**. The foundation houses an archive of photographs of Jorge Amado, as well as translations into numerous languages of the works of Bahia's best-known author. The second floor is given over to exhibitions of the work of local

and regional artists. A narrow sloping street adjacent to the museum leads to **Rua Gregório de Matos**, site of the headquarters of Brazil's best-known Afoxé, **Filhos de Gandhi**, a cultural association of Afro-Brazilian men that has been in existence for generations. The internationally renowned and prize-winning folklore theater company **Miguel Santana** has its offices and performance space on this street as well.

At the corner of Rua Gregório Matos and Rua Ãngelo Ferraz stands **Solar do Ferrão**, a mansion dating from 1690 that was originally a Jesuit seminary. Restored in 1976, it now houses the **Museu Abelardo Rodrigues**, which has the largest private collection of religious art in Brazil, including rare processional figures, paintings and sculptures.

The yellow construction on the right at the lower end of Largo do Pelourinho is **Senac** (State School of Gastronomy), which serves regional specialties. You can choose at will from a superb buffet, which means you can both procure and

Above: This Franciscan church is lavishly ornamented with gilding. Right: Young boys practicing capoeira techniques on Largo do Pelourinho.

subsequently savor these Afro-Brazilian dishes without having to resort to the medium of language. In the evenings there a variety of folklore performances are held in the courtyard, e.g., of capoeira, the ritualized fighting dance of the slaves.

The building adjacent to Senac is Pelourinho's calling-card; a blue church featuring twin towers known as **Nossa Senhora do Rosário dos Pretos** (Our Lady of the Rosary of the Blacks). Built and financed by slaves and freed slaves at the beginning of the 18th century, it is in the hands of an order of black priests to this day.

The restored colonial structure at the next corner is **Casa do Benin**, which was established on the initiative of the French ethnologist Pierre Verger to pay homage to the cultures of the many African peoples who were forcibly brought to Bahia from the former Dahomey. The museum documents the links between African and Bahian culture, and the restaurant provides visitors with the opportunity to sample a culinary potpourri of

dishes made of such exotic ingredients as coconut milk and palm oil.

Steeply inclined Ladeira do Carmo leads directly to the **Igreja Nossa Senhora do Paço** (1737), one of Salvador's 76 churches. Further along, Ladeira do Carmo intersects Rua do Carmo, where two Carmelite churches are to be found: the lay church of **Ordem Terceira do Carmo** and **Igreja do Carmo**, the cloister church. Especially noteworthy are the carved rosewood choir stalls. Each church also has a small museum whose most engaging works are Francisco Chagas' realistic sculpture of Christ being scourged (lay church), and a sacristy cloaked in sumptuous gilding (cloister church).

Venturing a bit farther down Rua do Carmo leads the visitor to a lesser-known upper city *bairro* (neighborhood), where small picturesque houses adorn quiet, archtypically quaint cobblestone streets. This romantic corner of Pelourinho provided an ideal backdrop for the screen adaptation of the Jorge Amado novel

Dona Flor and Her Two Husbands, in which Sonia Braga starred.

Praça Castro Alves and Largo da Piedade

Visitors can travel from the upper to the lower city without using the elevator by way of **Praça Castro Alves**, which is linked to Praça Tomé de Souza (see p. 144) by Rua Chile. In Praça Castro Alves stands a monumental statue of the Brazilian poet Antônio de Castro Alves (1847-1871), whose verse denounced the institution of slavery. The square also contains a bronze plaque with an engraving of a map of Salvador in colonial times; the map shows that part of the south city wall originally stood on this site. For many weekends previous to Carnival, and during the celebration itself,

Above: Carnival in Salvador is noisier and wilder than in Rio. Right: The pilgrimmage church of Bonfim is resplendent when illuminated at night.

this square is a central gathering place for samba dancers, thousands of whom step and sway to the rhythms of *trios eléctricos* – trucks filled to overflowing with loudspeakers. Below Praça Castro Alves, Ladeira da Gameleira leads (south) to a short street, Rua Santa Teresa, in which both the **Igreja Santa Teresa** and a former convent of the Carmelite order are located; the **Museu de Arte Sacra**, the largest collection of religious art in Brazil, is now housed here. The cloister is decorated with light blue glazed tiles, and the collection includes rare ivory carvings from the former Portuguese colonies of Goa and Macao.

Meandering southward down Rua do Sodré brings the visitor to Largo Dois de Julho, where Rua da Forca branches off to the left towards **Largo da Piedade**. Here, shoeshine boys await customers under shady trees on whose branches iguanas can sometimes be glimpsed skittering or sunbathing. The plaza is presided over by the pastel-hued **Gabinete Português de Leitura** (Por-

tuguese Literary Society), which has a library containing an extensive collection of reference works (some of historical nature), as well as periodicals.

A 20-minute stroll southward down the animated shopping street Av. 7 de Setembro leads to **Forte de São Pedro**, a colonial fortress that is now used as a military barracks. Just behind it lies Praça 2 de Julho, which Baianos call **Campo Grande**. This large green space contains a 26-meter-high memorial to the soldiers who, in 1823, marched victoriously into Salvador after lifting the Portuguese siege. The victorious native-born freedom fighters are symbolized by eagles and lions, and the defeated Portuguese by a snake.

The **Teatro Castro Alves**, a venue for classical music, dance and theater, is also located in the park. Behind it is a 6,000-seat open-air theater, the **Concha Acústica**, where such names in contemporary Brazilian music as Gilberto Gil, Caetano Veloso and Maria Bethânia, to name but a few, regularly perform.

Cidade Baixa – The Lower City

During the 18th century, the lower city was expanded onto landfill and is now comprised of a port, an industrial zone, and a commercial area. There are, nonetheless, places worth seeing, such as **Nossa Senhora da Conceção da Praia** (Our Lady of the Immaculate Conception on the Beach), which is situated near the Elevador Lacerda. When the church was built in the mid-18th century it stood closer to the shoreline than it now does, as the landfill had not yet distanced it from the water. Built according to a plan from Portugal, the church is made entirely out of Portuguese *pedra de lioz*, a marble-like stone that was used as ballast in the cargo holds of large sailing ships. Its monumental ceiling fresco dating from 1772 is the most outstanding work of its kind ever produced by the Bahia school. During the celebration of the Feast of the Immaculate Virgin, which begins a week early here (on November 30 rather than December 8), Bahian culinary specialties are sold from roadside stands, capoeira martial arts dancers display their skills, and Praça Cairu is full of sunbathers.

Mercado Modelo, which opened in 1971, is a tourist's shopping paradise housed in a sprawling two-story yellow building that was originally the customs office. Hammocks, musical instruments, embroidered blouses, T-shirts, and a potpourri of other merchandise are sold – but visitors who don't bargain will pay too much! The terraces on the two restaurants in the marketplace afford memorable views of the harbor. Boats to Itaparica and other islands leave from the **Terminal Marítimo**. Smaller boats next to the market building provide transportation to **São Marcelo**, a 17th-century Portuguese fort built to protect the harbor, and later used as a house of detention for political prisoners.

The lower city extends northward to **Peninsula Itapagipe**, where two pilgrimage churches of vital importance in the Bahian ecclesiastical calendar are located: Nosso Senhor do Bonfim and Boa Viagem. The fastest and safest way to reach them is by taxi. The 18th-century **Igreja do Bonfim** is of little art-historical interest. It is, however, among the churches in Brazil most frequented by pilgrims, and owing to its curious **Museu de Ex-Votos**, which features a varied collection of votive gifts, constitutes one of the highlights of a visit to Salvador. There is no avoiding the children who tie *fitinhas* (colored strips of cloth) with three knots in them around visitors' wrists, in exchange (the children hope) for some money. The knots symbolize three wishes that are supposed to be granted by the time the ribbons fall off.

The high point of the many religious feast days in Salvador da Bahias occurs in January on **Lavagem do Bonfim** (Church-cleaning Day), on which the women of the congregation wash down the broad staircase in front of the church after the procession from Igreja Conceição da Praia. Stefan Zweig, who witnessed this ritual, described it as follows: "The Church of Bonfim was originally a Negro church. Apparently, a parish priest told his flock that the proper thing to do on the day before the festival was to clean the church from top to bottom and wash down the floor with scrub brushes. The black Christians followed his instructions with pleasure, but in their naive, childlike way transformed the cleaning of the church into a festival. They tried to outdo each other in scrubbing and sweeping, as if it were their own sins they were trying to wash away. Thousands of them came from near and far, and their numbers increased from year to year. And from this custom a folk festival evolved."

The New Year's procession in honor of the patron saint of sailors wends its way to the aptly named **Igreja da Boa Viagem** (Church of the Safe Journey). Visitors can savor the pristine view of Salvador from **Igreja Nossa Senhora do Monte Serrat**, a former Benedictine hermitage perched on the western tip of the Itapagipe Peninsula. The Fort of Monte Serrat dates to the 16th century, and like the church, is not open to the public, as both are registered national monuments.

Another "sight" – and an important feature of the Itapagpipe Peninsula – are the **alagados** inhabited by Salvador's poorest citizens. *Algados* are rudimentary wooden shacks built on stilts above the surface of the often brackish water. These dwellings, as well as the people living in them, are regularly photographed by tourists. This can be dangerous and furthermore shows a lack of sensitivity; visitors should try to avoid such shameless gawking at poverty.

Salvador's Beaches

Salvador's extensive beaches, some of which are graced with coconut palms, offer delightful swimming almost year-

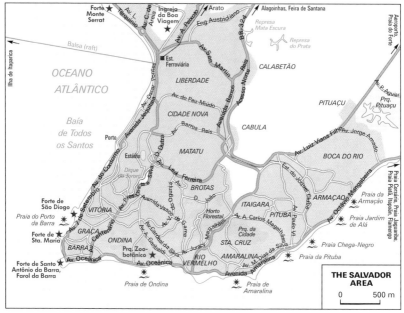

Forte Monte Serrat ★
Av. L. Tarquínio
Av. Cidade Areia
Ingreja da Boa Viagem ★
Av. A. Peixoto
Arato
Alagoinhas, Feira de Santana
Aeroporto, Praia do Forte
Eng. Austricliano
Balsa (raft)
BR-324
Represa Mata Escura
Represa do Prata
Est. Ferroviária
Av. Sen. Martim
OCEANO ATLÂNTICO
LIBERDADE
Reis
Nasso Norte
CALABETÃO
Ilha de Itaparica
Av. do Pau-Miúdo
Av. Oscar Pontes
Avenida Jequitaia
CIDADE NOVA
Av. P. Aguiar
Prq. Pituaçu
PITUAÇU
Baía de Todos os Santos
Porto
Barros Reis
Avenida Barros Reis
CABULA
Av. Luiz Viana Filho
Av. Jorge Amado
Estádio
Dique do Tororó
MATATU
BOCA DO RIO
Av. Zte Setembro
Av. do Contorno
D. Dutra
Leão
S. Silva
Ferreira
BROTAS
Est. do Joanes Cabrit
Praia Corsário, Praia Jaguaribe, Praia Piatã, Itapoan, Flamengo
Forte de São Diogo ★
VITÓRIA
Alves Silva
Arindo Braga
Avenida Vasco
D. João
ARMAÇÃO
Praia da Armação
Praia do Porto da Barra
Horto Florestal
ITAIGARA
Av. Octávio Mangabeira
Av. A. Carlos Magalhães
PITUBA
Praia Jardim de Alá
Forte de Sta. Maria ★
GRAÇA
Centro
Av. Cardeal da Silva
da Gama
ONDINA
Marquês
Pq. da Cidade
Av. Paulo VI
Av. C. Gnabaldi
Prq. Zoo-botânico
Av. Juraci
STA. CRUZ
Dias da Silva
Praia Chega-Negro
BARRA
Forte de Santo Antônio da Barra, Farol da Barra
Av. Oceânica
RIO VERMELHO
AMARALINA
Av. Amaralina
Praia da Pituba
Av. Oceânica
Avenida
Praia de Ondina
Praia de Amaralina

THE SALVADOR AREA
0   500 m

round. As a general rule, the farther from a large urban area a beach is situated, the cleaner and less crowded it will turn out to be. However, even on deserted-looking beaches, visitors should exercise caution by carrying as little cash as possible, depositing valuables and travel documents (e.g., passport, airline tickets) in the hotel safe, and leaving their room keys at the reception desk. Beaches are of course more populated on weekends, as well as during Christmas, Carnival and summer vacation (December through February).

Mingling with Brazilians on the beach can be a delightful experience, but visitors should not expect that experience to include having a secluded stretch of sand all to themselves in a city the size of Salvador! The various buses that ply the coastal road have a sign at the front indicating the name of the beach they are going to. Each beach also has a sign posted with its name and the words *própria* or *imprópria*, i.e., suitable for swimming or unsuitable for swimming.

A cultural tip: Baianos customarily don their swimming suits at home, and visitors are advised to do likewise.

If you wish to tour all the beaches along Salvador's coastline and get in some sightseeing while you're at it, the best place to start is at the **Igreja Santo Antônio da Barra** in the **Barra** quarter (buses in Barra leave from Campo Grande). The Church of St. Anthony is situated on a rise adjoining **Forte de São Diogo**, from both of which 16th-century structures there is a spectacular panorama of the bay and the Barra quarter. The beach you first encounter, **Praia do Porto da Barra**, is adjacent to the fort and always very crowded. Next comes the 17th-century fort, **Santa Maria**, a reminder of the designs the Dutch had on Salvador in colonial times.

Two coastal kilometers later comes yet another fort, **Santo Antônio da Barra**, and the lighthouse **Farol da Barra**, a "must" for all bearers of cameras: to the right lies All Saints' Bay, and to the left the Atlantic, with its white sand beaches

153

and rocky cliffs rising dramatically from the ocean depths. After taking their photographs, visitors can purchase cold beer or chilled coconut from a mobile vendor. The **Museu Hidrográfico de Salvador**, which is located inside the fort, features displays of model ships and nautical charts. The entire shore avenue in Barra abounds in hotels, restaurants, and bars, some of which stay open all night. None could be classified as four-star establishments, but the seafood dishes are always made from freshly caught fish or shellfish.

Barra is followed by **Ondina,** where the road turns inland. Several of the large hotels here are situated directly on the beach. At **Rio Vermelho** the swimming is not all it could be, but by way of compensation the nightlife is classier and the beach, **Praia da Santana**, is the scene of a seaside procession every February 2, during which thousands of Baianos make

Above: Porto da Barra is one of Salvador's most popular beaches.

offerings to Yemanjá, the goddess of the sea. Next to a small church in an unremarkable structure stands an altar at which fishermen and Candomblé priests ask Yemanjá to intercede on their behalf.

The next beaches are **Amaralina** and **Pituba**, neither of them particularly wide or clean. **Chega Negro** beach derives its name from the transporting of slaves from Africa. It means, literally, "Here come the Negroes," since it was here, sadly, that human "cargo" reached shore. Swimming at this beach is inadvisable, as the river empties raw sewage into the sea here. Next comes **Jardim de Alá** (Garden of Allah), where tall coconut palms cast cooling shade. It occasionally happens that visitors can arrange to have a freshly-picked coconut delivered right to their beach towel – in exchange for a small gratuity, of course.

Praia de Armação is surfer heaven. One stretch, Praia dos Artistas, is used by a local athletics association whose clubhouse is on the beach. Because they lie outside of Salvador, **Corsário**, **Jag-**

uaribe and **Piatã** are perfect for a day of relaxation or sports. Exercise machines are available, and on weekends many local residents come to the beach to play volleyball or beach football. Along the entire shore avenue there is a very safe bicycle path, something Bahia had long before Rio (cf. p. 50 and 54). **Itapoãn**, a suburb, has a long beach, a lighthouse and a reef, inside of which a small pool perfect for splashing around in forms at low tide. The last beach within the city limits is **Flamengo**.

Visitors can take an excursion inland from Itapoãn to **Lagoa de Abaeté**, a nature reserve with a lagoon idyllically set in the middle of pristine white sand dunes. Salvador's international airport, Dois de Julho, is a few minutes' drive away; its access road is lined with massive bamboo trees.

Praia do Forte

A 50-kilometer drive north from the Bahia airport by way of **Estrada de Coco** rewards the visitor with the luxuriant beaches of **Ipitanga** and **Arembepe**, as well as the fishing village of **Praia do Forte**. In 1972, a German industrialist purchased Praia do Forte – 7,000 hectares of tropical rain forest, a ruined building, and in a sense, its inhabitants, too – with a view to developing ecotourism; at the time still regarded as utopian. The practice of collecting tortoise eggs was banned, as was capturing songbirds or erecting any structure taller than a coconut palm. Permits were required to fell trees, and the fencing off of property was discouraged. And to prevent speculation, foreigners were not allowed to buy houses in the village.

The 200 apartments of the **Praia do Forte Resort** were built in the local style. Half of them are "eco-apartments," i.e., they have neither air-conditioning, televisions, nor radios. The restaurant is also free of air-conditioning, which means

visitors can savor the copious breakfast buffet and excellent cooking without running the risk of catching a cold. The beach is right outside the hotel door, and the village and its numerous small restaurants are no more than a 15-minute walk away. The white sand beach, which is over 12 kilometers long (and on which the Tamar Project carries out its work of protecting sea turtles), is dotted with coconut palms, reefs and lagoons.

Ilha de Itaparica

Itaparica – with an area of 239 square kilometers, Brazil's largest Atlantic island – lies 17 kilometers off the coast of Salvador in All Saints' Bay and functions as a breakwater in the open sea. A number of companies provide regularly scheduled ferry service to the island, travel time to which varies from 20 to 50 minutes according to the type of boat you take. The island's heavy tourist traffic notwithstanding, its land is used primarily for agricultural purposes: fishing, cattle raising, and mango and cashew fruit growing are the main sources of income for Itaparica's 15,000 inhabitants. Most beaches and other tourist facilities, including the ferry terminal and **Club Med**, are concentrated on the southeast side of the island. A day's outing to Itaparica is certainly a worthwhile enterprise, although less so for visitors who favor the beach.

RECÔNCAVO
Hinterland Traditions

The literal meaning of *recôncavo* is "behind the concave forms," a reference to the topographical contours around All Saints' Bay. Salvador's backlands have been farmed since the colonial era, its fertile soil providing the basis for the production of sugar cane and tobacco. But business eventually moved south, leaving behind – and well preserved – the large plantations and small-town charm of the colonial past, which is particularly well represented by the Baroque town of Cachoeira.

After driving north out of Salvador on the BR 324 towards Feira de Santana for about 40 kilometers, turn west, which takes you directly into **Santo Amaro**. This small town has several colonial structures, among them a 17th-century parish church, **Nossa Senhora da Purificação**, which is decorated with azulejos (tiled murals). Santo Amaro is dear to the hearts of afficionados of alcoholic beverages owing to its cachaça (sugar-cane spirits). To music buffs, it is known as the birthplace of Caetano Veloso and Maria Bethânia (see p. 227).

Another 40 kilometers to the west is Rio Paraguaçu, on whose banks the towns of **Cachoeira** and **São Félix** lie opposite each other. In colonial times, gold prospectors and merchants came here by boat and then loaded their possessions onto oxcarts. On the return trip, the valuable finds they unearthed in the interior were placed on ships that sailed from here directly to Lisbon. In addition to colonial structures, these two towns have also preserved their *Candomblé* temples, where the descendants of slaves still carry on their religious traditions to this day (see p. 226). The *Irmandade da Nossa Senhora da Boa Morte* (Sisterhood of Our Lady of the Good Death), founded in the 19th century, worked for the abolition of slavery and tried to make life easier for the children of slaves. Each year the church holds a traditional (and well-attended) Afro-Bahian celebration on Assumption Day.

A market featuring a wide range of tropical fruits and spices is held on Saturdays in Cachoeira's main square, **Praça Maciel**. Following Rua Lauro de Freitas

Right: The "Sisterhood of Our Lady of the Good Death" celebrates Assumption Day each year with a procession.

eastward takes you to Rua Ana Nery and the 17th-century **Nossa Senhora do Rosário** with its handsome tiled murals. Next door stands the birthplace of Ana Nery, a nurse who is honored as the "Mother of all Brazilians" for having served as a volunteer on the front lines during Brazil's war with Paraguay in the 19th century. Her former home is the site of the **Museu Hansen Bahia**, whose story is as follows: Karl-Heinz Hansen, a 40-year-old sailor from Hamburg, came to Bahia and discovered that he had artistic talents. He returned to Europe and subsequently obtained a teaching position in Addis Abbaba, where he became well known for his wood engravings. But his heart belonged to Bahia, and he eventually returned to São Félix where he set up his dream studio. He worked there until his death in 1978, producing over 3,000 paintings and wood carvings, some of which are on display in the museum.

Another internationally-renowned artist from Cachoeira is *O Louco* (The Madman), whose given name was Bonifacio Silva Filho. A trained barber, he initially carved bowls for tobacco pipes, but later primarily made devotional objects in rosewood. His Last Supper is in the Museum of Folk Art in Vienna.

The neighboring **Praça da Aclamação** is the site of **Casa da Câmara e Cadeia**, the historic city hall and prison. It is here that citizens gathered on June 25, 1822, to call for Brazil's independence, which is how the plaza acquired its name: *aclamação* means "to call for." A few meters away stands a former Carmelite convent, the **Convento Nossa Senhora do Carmo**, which was commandeered first as a barracks, and then a hospital, during Brazil's war of independence. It now houses the only good hotel in either Cachoeira or São Felix, with a cozy courtyard, swimming pool, and a fine restaurant. Religious services are still held in the **Capela da Ordem Terceira do Carmo**, whose admirable rosewood

cross (in the sacristy) and figures from Macao representing the Passion of Christ are well worth seeing.

The picturesque riverside **Praça Teixeira de Freitas**, which can be accessed from Rua 25 de Junho, features many handicrafts shops that sell the wood carvings for which this area is famous. Continuing north along the Paraguaçu, you reach a 100-year-old iron bridge from England, **Ponte Dom Pedro II**, which links the two sister cities and is well worth seeing in its own right. The **Centro Cultural Dannemann** on the opposite bank in São Félix is also an engaging place to visit. Named after a merchant from Bremen, Gerhard Dannemann, who in 1872 came in search of quality tobacco and later became mayor of São Félix, the center's focus is on contemporary Bahian art. Visitors can also watch the world-famous cigars being made.

On the way back to Salvador – the quickest route being the BR 324 – one plausible option is to take a brief detour (about 15 kilometers from the main road) to visit **Feira de Santana**. Located 116 kilometers (two hours by bus) from Salvador and known as a somewhat disreputable entrepôt for the interior and coastal areas of Brazil, Feira de Santana is not nearly as tourism-oriented as Salvador. *A feira*, the daily market, is of little interest, but *Feira de Gado e Couro*, the cattle and leather market, is another story. At this event, leather goods of every description are sold along with cattle-breeding products, while at the same time the fascinating commerce in cows is played out all around the visitor, who can wander at will amongst the cattle merchants and drovers. There are plenty of photo opportunities, but take care not to end up shooting from beneath any cow hooves!

Parque Nacional da Chapada Diamantina

Situated 310 kilometers west of Feira da Santana, **Lençóis** grew rich from diamond prospecting in the 19th century,

157

and today is a jumping-off point for visits to the 152,000-hectare national park nearby that was founded in 1985. Although Lençóis can be reached by bus from Salvador, a car is indispensable for exploring the park. Car-pooling services are available, but primarily on weekends, when Baianos turn out in droves.

The main attraction of the park is the loveliness of its topographical features, including table mountains, canyons, cascades and caves. Sixty varieties of orchid and rare bromelia, such as ortophytum, the only one of its species with leaves on its shoots, are also found here. And visitors may occasionally catch sight of parakeets, hummingbirds or rare species of finch. The wild animal population in the park has been drastically reduced, however, by poaching.

The park is traversed by the 140-kilometer-long Serra do Sincorá. Most areas

Above: Parrots are among the many attractions at Chapada National Park. Right: Lençois has many colonial buildings.

of the facility lie at 800 meters above sea level, making for agreeable temperatures. **Pico da Barbado**, one of the peaks of the Serra do Sincorá and the highest in Bahia, reaches 2,033 meters. Chapada's emblem is the spectacular table mountain **Morro do Pai Inácio**, which can be climbed, albeit with some effort. **Gruta de Lapão**, a one-kilometer-long quartzite cave (the largest in Brazil), is five kilometers from Lençóis.

A much-frequented hiking trail leads to the highest waterfall in Brazil, **Cachoeira da Fumaça**, which means "smoke waterfall." It is probably so named because the water tumbles from a height of 422 meters and breaks into smoke-like spray when it hits the rocks below. Outside of the rainy season, which lasts from November to February, Cachoiera sometimes dries up, as average annual precipitation in this area is only 700-1000 mm. The pathway to the falls begins at Weiler Capão, and the hike in takes about two hours. During the rainy season, the large purple blossoms of the *quaresmeiras* (Lenten rose) are everywhere in evidence. These hellebores are typical of secondary growth, i.e., they flourish where primary growth decomposes rapidly.

SOUTHERN BAHIA
History and Cocoa

Ilhéus

The 460 kilometers separating Salvador from the port city of **Ilhéus** (population 250,000) can be covered in seven hours by bus or 40 minutes by plane. Driving can be arduous, however, as there is no through coastal highway or other road linking the two cities. Ilhéus, founded in 1534, grew rich from cocoa production during the 18th century. The region around Ilhéus now accounts for 90 percent of Brazil's total output of cocoa, which in 1994 was 344,000 tons, making

Brazil the world's second-largest pro-ducer. The **Museu Regional do Cacau** makes abundantly clear the importance of cocoa beans for this region, and Jorge Amado, who was born in nearby Pirangi, has immortalized Ilhéus and the entire cocoa-producing region in his books. Ve-zúvio, a bar depicted in his novel *Gab-riela, Cinnamon and Cloves*, is still in existence.

Tourists come here primarily for the city's seemingly endless string of perfect and – good news for devotees of deserted stretches of sand – often difficult-to-access beaches that extend to the north and south farther than the eye can see. Located in a palm grove on an island in the Atlantic 81 kilometers south of Il-héus, the 250-room resort **Transamérica Ilha de Comandatuba** is one of Brazil's most exclusive beach hotels.

Porto Seguro

In 1500, Pedro Álvares Cabral landed 730 kilometers south of Salvador at this "safe harbor," thereby making this the first place in Brazil ever to be visited by a European. A marble stela erected in 1504 in commemoration of this event still stands in the upper city.

Porto Seguro is divided into a historic upper city and a business- and tourism-oriented lower city. The *Cidade Alta* con-tains the oldest preserved church in Brazil, the **Igreja da Misericórdia**, built in 1526 and later remodeled in Baroque style. Still older, but now only a ruin, is the Igreja da Gloria. **Nossa Senhora da Penha**, which dates from 1535, is signifi-cant from an art-historical standpoint, as it contains the oldest sacred image in Brazil, a painting of St. Francis of Assisi that was brought to Brazil by a Portugese expedition in 1503.

During the vacation months, both Porto Seguro and its neighbors to the south, **Arraial d'Ajuda** and **Trancoso**, become holiday centers for legions of young southern Brazilians. En route to the latter two cities, visitors take a ferry across the Rio Buranhém.

159

SALVADOR DA BAHIA (Area Code 071)
Accommodation
EXPENSIVE: **Meridien Bahia**, Rio Vermelho, R. Fonte do Boi 216, tel. 335-8011, fax 334-1072. Extremely well managed 400-room hotel on a rise overlooking the sea. Pool, sauna, fitness room, tennis, room safes, non-smokers' rooms.
MODERATE: **Catussaba**, Itapoã, Al. da Praia de Guaritá 101, tel. 374-0555, fax 374-4749. Beach hotel, 25 km from center of town. Shuttlebus, pool, sauna, beach service, fitness room, room safes, non-smokers' rooms; **Tropical da Bahia**, Praça 2 de Julho 2, tel. 336-0102, fax 336-9725. Varig chain hotel centrally located on Campo Grande. Pool, sauna, room safes, non-smokers' rooms; **Do Farol**, Barra, Av. Pres. Vargas 68, tel. 336-6611, fax 245-4436, near the beach, pool; **Pituba Plaza**, Pituba, Av. Manoel Dias da Silva 2495, tel. 248-1022, fax 240-2493, pool, two blocks from beach; **Vilamar**, Av. Amaralina 111, tel. 248-4428, fax 248-2099, on the coastal road at Amaralina beach, pool.
BUDGET: **Villa Romana**, Barra, Rua Prof. Lemos de Brito 14, tel. 336-6522, fax 247-6748, pool; **Mar à Vista**, Ondina, near the beach, Rua Helvécio Carneiro Ribeiro 1, tel./fax 247-3866; **Corsário Tropical**, Av. Otávio Mangabeira 7549, tel. 231-6591, fax 231-8990, at Corsário beach, pool.

Restaurants
REGIONAL: **Senac**, Largo do Pelourinho 13, tel. 321-5502, school of gastromony in Pelourinho; **Tempero da Dadá**, Pelourinho, Rua Frei Vicente 5, tel. 321-5883. The chef makes masterful Bahian specialties, closed Mondays.
AFRO-BRAZILIAN: **Casa da Gamboa**, Pelourinho, Rua João de Deus 32, tel. 321-3393. Colonial atmosphere, the best Afro-Brazilian restaurant; **Uauá**, two branches in Pelourinho: Rua Gregório de Matos 36, tel. 321-3089, and at Itapoá Beach, Av. Dorival Caymi 46, tel. 249-9579. Northeast specialties, closed Mondays; **Casa do Benin**, Largo do Pelourinho 17, tel. 326-3127. Formal, expensive.
ITALIAN: **Casa d'Itália**, near Hotel da Bahia, Av. 7 de Setembro 279, tel. 321-1505, on Tuesdays only open for lunch; **Don Vitellone**, Barra, Rua Dr. Marcos Teixeira 25, tel. 235-7274.

Museums
Palácio Rio Branco, Praça Tom de Souza, tel. 243-4129, Mon-Fri 2 to 5 pm; **Museu da Cidade**, Largo do Pelourinho 3, Tue-Fri 10 am to 6 pm, Sat-Sun 1 to 5 pm; **Casa de Jorge Amado**, Largo do Pelourinho 1, tel. 321-0122, Mon-Fri 9 am to 6 pm; **Museu Abelardo Rodrigues**, Rua Gregório de Mattos 45, tel. 321-0222, Tue-Fri 9 am to 6:45 pm, Sat-Sun 11 am to 5 pm; **Igreja do Carmo**, **Igreja Ordem Terceira do Carmo**, Largo do Carmo, daily 9 am to noon, 2 to 6 pm; **Museu de Arte Sacra**, Rua do Sodré 276, tel. 243-6310, Mon-Fri 1 to 5 pm; **Museu de Ex-Votos**, Largo do Bonfim, tel. 312-0196, Tue-Sun 9 am to noon, 2 to 5:30 pm; **Museu Hidrográfico**, Forte St. Antônio da Barra, tel. 245-0539, Tue-Sun 11 am to 5 pm; **Theater Miguel Santana**, R. Gregório de Mattos, tel. 321-1155. An introduction to Candomblé that is also a performance, begins at 8 pm.

Candomblé
Visitors can attend certain religious ceremonies during non-Lenten periods. Schedules available from Bahiatursa, or ask the *terreiros* themselves for information. All forms of photography are strictly forbidden, as are shorts! **Axé Opô Afonjá**, Cabula, Estrada de São Gonçalo do Retiro 245, tel. 384-9801; **Casa Branca**, Vasco da Gama, Av. Vasco da Gama 463; **Casa Oxumaré** Vasco da Gama, Av. Vasco da Gama 343, tel. 237-2859.

Transportation
BUS STATION: Terminal Rodoviária, Pituba, Av. Antônio Carlos Magalhães, tel. 358-0765. *SHIPS:* Ferries to Itaparica: *Balsa para Bom Despacho*, Terminal Turístico Marítimo de São Joaquim, Av. Oscar Pontes 1051, tel. 320-9111, daily 6 am to 10 pm; *Mar Grande, Itaparica*: Terminal Turístico Marítimo, Av. da França, tel. 243-0741, daily 6:30 am to 7 pm. *TAXIS:* **Alôtaxi**, tel. 381-4411; **Teletaxi**, tel. 321-9988. *RENTAL CARS:* **Avis**, Ondina, tel. 245-2000; **Localiza**, tel. 241-2266.

Post Office
Av. Estados Unidos/Rua P. Martins, Lower City, Rua Alfredo Brito, Pelourinho.

Tourist Information
Bahiatursa: Praça da Sé, tel. 322-2402/2409, 8 am to 6:30 pm; Terminal Rodoviária, tel. 358-0871, 8:30 am to 9:30 pm; Aeroporto, tel. 204-1244.

PRAIA DO FORTE (Area Code 071)
Accommodation
EXPENSIVE: **Praia do Forte Resor**t, Estrada do Coco, tel. 876-1111, 0800-11-8289 (toll-free), fax 876-1112. Exclusive, four pools, tennis, windsurfing.
MODERATE: **Sobrado da Vila**, Al. do Sol, tel./fax 876-1088, 15 rooms, kitchenettes, centrally located. *BUDGET:* **Pousada Tatuapara**, Praça dos Artistas, tel. 876-1015, fax 879-0281.
Restaurants
Bombordo, Rua da Aurora 20, tel. 876-1011, fish.

ITAPARICA (Area Code 071)
Accommodation
EXPENSIVE: **Club Méditerranée**, Praia da Conceição, tel. 880-7141, fax 880-7165. Beach hotel, pool, sauna, fitness room, tennis, golf, room safes.
MODERATE: **Village Sonho Nosso**, Estrada para Cacha Pregos km 9, tel. 837-1040, fax 837-1041. 16

beach bungalows, sauna, dinner included, reasonably priced.
BUDGET: **Pousada Arco-Iris**, Mar Grande, Estrada da Gamboa 102, tel. 833-628, park, pool.

Tourist Information
Informações Turísticas, Mar Grande, Rua São Bento, tel. 833-1324, daily 8 am to 5 pm.

RECÔNCAVO (Area Code 075)
Cachoeira
Accommodation / Restaurants
Pousada do Convento, Rua Inocêncio Boaventura, tel./fax 725-516, pool, playground.

Museums
Museu Hansen Bahia, Rua Ana Nery, Mon-Sat 8 am to noon, 2 to 5 pm, Sun 8 am to noon; **Centro Cultural Dannemann**, São Félix, Av. Salvador Pinto 29, tel. 725-2202, Tue-Sat 8 am to 5 pm, Sun 1 to 5 pm.

FEIRA DE SANTANA
Accommodation
MODERATE: **Feira Palace**, Av. Maria Quitéria 1572, tel. 221-5011, fax 221-5409, restaurant, pool.
BUDGET: **Senador**, Rua Sen. Quintino 10, tel./fax 623-5111.

Restaurants
O Picuí, Rua Maria Quitéria 2463, tel. 221-1018, regional cuisine.

Bus Station
Av. Pres. Dutra, tel. 623-3667.

LENÇÓIS (Area Code 075)
Accommodation
MODERATE: **Pousada de Lençóis**, Rua Altina Alves 747, tel. 334-1102, fax 334-1180, restaurant, pool; **Pousada Canto das Águas**, Av. Sr. dos Passos, tel. 334-1154, fax 334-1188. Exquisite riverside location, restaurant, pool, noisy on weekends.
BUDGET: **Fazenda da Parque**, BR 242 km 2, tel. 071-248-8967, pool; **Colonial**, Praça Otaviano Alves 750, tel. 334-1114, centrally located.

Restaurants
Os Artistas da Massa, Rua da Baderna 111, Italian cuisine; **Lajedo**, Rua Cajueiro, regional cuisine.

Bus Station
Av. Sr. dos Passos.

Tourist Information
Av. Sr. dos Passos, tel. 334-1121.

Parque Nacional Chapada Diamantina
Info from **Ibama**. In Salvador, Av. J. Magalhaes Jr. 608, tel. 071-240-7343, in Palmeiras, tel. 332-2175.

ILHÉUS (Area Code 073)
Accommodation
EXPENSIVE: **Transamérica Ilha de Comandatuba**, Estrada para Canavieiras km 81, tel. 613-

1122 and 0800-12-6060 (toll-free), fax 613-1114. Island hotel, windsurfing, boats, jet-skiing, heliport, pool, sauna, bikes, tennis, fitness room, room safes, good restaurants; **Jardim Atlântico**, Estrada para Olivença km 2, tel. 632-2222, fax 632-2223. Beach hotel, pool, sauna, tennis, fitness room, room safes.
MODERATE: **Pousada Morada do Cristo**, Av. 2 de Julho 179, tel./fax 231-3156. Beautiful location, only seven rooms, pool; **Pousada do Sol**, Estrada para Olivença km 2.5, tel./fax 632-7000. Beach hotel with 100 rooms, pool, room safes.
BUDGET: **Pousada Encontro das Águas**, Av. 2 de Julho 393, tel. 634-8746, pool; **Pousada Praia dos Milagres**, Estrada para Una km 18, tel./fax 269-1140, pool.

Restaurants
Os velhos Marinheiros, Av. 2 de Julho, tel. 231-6771. Good fish, on the beach; **Alfama**, Av. Itabuna 159, tel. 231-2810, closed Sun, Portuguese cuisine; **Bar Vezúvio**, Pça. Dom Pedro, tel. 231-2338.

Museums
Museu Regional do Cacau, Rua Antônio de Lemos 126, Mon-Fri 2 to 6 pm.

Transportation
BUS STATION: Est. para Itabuna km 4, tel. 231-4221. *RENTAL CARS:* **Localiza**, tel. 212-5833; **Unidas**, tel. 231-8572.

Tourist Information
Ilheustur: Praça Castro Alves, tel. 231-661.

PORTO SEGURO (Area Code 073)
Accommodation
MODERATE: **Porto Seguro Praia**, Praia de Curuípe km 3.5, tel. 288-2321, fax 288-2069. Park, pool, sauna, fitness room, room safes; **Portobello Praia**, Praia de Taperapuã, tel. 879-2911, fax 879-2320. Beach hotel, pool, sauna; **Porto Príncipe**, Av. dos Navegantes 82, tel. 288-2721, fax 288-2327, pool, sauna, room safes; **Shalimar**, Praia do Cruzeiro km 1, tel./fax 288-2001, pool, sauna.
BUDGET: **Alegrete Porto**, Av. dos Navegantes 567, tel./fax 288-538, pool; **Pousada do Cais**, Av. Portugal 382, tel. 288-2112, fax 288-2540.

Restaurants
Anticaro, Rua Assis Chateaubriand 26, tel. 288-2683, international cuisine; **Cruz de Malta**, Av. Getúlio Vargas 358, tel. 288-2399, seafood; **Oxalá**, Av. Portugal 516, tel. 288-1520, regional cuisine.

Transportation
BUS STATION: Upper city, BR 367 km 1.5, tel. 288-1039, 288-2707. *FERRIES* to Arraial d'Ajuda (every 15 minutes), Praça dos Pataxós, tel. 288-3177. *RENTAL CARS:* **Localiza**, tel. 288-1488. *MOTORBIKES:* **Bem Brasil**, tel. 288-2532.

Tourist Information
Informações Turísticas, airport, tel. 288-1428.

PERNAMBUCO

Situated in relatively densely populated eastern South America, the 98,000-square-kilometer state of **Pernambuco** still bears the indelible imprint of colonial Portugal and Holland, in the form of the slave trade and sugar-cane plantations on the one hand, and European culture on the other. Recife, the "Venice of Brazil," and its sister city of Olinda, both have superb national monuments. Moreover, thanks to inexpensive charter flights, their breathtaking beaches play host to tens of thousands of tourists each year. The state as a whole has two distinct seasons: rainy from March to July, and dry during the remainder of the year.

Government regulations requiring that ethyl alcohol be used to power automobiles have led to an increase in sugarcane production over the past few decades, and Brazil is currently, along with India, the world's leading producer of sugar cane. A substantial amount of this commodity is grown in Pernambuco: fields with long green stalks of sugar cane stretch far into the interior, all the way to the Sertão. Other mainstays of the state's economy include tropical and semitropical fruits (bananas, oranges, coconuts), livestock raising, fishing, and along the coast, tourism.

RECIFE – The Gap in the Reef

"Recife" means "reef": it was in this place, during the 16th century, that Portuguese sailors discovered an opening in the coral reef, and thereby an ideal location for a much-needed harbor. Until the arrival of the Dutch in the 17th century, Recife, which today has a population of over one million, was merely a port for Olinda, the wealthy administrative capi-

Left: The abundant aquatic life off the coast of Pernambuco provides inhabitants with a modest livelihood.

tal of the Pernambuco captaincy. But the originator of Recife's nickname, "the Venice of Brazil" surely never set foot in the Italian city. A more appropriate name for Recife might be the "Manhattan of the Northeast" or perhaps the "Amsterdam of Brazil." The modern-day capital of Pernambuco owes its canals and 39 bridges to the Dutch, who, in 1630, at the behest of Prince Moritz of Nassau, drained the swamps, dug the canals, and built the marvelous gabled houses, *sobrados magros*, modeled on those the settlers had left behind in the Netherlands.

The picturesque Old Town is situated on the islands lying at the mouth of the two rivers, Rio Capibaribe and Rio Beberibe. **Boa Viagem Beach**, which is on the mainland, is also called the "Copacabana of Pernambuco," and is known both for its hotels and its red-light district.

The Historic Old Town

The historic districts of Santo Antônio and São José, which are best toured on foot, can be found on the northern half of the elongated **Ilha Joana Bezerra**, the northern tip of which is occupied by the flamboyantly yellow **Palácio das Princesas** in **Santo Antônio** on **Praça da República**. **Teatro Santa Isabel** (in front of the palace) also makes its quieter, neoclassical presence felt. Built by the French architect Luis Vauthier in 1850, it is open to the public.

Though obscured from view by highrise buildings, diagonally across from the Teatro is the **Capela Dourada**, in the **Convento de Santo Antônio**, the oldest cloister and most brilliant jewel in Recife's architectural crown. Founded in 1606, the church was not actually completed until the beginning of the 18th century, and over the course of the next hundred years the majority of its furnishings were lost. However, the cupola, tiled in Moorish style, and the azulejos in the cloister have been preserved. Not to be

missed on any account is the "gilded chapel," which is separated from the church only by a grating. Commissioned by a sugar baron to prove to the motherland that culture was thriving in Brazil, this most striking of Baroque spaces in Brazil was created between 1696 and 1724 by the master church builder Antônio Fernandes Matos and the wood-carver Antônio Santiago. The most impressive of the murals depicts the martyrdom of the missionaries in the Far East, while the chapel's prodigal gilding creates an atmosphere of harmonious unity.

South of the cloister at **Praça da Independência** stands **Santíssimo Sacramento** (parish church of the Santo Antônio district), which dates from the 18th century. Its deftly executed hand-carved filigreed stone façade is a visual delight.

Recife boasts 62 churches, too many for even the most ardent of art history afi-

cionados to visit, especially in the intense heat of the tropical day. But no visitor should leave without having admired the cathedral located in the São José district. On the way there, you pass the Baroque Carmelite church of **Igreja do Carmo**, from which **Pátio de São Pedro** (St. Peter's Courtyard), the colonial showpiece of the Old Town, can be reached. This "courtyard" is actually an enclosed colonial plaza with the **Catedral de São Pedro dos Clárigos** as its focal point. Consecrated in 1782 and restored in 1858, it is the only church in the northeast with an octagonal interior. The feeling of spaciousness within is enhanced by João de Sepúlveda's superb ceiling frescos. The choir stalls are made of cedar, while the sacristy has masterfully carved rosewood commodes and closets.

The side streets of Recife's Old Town are packed with small stores, bars, street vendors and hustlers. In the evening, the outdoor cafés on Pátio de São Pedro are popular places for relaxing. Weekends bring performances by folklore and

Above: Recife's lovely historic Old Town.
Right: Enthusiastic soccer fans at the stadium in Recife.

samba groups, as well as rehearsals by Carnival associations.

Further east on **Travessa do Macedo** lies São Jose's market hall, **Mercado São José**, an ironwork structure by the French architect Luis Vauthier that harks back to Parisian markets of a bygone era.

Perched on *Bacia do Pina* and bearing silent testimony to the Dutch military presence of centuries ago is **Forte das Cinco Pontas**, which the Portuguese took over from the besieged occupiers. On the way back to the mainland, one option is to stop by at **Casa da Cultura**, situated on the opposite shore of the island. Here, the entrepreurnial acumen of the *Pernambucanos* is clearly in evidence: they even promote art in a dungeon, which is what the "House of Culture" originally was.

Museums and Beaches

There are two notable museums at Rio Capabaribe on the mainland in the northern part of the city. The **Museu do Es-tado de Pernambuco**, three kilometers from the center of town in the **Graças** district, has on display furniture from the colonial era and the time of the Emperor's reign, as well as handcrafts and paintings.

Located three kilometers to the west is the **Museu do Homem do Nordeste**, Brazil's preeminent anthropological museum, founded by Gilberto Freyre, one of the country's foremost practitioners of this discipline. Among the diverse cultural phenomena documented by this institution are the treatment of slaves, folklore, handicrafts, sugar refining, and the musical instruments and dress of the people of the Northeast. *Literatura de Cordel*, "literature on a string" (see p. 232) – novels and pamphlets that can be bought or borrowed that hang from a string when on display – intrigue many visitors to the museum, as does pottery produced in the region. In his book *The Mansions and the Shanties*, Freyre gives an empathic and comprehensive account of Brazilian sociocultural history.

Of great importance for Brazilian national consciousness is the **Parque Histórico Nacional dos Guararapes**, 14 kilometers south of Recife. It was here in 1648 and 1649 that the Dutch were defeated in decisive battles with Portuguese and Brazilian troops, which led to the Treaty of Independence of 1654 and the withdrawal of the occupying forces. In 1656, **Nossa Senhora dos Prazeres** was built to commemorate this event. The church is decorated with tiled murals, as well as altars that are decorated with striking overlays of carved wood.

Piedade, **Candeias**, **Porto de Galinhas** and **Tamandar**, Pernambuco's southern beaches – 100 kilometers from Recife – are among the best places to swim in the northeast. At low tide you can wade to the coral reef, and when the tide comes in you can sometimes hitch a ride on a *jangada*. These balsa-wood rafts that fishermen sail on the open sea are held together with lashing and propelled by a single triangular lateen sail.

OLINDA
Beautiful and Protected Monuments

"*O linda situação para uma vila*" ("What a beautiful place for a city"): These are the words Duarte Coelho is supposed to have uttered upon founding a Portuguese colony here in 1535 – whence, it is believed, came "O linda" and with it the city's name. There exists another plausible explanation for the appellation: The name "beautiful one" is also apt, as this city of 350,000 inhabitants, located seven kilometers north of Recife, has been declared a UNESCO World Heritage Site. The "beauty" in the name suits Olinda's enchanting (and coastal) Old Town, although the city has of course undergone considerable change since colonial days.

A good starting point for a walking tour is the bus station at **Praça do Carmo**. With the sea at your back, look

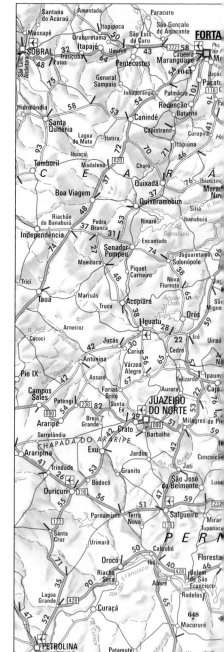

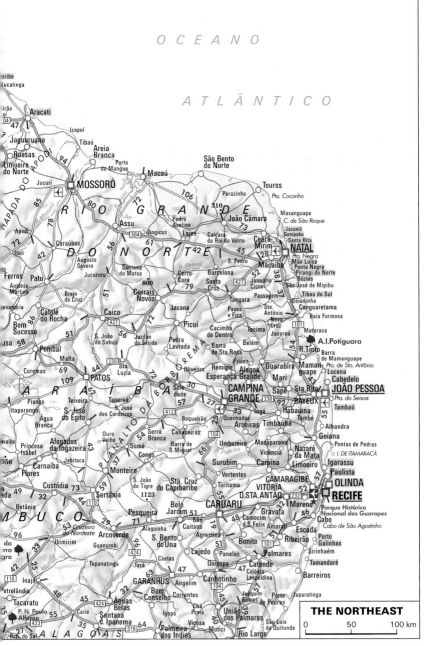

O C E A N O

A T L Â N T I C O

aribe
Sucatinga

irão
o 04 47
Aracati
Icapuí
Jaguaruana
Russas
Tibaú
Areia
Branca
Porto
do Mangue
Macaú
São Bento
do Norte
Limoeiro
do Norte
Jucuri
MOSSORÓ
Touros
Pta. Coconho
Parazinho
Assu
Pedro
Avelino
João Câmara
Maxanguape
C. de São Roque
Angicos
Lajes
Caiçara
do Rio do Vento
Jacumã
Genipabu
Santa Rita
Ceará-
Mirim
NATAL
Caraúbas
Augusto
Severo
Santana
do Matos
Cerro-
Corá
S. Pedro
Barcelona
Santa
Cruz
Macaíba
Januário
Cicco
Pta. Negra
Mãe Luísa
Ponta Negra
Pirangi do Norte
Búzios
São José de Mipibu
Ferros
Patu
Jucurutu
800
79
Currais
Novos
Jacana
Passagem
Tangara
Passa
e Fica
Sto.
Antônio
Nova
Cruz
Tibaú do Sul
Goianinha
Canguaretama
Baía Formosa
Brejo
do Cruz
exandria
Catolé
do Rocha
Caicó
427
72
Picuí
Cacimba
de Dentro
Jardim
do Sérido
Pedra
Lavrada
Jacaraú
Mataraca
A.I.Potiguara
R.Tinto
Barra
de Mamanguape
Pta. de Sto. Antônio
Bom
Sucesso
usa 58
Pombal
Malta
Coremas
69
109
PATOS
230
Sta.
Luzia
S. João
do Sabují
Olivêdos
Barra
de Sta.Rosa
Pilões
Remígio
Esperança
Alagoa
Grande
Mari
Guarabira
Lucena
Cabedelo
Mamanguape
JOÃO PESSOA
Pta. do Seixas
Tambaú
Piancó
Teixeira
Taperoá
S. José
dos Cordeiros
412
57
27
Solê-
dade
CAMPINA
GRANDE
230
Sapé
BAYEUX
92
Itaporanga
Água
Branca
S. José
do Egito
Boqueirão
Queimadas
Ingá
Itabaiana
Tombé
Alhandra
Afogados
da Ingazeira
Ouro
Velho
Sumé
Serra
Branca
Cabaceiras
104
Umbuzeiro
Aroeiras
Timbaúba
Goiana
Pontas de Pedras
I. DE ITAMARACÁ
Princesa
Isabel
Jabitaca
Congo
Barra de
S. Miguel
Vicência
Macaparana
Nazaré
da Mata
Igarassu
Carnaíba
Flores
Monteiro
Surubim
Carpina
Limoeiro
Paulista
OLINDA
Custódia
73
Sertânia
S. João
do Tigre
1123
Sta. Cruz
do Capibaribe
Vertentes
Toritama
CAMARAGIBE
VITÓRIA
D.STA.ANTÃO
232
52
RECIFE
Betânia
110
Pesqueira
Belo
Jardim
51
CARUARU
Gravatá
Moreno
Parque Histórico
Nacional dos Guarapes
Cabo
Cruzeiro
do Nordeste
Arcoverde
29
71
São
Caitano
Agrestina
Camocim
d.S.Félix Amaraji
Escada
Cabo de São Agostinho
Porto
de Galinhas
Ibimirim
Guanumbi
424
Alagoinha
S. Bento
do Una
Bonito
101
Ribeirão
Sirinhaém
Inajá
Tupanatinga
Tará
Cáetas
Lajedo
Panelas
47
Palmares
Tamandaré
etrolândia
63
Quipapa
Catende
Colônia
Leopoldina
Barreiros
Tacaratu
P. N. Paulo
Afonso
423
45
424
Águas
Belas
Carié
GARANHUS
Bom
Conselho
Santana
d. Ipanema
316
Angelim
Correntes
Igapó
Canhotinho
104
Chã
Preta
União
dos Palmares
Joaquim
Gomes
Porto
de Pedras
Japaratinga
Rch. do Sat
A L A G O A S
35
64
Palmeira
dos Índios
Viçosa
Mutici
São Luís
da Quitunde
Rio Largo

THE NORTHEAST
0   50   100 km

to the left for Nossa Senhora do Carmo, the oldest Carmelite church in Brazil. It will be familiar to anyone who has seen the Dutch artist Franz Post's painting that made the church famous. Ironically, it was burnt down by the Dutch in 1631, then rebuilt in 1720, and completely restored at the end of the 20th century.

Proceeding to the right down Rua São Francisco, you reach the Franciscan cloister **Convento de São Francisco**, which was founded in 1585. The glorious view of the sea from this location is indicative of the good taste of the members of the order, which is still quite active throughout northeastern Brazil. In view of the prevailing hot and humid climate, the reason why **Nossa Senhora das Neves** ("Our Lady of the Snow") was so named remains something of a mystery. Like Nossa Senhora do Carmo, it was

Above: Colonial relics of Olinda's glory days contrast sharply with Recife's modernist skyline. Right: The Franciscan convent in Olinda.

also destroyed by the Dutch occupying forces, and then rebuilt during the next century. Inside the church are arresting ajulejos that narrate the life of the Virgin Mary; the life of St. Francis is similarly depicted in the cloister. Equally impressive are ceiling frescos in the meeting room and sacristy.

Continuing uphill on Rua Bispo Coutinho, the visitor will come upon (on a rise off to the right) the Jesuit church of **Nossa Senhor da Graça**, which was designed by Francisco Dias, the founder of ecclesiastical architecture in Brazil. It is also the site of a seminary for the diocese, whose archbishop, Dom Helder Câmara, is a world-famous proponent of liberation theology.

Alto da Sé – Cathedral on a Hill

Even visitors who have vowed they will visit no churches while in Brazil should make the short climb up this hill, if only for the view. Standing before the cathedral looking out over the palm and

rosewood trees and down to the sea below, one senses the distinctive atmosphere of this historic city. During the day, the plaza is frequented by the inevitable souvenir vendors. In the evening, visitors can sit outdoors nibbling cheese smoked on a spit and sipping ice-cold coconut milk or beer.

Unfortunately, numerous attempts at restoration have diminished the art-historical interest of the **Igreja da Sé São Salvador do Mundo**, founded as Olinda's first parish church in 1537. The view of the former Episcopal Palace (17th century) next door is obscured by a white architectural monstrosity, a water tower by Oscar Niemeyer that many people would like to see torn down. Today, the palace houses the religious and folk art collections of the **Museu de Arte Sacra de Pernambuco**.

Further to the north lies Largo da Misericórdia, on whose corner stands the **Igreja da Misericórdia** (1540), which contains striking tile work and a splendid pulpit. You now pass the Igreja Nossa Senhora do Amparo on Rua São Martinho and then climb Rua do Amparo, where the former bishop's residence (today a regional museum) is to be found, along with several well-preserved **sobrados** – two-story colonial houses with balconies and *muxarabi*, Moorish-style latticework.

Rua 13 de Maio leads to the former *Cadeia Pública* (prison), now the **Museu de Arte Contemporânea**. The plaza in the next street over (to the east), **Mercado da Ribeira**, was the slave market in the 17th century, and today is the site of a handicrafts market at which, on Sundays at 8 p.m., folklore groups also perform. Further south on Rua São Bento stands the **Palácio Governadores**, the former Governor-General's Palace dating from the 17th century and now the prefectural seat.

It's only a short walk from here to **Mosteiro de São Bento**, a Benedictine monastery with tall and shady palm trees in its forecourt. The cloister church, consecrated in the 16th century, underwent

considerable change during reconstruction after being destroyed by Dutch troops. Of greatest interest inside the church are its wood carvings based on Portuguese motifs and a high altar dating from the 18th century.

A few minutes' walk takes you to the river road. The beach close to town is not suitable for swimming, but the simple oceanfront restaurants there serve delicious seafood dishes.

Swimming Beaches

The best swimming beaches in this area are situated eight kilometers north of the village of **Paulista**, where, in 1719, the Portuguese constructed a fort on the beach at **Pau Amarelo**. Further north, in **Maria Farinha**, visitors can marvel at extensive stands of mangrove trees. This

Above: Baroque splendor at the cloister church of São Bento in Olinda. Right: The northeast's palm-lined beaches attract large numbers of visitors.

is also an ideal locale for water sports such as windsurfing and water-skiing.

Forty-five kilometers north of Recife lies **Insel Itamaracá**, which is linked to the mainland by a bridge. Visitors to this island can not only revel in its vast expanses of pristine white sand, but can also laze away part of the day on the open sea in a catamaran. The trip lasts approximately four and a half hours, and the Hotel Amoaras in Maria will supply you with all the pertinent information.

Igarassu

This small village, which is located 39 kilometers north of Recife, was founded even earlier than Olinda, in 1530. Devotees of religious art will find a trip here well worth their while; some *sobrados* (colonial houses) have also been preserved. **São Cosme e São Damião**, the main house of worship in the village (on the eponymous square), is thought to be one of the oldest stone churches in Brazil. Frans Post also immortalized it in one of his paintings.

Santo Antônio, the Franciscan convent on Rua Barbosa Lima, was founded in 1588 and subsequently burned down by the Dutch; it was not rebuilt until the 18th century. This single-nave structure is decorated with lovely painted tiles inside, and a handsome vestment cupboard in the sacristy. Unusual and worth seeing is the **Pinacoteca**, a collection of paintings by anonymous masters, including mural paintings of saints and a depiction of the plague in Olinda in 1685, which miraculously left Igarassu untouched.

JOÃO PESSOA

Although **João Pessoa**, capital of the small state of **Paraíba**, contains its share of interesting churches and cloisters, it is best known for the futuristic-looking hotel located seven kilometers to the east, in **Tambaú**. The **Hotel Tropical Tam-**

baú, a round structure with a tower set in the middle, bears a striking resemblance to a rocket launching pad. The architect, Sergio Bernardes, also designed the hotel in such a way that half of the structure sits directly over the water.

João Pessoa is located not on the sea but rather on the banks of the Rio Paraíba. Upon being founded in 1585 it was granted a town charter, making it the third-oldest city in Brazil. If they wish, early risers can be the first on the South American subcontinent to see the sun come up: beyond Cabo Branco (White Cape) lies **Ponta do Seixas**, the easternmost point in the Americas.

An appealing day-trip option is Cabedelo, a spit of land just north of João Pessoa. Visitors can sail from **Praia do Poço** to **Ilha da Areia Vermelha** ("Island of the Red Sands") on *jangadas* – but only in summer at low tide when the island emerges from the sea. Other superb beaches await visitors north of João Pessoa at **Lucena** and **Tambaba** (29 and 35 kilometers north respec-

tively). Both of these locales feature cliffs, natural swimming pools, and – a rarity in Brazil – nude bathing.

Well worth taking time out for in the center of this town of 500,000 is a leisurely stroll through the **Parque Sólon de Lucena**, which leads past an artificial lake and towering coconut palms to the **Convento de Santo Antônio**, a Franciscan monastery in Baroque style that through the years has been put to various uses: seminary, hospital, school, administrative building, and (today) **Museu Sacro e de Arte Popular**, a museum of religious and folk art.

The convent church of **São Francisco**, which was constructed between 1701 and 1734, is a magnificent edifice that features an ornate triangular façade and a portico with five arches. The interior walls are decorated with azulejos, and there is a striking illusionistic ceiling fresco depicting the Mother of God and canonized Franciscans. The extensively gilded interior of this church has earned the adjoining **Capela de Ordem Ter-**

ceira de São Francisco the byname *Capela Dourada*, or "Golden Chapel."

NATAL

Just under 300 kilometers north of Recife and a long 2,625 kilometers from Rio lies **Natal** (population 650,000), the capital of the state of **Rio Grande do Norte**. The city derives its name, as do so many others in Brazil, from the ecclesiastical calendar: it was founded in 1599 during Christmas, for which the Portuguese word is *Natal*. Visitors will find no religious art here: being at such a great distance from the center of colonial power kept the wealth enjoyed by other Brazilian cities at a distance as well.

Natal does nonetheless have several interesting sights to offer. The largest saltworks and cotton plantation in Brazil are located nearby; and rocket research is carried out 20 kilometers south of the city at **Barreiro do Inferno** (The Gates of Hell), so named owing to the reddish sand dunes near the facility, which visitors can tour on Wednesdays by prearrangement.

Natal has evolved from a riverine port on the Rio Potengi to a coastal harbor, and is no longer sandwiched between fresh and salt water. In 1598, the Portuguese built **Forte dos Reis Magos** (Fort of the Magi) at the northern tip of the city, naming it after the feast day in the ecclesiastical calendar (Epiphany; January 6) on which work was begun on it. The fort, built to a star-shaped plan, has five bastions and was erected as protection against the French. Today it is the city's biggest tourist attraction. A tour guide regales visitors with dramatic accounts of the taking of important prisoners, and of the 20-year-long siege of the fort by the Dutch.

Right: Visitors to the beach at Genipabu can go for a stroll along the dunes or sign up for a boat excursion.

Casa de Dentenção, originally a prison, is now a tourist center featuring crafts shops, art galleries and restaurants. The city also has one museum that is worth a brief visit: the **Câmara Cascudo**, in the Tirol district east of the upper part of the city, features anthropological and ethnological exhibits, as well as displays of religious art and a sugar mill.

Beaches to the South

On the beach at **Mãe Luisa**, four kilometers south of Natal, visitors have the rare opportunity to climb to the top of a lighthouse (open Sundays from 2 to 5 p.m.). In **Ponta Negra**, 10 kilometers further south, you can marvel at **Morro do Careca**, a 120-meter-high sand dune that is part of a unique landscape best toured in a dune buggy, which can be rented in Natal.

The next attraction south (28 kilometers), in **Pirangi do Norte**, is from the plant kingdom: **O Cajueiro**, a gigantic cashew tree which has as an appendage a large accessory fruit, the bitter cashew nut, which can only be eaten after being roasted. The crowns of these magnificent trees are estimated to measure about 7,000 square meters. Boat excursions that follow the coastline leave from the dock near the beach.

A perfect scuba-diving and surfing area awaits water-sports enthusiasts in nearby **Búzios**. Surfers will also be highly pleased with **Barra da Tabatinga** (at kilometer 40), an ideal place to ride the waves, situated as it is between cliffs and a reef. The coastal highway ends 50 kilometers south of Natal at **Camurupim**, where superb white sand dunes and natural swimming pools provide the perfect backdrop for a memorable beach holiday. This Edenic coastal environment is best explored in a dune buggy. Visitors can make the crossing to **Tibau do Sul** in a tiny ferry. **Pipa**, 90 kilometers from

Natal, is a locale where the young, rich and beautiful frolic.

Genipabu – Beaches to the North

After traversing the broad mouth of the Rio Potenji, five kilometers west of Natal, you come to the beach, dunes and coral reef of **Santa Rita**, 11 kilometers beyond Redinha. Visitors without cars can take the ferry from the port at Rio Potenji in Natal.

Genipabu is a ten-minute ferry ride or a 24-kilometer drive from **Praia da Redinha**. The town is known for its exquisite lagoon surrounded by huge sand dunes and cashew trees. Boat excursions that depart right from the silky sands of the dunes are also available, as are sightseeing flights in ultralight aircraft. Farther to the north in the fishing village of **Graçandu** visitors will find natural seawater pools to swim in, and snorkeling devotees will relish the scrumptiously colorful marine life in the lagoon **Lagoa de Pitangui**. Amidst the dunes and reefs of

Jacumã, 50 kilometers north of Natal, both scuba divers and fishermen will find conditions well suited to their respective pursuits.

FORTALEZA
Fortified and Embattled

In 1603, Martim Soares Moreno was instructed by the Portuguese Governor-General to pave the way for settlement of the coast of **Ceará**, and to "pacify" the indigenous inhabitants. After many years of conflict and numerous setbacks, an alliance was made with the Jaguaribe, and a fort was built at the mouth of the Rio Ceará that, with native help, successfully held off French attacks. But in 1649 the Dutch seized control of the tiny settlement and built a new fortification, Fort Schoonenborch, and at the same time laid the cornerstone for a new city.

When, in 1654, the Portuguese wrested control of the entire northeast coast from the Dutch, the fort was renamed Fortaleza de Nossa Senhora da Assunção.

173

Fortaleza, (Fort) then became the (shortened) name of this city, the fifth largest in Brazil and capital of the state of Ceará, where much of daily life is dominated by the semi-arid climate of the Sertão. The state's economic mainstays include cotton and cashews, livestock raising, the textile industry and tourism.

In 1884, four years before slavery was officially abolished by Princess Isabel, Ceará became the first Brazilian state to ban the buying and selling of human beings (although the practice was not very widespread in Ceará to begin with). The bulk of the population is comprised of *morenos* and *mulatos* (descendants of Europeans and black Africans), and *caboclos* (descendants of Europeans and indigenous peoples).

The fort in the town center is still used as a military barracks and can be visited, but only by special arrangement. An ar-

*Above: Traditional fishing methods in Natal.
Right: Lacemakers offer their work for sale in Aquiraz.*

resting edifice in Fortaleza is the muncipal theater, **Teatro José de Alencar**, an Art Nouveau iron structure whose components were brought over from England. Its official opening took place in 1910. The theater bears the name of the city's most famous poet; its box seats bear the titles of his works; and a monument to the poet stands in **Praça José de Alencar**, the plaza in front of the theater. In novels such as *The Guarani* and *Icarema*, Alencar avoided falling into the trap of romanticizing the indigenous peoples of Brazil, and instead tried to see them objectively as an integral and real part of Brazilian life. Alencar was born in 1829. His father was a senator, and he himself became Brazilian Minister of Justice when he was only 39 years old.

Visitors who love markets won't want to miss the **Mercado Central** on Rua Conde, across from the Neo-Gothic cathedral. In addition to a cornucopia of vegetables, fruit, fish and spices, the marketplace affords visitors the opportunity to purchase the much-prized work of lacemakers. Coverlets and tablecloths are painstakingly produced in coastal villages, mostly by older women who are the wives of fishermen. Prices are reasonable considering the amount of arduous work involved. Lace can also be purchased in a more comfortable setting, albeit at higher prices, in the **Centro de Turismo** (Rua S. Pompeu), which was originally a prison and is located in a district rich in historical lore.

Excursions from Fortaleza

Trains for the two-and-a-half-hour trip to **Baturite** – an important regional commercial center in the highlands that was founded in 1745 – depart on Saturdays and Sundays from *Estação Ferroviária*. Conveniently grouped at Praça Matriz visitors will find the Baroque Nossa Senhora da Palma, Palácio Entre-Rios, and other stately colonial buildings.

Do not interpret the heart-gladdening sight of throngs of children playing on the beaches near Fortaleza to mean that those sandy stretches are clean, because they are in fact extremely dirty and not suitable for swimming. But don't despair either: there is a beach in your future, appropriately named **Praia do Futuro** (Beach of the Future), and it is located in **Porto das Dunas**, eight kilometers southeast of town. In addition to handsome palm groves and sensuous sand dunes, the beach features boats you can rent, dune buggies, horses and surfboards you can ride, and ultralight aircraft you can sightsee from the air in.

Two kilometers away lies the town of **Aquiraz** (population 50,000), where some fine examples of colonial architecture are to be found. At **Centro de Rendeiras da Prainha**, visitors can watch bobbin lace makers (*rendeiras*) at work, and can also purchase the lovely fruits of their labors.

Beberibe, 78 kilometers from Fortaleza, is justifiably renowned for its de-

lectable lobsters and delightful beach, **Morro Branco**. Two good reasons to venture 10 kilometers further down the road to **Praia das Fontes** are the freshwater cascade at the beach and the "water" cave, Mãe d'Água, which is only visible at low tide, however. This dreamscape of lagoons, dunes and pretty beaches extends as far as **Arcati**, 142 kilometers southeast of Forteleza, encompassing the sand- and sun-drenched swimming paradises of **Fortim** and **Canoa Quebrada** as well.

SÃO LUÍS

International tourists have thus far paid little heed to this city of 800,000 and the state, **Maranhão**, of which it is capital. For three years in the early 17th century **São Luís** was used as a base by the French, and then came under Dutch control for an equally short period (1641-1644). The architecture in the historic town center, a registered national monument, is predominantly Portuguese, with

façades featuring Portuguese azujelos that help keep the buildings cool.

São Luís is a port city situated on a pensinsula that it shares with the towns of Paço do Lumiar, São José do Ribamar, Anil and Itaqui. The latter has a time-saving car-ferry service to **Itaúna**, from which you can easily drive to the neighboring city of Pará.

Visitors wishing to take a day trip to **Alcântra** can choose between the aging passenger ferries or the more modern *aerobarco* craft at the dock in São Luís, from whence they are whisked in 75 minutes to this 17th-century colonial village, which lies on the opposite (mainland) shore. Electricity only arrived in this dilapidated village in 1988 after the Brazilian government began building a rocket base nearby. Some buildings in the village were never completed, among them the parish church, Matriz de São Matias, whose walls, made using whale

oil, collapsed before so much as one mass was celebrated. The palaces of two families who were vying with each other to pay homage to Emperor Dom Pedro II upon the occasion of his visit also remained unfinished, because the Emperor angrily decided not to come after all.

During the second half of June, life in Maranhão, and especially in São Luíz, centers around the effervescent festival of São João, during which joyful throngs drum, sing and dance their way through the Old Town, exuberantly acting out the pageant-cum-dance known as **Bumba-meu-boi**. A dancer portraying the bull, *boi estrela*, symbol of wealth, dressed in a papier-mâché costume decorated with glass pearls and sequins, is exposed to various dangers that are depicted in a farcical style. The loud and boisterous Bumba-meu-boi spectacle has its origins in protests against Portuguese and ecclesiastical domination during colonial times. But for modern-day participants it's just *a brincadeira mais linda*: "pure unadulterated fun."

Above: A young fisherman learns how to handle a lateen sail (near São Luis).

RECIFE
Area Code 081
Accommodation
EXPENSIVE: **Caesar Park Cabode de Santo Agostinho**, Vila Suape, 45 km south of Recife, Av. Beira Mar 750, tel. 521-6000, fax 521-6010. Recently opened beach hotel with every imaginable comfort; **Sheraton Petribu**, Piedade, 20 km south of town, Av. Bernardo Vieira de Melo 1624, tel. 468-1288 and 0800-11-6000 (toll-free), fax 468-1118. Beautifully situated beach hotel with pool, sauna, tennis, room safes, non-smokers' rooms.

MODERATE: **Atlante Plaza**, Boa Viagem, Av. Boa Viagem 5426, tel./fax 462-3333. Ocean view, pool, room safes, non-smokers' rooms, very good restaurants; **Fator Palace**, Boa Viagem, R. dos Navegantes 157, tel./fax 465-0040, pool, sauna; **Novotel Chaves Recife**, Piedade, Av. Bernardo Vieira de Melo 694, tel. 468-4343 and 0800-11-1790 (toll-free), fax 468-4344. Beach hotel, pool, room safes; **Onda Mar**, Boa Viagem, R. Ernesto de Paula Santos 284, tel./fax 465-2833, pool; **Savaroni**, Boa Viagem, Av. Boa Viagem 3772, tel. 465-4299, fax 326-4900, pool, family atmosphere, kids welcome.

BUDGET: **Aquamar Praia**, Boa Viagem, Rua dos Navegantes 492, tel. 326-4604, fax 326-4317, near the beach; **Arcada**, Boa Viagem, Av. Cons. Aguiar 3500, tel./fax 465-6499, room safes; **Vila Rica Ideale**, on the road to Boa Viagem, Av. Boa Viagem 4308, tel. 465-8111, fax 465-0477, pool.

Restaurants
CHURRASCARIAS: **Porcão**, Boa Viagem, Av. Eng. Domingos Ferreira 4215, tel. 465-3999, *rodízio*; **Spettus**, Derby, Av. Agamenon Magalhães 2132, tel. 423-4122, *rodízio*.

SEAFOOD: **Lobster**, at the Capibaribe River, Av. Rui Barbosa 1649, tel. 268-5516. In a colonial building dating from 1813. Lobster and shellfish, live music; **Cícero Rei do Camarão**, Boa Viagem, Av. Boa Viagem 5476, tel. 462-3656.

PORTUGUESE: **Tasca,** Boa Viagem, Rua Dom José Lopes 165, tel. 326-6309, closed Mondays, dried cod and crab dishes; **Recanto Lusitano**, Boa Viagem, Rua Antônio Vicente 284, tel. 462-2161. Specialities from the Minho region of Portugal, also Portuguese wines. On Sundays only open for lunch, closed Mondays.

INTERNATIONAL: **Chez Georges**, Pina, Av. Antônio de Góes 183 A, tel. 326-2768. Superb meat and seafood dishes including wild boar cutlet in wine sauce, expensive, open for dinner only. Closed Sun-Mon; **Costa Brava**, Boa Viagem, Rua Barão de Souza Leão 698, tel. 341-3535.

Sights
Teatro Santa Isabel, Praça da República, tel. 224-1020, Mon-Fri 1 to 5 pm; **Convento de Santo Antônio**, Rua do Imperador 206, tel. 224-0530, Mon-Fri 8 to 11:30 am and 2 to 5 pm, Sat 8 to 11:30 am; **Casa da Cultura**, Santo Antônio, Rua Floriano Peixoto, tel. 224-2850, Mon-Sat 9 am to 7 pm; **Forte das Cinco Pontas**, Largo das cinco Pontas, tel. 224-8492, Mon-Fri 9 am to 6 pm, Sat-Sun 2 to 5 pm; **Museu de Estado de Pernambuco**, Graças, Av. Rui Barbosa 960, tel. 222-6694, Tue-Fri 9 am to 5 pm, Sat-Sun 2 to 6 pm; **Museu do Homem do Nordeste**, Casa Forte, Av. 17 de Agosto 2187, tel. 441-5500, Tue-Fri 11 am to 5 pm, Sat-Sun 1 to 5 pm.

Transportation
BUS STATION: **TIP**, *Terminal Integrado de Passageiros*, Curado, BR 232 km 15, tel. 452-1999. Can be reached by train from the station in São José, *Estacão Ferroviária*, Rua Floriano Peixoto, tel. 955-4533.

RENTAL CARS: **Avis**, tel. 341-2542; **Unidas**, tel. 461-1300 (in town center), 465-0200 (Boa Viagem).

Post Office
Av. do Sol, Santo Antônio, next to the bridge, Ponte D. Coelho.

Tourist Information
Empetur, Centro de Convenções, tel. 241-2111.

OLINDA
Area Code 081
Accommodation
MODERATE: **Amoaras**, Rua Garoupa 525, tel. 436-1331, fax 435-1880. Beach hotel, 20 km north of town. At Praia do Pontal de Maria Farinha, pool, sauna, room safes, large sports complex.

BUDGET: **Costeiro Olinda**, Bairro Novo, Av. Min. Marcos Freire 681, tel. 429-4877, fax 429-3904, pool, room safes; **Chalet de Maria Farinha**, Av. Cláudio José Gueiros Leite 10336, tel. 435-1240, fax 435-1696, 19 bungalows right on the beach; **Pousada d'Olinda**, Carmo, Praça João Alfredo 178, tel./fax 439-1163, pool; **Pousada dos Quatro Cantos**, Rua Prudente de Morais 441, tel. 429-0220, fax 429-1845, 15 nice rooms (with safes).

Restaurants
Oficina do Sabor, Amparo, Rua do Amparo 335, tel. 429-3331, regional cuisine and shellfish, on Sunday only open for lunch, closed Mondays; **Mourisco**, Carmo, Praça Cons. João Alfredo 7, tel. 429-1390, seafood, closed Mondays.

Sights
Museu de Arte Sacra de Pernambuco, Rua Bispo Coutinho, tel. 429-0032, Mon-Fri 8 am to 12:30 pm; **Museu de Arte Contemporânea**, Rua 13 de Maio, tel. 429-2587, Tue-Fri 9 am to 1 pm, Sat-Sun 2 to 5 pm; **Mercado da Ribeira**, Rua Bernardo Vieira de Melo, tel. 231-7172; **Palácio dos Governadores**, Rua São Bento, Mon-Fri 8 am to noon and 2 to 5 pm.

Transportation
BUS STATION: Praça do Carmo.
CATAMARAN TRIPS to Ilha de Itamarac: Hotel Amoaras, tel. 436-1331.

Tourist Information
Secretaria de Turismo, Varadouro, Rua de São Bento 160, tel. 439-1927.

Igarassu
Convento Santo Antônio, Pinacoteca, Rua Barbosa Lima, Tue-Fri 9 am to 2 pm.

JOÃO PESSOA
Area Code 083

Accommodation
MODERATE: **Tropical Hotel Tambaú**, Av. Alm. Tamandar 229, tel. 247-3660, fax 226-2390. Beach hotel, pool, sauna, room safes, tennis, kayaking; **Ponto do Sol**, Praia de Manaíra, Av. João Maurício 1861, tel. 246-3100, fax 246-2782. Lovely location, pool; **Xênius**, Cabo Branco, Av. Cabo Branco 1262, tel. 226-3535, fax 226-5463, beach hotel, pool.
BUDGET: **Paraíba Palace**, Ponto dos Cem Ris, Praça Vidal de Negreiros, tel. 241-4503, pool; **Dom Felipe Praia**, Tambaú, Rua Isidro Gomes 257, tel. 247-1240, fax 247-1708; **Solar Praia do Seixas**, beach hotel in Ponta do Seixa, Av. dos Pescadores, tel. 247-1463.

Restaurants
Gulliver, Tambaú, Av. Olinda 590, tel. 226-2504, int'l; **Elite**, Tambaú, Av. João Maurício 33, seafood; **Olho de Lula**, Cabo Branco, Av. Cabo Branco 2300, tel. 226-2328, closed Mondays, international; **Tábua de Carne**, Tambaú, Av. Rui Carneiro 648, tel. 226-3871, regional cuisine (*carne do sol*).

Museum
Museu Sacro e de Arte Popular, Praça São Francisco, tel. 221-2840, Tue-Sun 8 to 11 am, 2 to 5 pm.

Excursions
Ilha da Areia Vermelha, Praia do Poço, tel. 226-6321; **Praia do Jacaré**, three-hour boat trip, tel. 981-6165; **Praia do Bessa**, sightseeing flights in ultralight aircraft, tel. 246-2202; **Tambaú**, outings to tidal pools in Picãozinho, tel. 226-4859.

Transportation
BUS STATION: Varadouro, Rua Francisco Londres, tel. 221-9611.
RENTAL CARS: **Localiza**, tel. 232-1130; **Locarauto**, tel. 226-3335.
TAXIS: **Rádio Taxi**, tel. 221-6500; **Teletáxi**, tel. 222-3765.

Post Office
Praça Pedro Américo.

Tourist Information
PBTUR, Centro Turístico Tambaú, Av. Alm. Tamandar 100, tel. 226-7078, 8 am to 8 pm.

NATAL
Area Code 084

Accommodation
MODERATE: **Vila do Mar**, Praia de Barreira d'Água, Via Costeira, km 8, tel. 211-6000, fax 221-6017. Beach hotel, good restaurants, pool, sauna, room safes, tennis; **Parque da Costeira**, Via Costeira km 5.5, tel. 211-8494, fax 222-1459. Beach hotel, views, pool, waterslide, room safes; **Novotel Ladeira do Sol**, Praia das Artistas, R. Fabrício Pedrosa 915, tel. 202-1133, fax 202-1688, pool, room safes; **Swiss Oasis**, Petrópolis, R. Joaquim Fabrício 291, Casa 06, tel. 202-2455, fax 202-2766, centrally located, under Swiss management.
BUDGET: **Pousada Pontal do Atlântico**, Ponta Negra, Rua Elia Barros 9036, tel./fax 219-3582, pool; **Varandas de Búzios**, Praia de Búzios km 36, tel. 239-2121, 10 bungalows on the beach, pool.

Restaurants
CHURRASCARIA: **Tererê**, Ponta Negra, Estrada de Pirangi 2316, tel. 219-4081, *rodízio*.
SEAFOOD: **Camarões**, Ponta Negra, Av. Eng. Roberto Freire 2610, tel. 219-2424. On Sundays only open for lunch; **Moqueca Capixaba**, Praia de Areia Preta, Av. Gov. Sílvio Pedrosa 266, tel. 211-5683, near town; **Peixada da Comadre**, Praia dos Artistas, Rua Dr. Jos Augusto Medeiros 14, tel. 222-7629, breathtaking location, superb food. On Sundays only open for lunch, closed Tuesdays.
INTERNATIONAL: **Xique-Xique**, Petrópolis, Av. Afonso Pena 444, tel. 211-5545, centrally located, closed Sundays; **Chaplin**, Praia dos Artistas, Av. Pres. Café Filho 27, tel. 202-4253, superb view, fine cooking, popular place.

Sights
Museu Câmara Cascudo, Tirol, Av. Hermes da Fonseca 1398, tel. 222-0923. Mon 2 to 5 pm, Tue-Fri 8 to 11 am and 2 to 5 pm, Sat 10 sm to 4 pm; **Forte dos Reis Magos**, Praia do Forte, daily 8 am to 4:45 pm; **Barreira do Inferno**, rocket center, tel. 211-4799, tours Wed only at 2 pm, reservations required.

Transportation
BUS STATION: Cidade da Esperança, Av. Cap. Mor Gouveia 1237, tel. 231-1170.
ULTRALIGHT AIRCRAFT: Circulo Militar, Av. Praia do Forte, tel. 222-0092/2144. 15-minute sightseeing flights over the north and south coasts.
BOAT EXCURSIONS: Pirangi do Norte, Albacora Azul, tel. 238-2204, Marina Badauê, tel. 238-2066.
RENTAL CARS: **Locarauto**, tel. 211-5195; **Unidas**, tel. 157-5300.
BUGGYS: **Dunna Rent-a-Buggy**, tel. 217-8242.
TAXIS: **Cooptax**, tel. 223-8366; **Natal-Táxi**, tel. 223-6800.

Post Office
In the center of town, on Avenida José Clemente.

Tourist Information
Centro de Turismo, in Casa de Detenção, Rua Aderbal de Figueiredo 980, tel. 212-2267.

GENIPABU
Area Code 084
Accommodation
MODERATE: **Genipabu,** Estrada para Natal, tel. 225-2063, fax 225-2072; dunes, 24 rustic rooms, 5 km from the beach (shuttle service); pool; **Extremoz Laguna**, Rua Raimando B. Cavalcante 522, tel./fax 279-2256, beautiful location, pool.
Restaurants
Itxas-Haizea, Praia de Genipabu, tel. 225-2013. Spanish cuisine, right at the beach; **Da Guiomar**, at Muriú beach, tel. 228-2164, 12 to 5 pm, cafeteria-style seafood restaurant.
Transportation
FERRIES to Natal: **Balsa**, Redinha, 6 am to 6 pm. *BUGGY RENTALS:* **Associação dos Bugueiros**, tel. 225-2077; **Aprotur**, tel. 225-2154.

FORTALEZA
Area Code 085
Accommodation
EXPENSIVE: **Caesar Park**, at Mucuripe Beach, Av. Beira Mar 3980, tel. 263-1133, 800-2202 (toll-free), fax 263-1444, best hotel in town, very good restaurants, pool, sauna, fitness center, safes.
MODERATE: **Imperial Othon** Palace, at Meireles beach, Av. Beira Mar 2500, tel. 244-9177, fax 224-7777. An evening handicrafts market right out in front of the hotel. Lively atmosphere, pool, sauna, room safes; **Praia Centro, Iracema**, Av. Mons. Tabosa 740, tel. 211-1122, pool, room safes, centrally located; **Praiano Palace**, Meireles, Av. Beira Mar 2800, tel. 244-9333, fax 244-3333, superb view, pool; **Magna Praia**, Icarema, Av. Historiador Raimando Girão 1002, tel./fax 244-9311, good location, pool, room safes; **Ibis**, Icarema, Rua Atualpa Barbosa Lima 660, tel. 252-2044, fax 226-8621, beautiful view, pool; **Toaçu Praia**, Praia do Futuro, 13 km south of town, Av. Dioguinho 3100, tel./fax 234-7500, pool.
BUDGET: **Abrolhos Praia**, Meireles, Av. da Abol oção 2030, tel./fax 261-1217; **Fortaleza Praia**, Praia do Futuro, Rua Geminiano Jurema 68, tel. 234-6868, pool, sauna; **Atlântico**, Aldeota, Rua Tibúrcio Cavalcante 451, tel./fax 224-6566.
Restaurants
SEAFOOD: João Branco, Mucuripe, Rua Olga Barroso 404, tel. 263-1401. Small restaurant with superb quality seafood and shellfish, closed Mondays; **Al Mare**, Meireles, Av. Beira Mar 3821, tel. 263-3888, at the beach; **Tudo em Cima**, Mucuripe, nice view, Rua do Mirante 107, tel. 263-2777.

INTERNATIONAL: **Le Caesar**, in Hotel Caesar Park, tel. 263-1133, exclusive atmosphere, house speciality is a shellfish platter; closed Mondays; **Le Dinner**, Aldeota, Rua Afonso Celso 1020, tel. 224-2627, French-Asian cuisine with local ingredients, open for dinner only, closed Sundays; **Cantinho do Faustino**, Varjota, Rua Pereira Valente 1569, tel. 267-5348, beef, lamb, crab dishes, closed Mondays.
REGIONAL: **Colher de Pau**, Iracema, Rua dos Tabajaras 412, tel. 221-4097; **Panela de Barro**, Aldeota, Av. Eng. Santana Jr. 1410, tel. 234-0635.
ITALIAN: **Pulcinella**, Aldeota, Rua Osvaldo Cruz 640, tel. 261-3411. Specialties made with partridge, homemade ravioli.
Sights
Theatro Jos de Alencar, Praça Jos de Alencar, tel. 252-2324, Mon-Fri 8 to 11 am and 2 to 5 pm; **Centro de Turismo**, Rua Senador Pompeu 350, tel. 253-1522, Mon-Sat 8 am to 6 pm, Sun 8 am to noon.
Transportation
BUS STATION: **Fátima**, Av. Borges de Melo 1630, tel. 272-1566. *TRAINS: Estação Ferroviária João Felipe*, Rua Senador Jaguaribe, tel. 221-3090, Sun 7 to 10 am only. *RENTAL CARS:* **Avis**, tel. 224-1989; **Localiza**, tel. 272-2294. *BUGGYS:* **Buggy Tur**, tel. 261-5036; **Locabuggy**, in Hotel Othon Palace, tel. 261-6945. *TAXIS:* **Radio Táxi**, tel. 221-5744; **Rodotáxi**, tel. 252-1866.
Post Office
Rua Senador Alencar.
Tourist Information
Setur, Centro de Turismo, Rua Senador Pompeu 350, tel. 253-1522.

BEBERIBE
Area Code 085
Accommodation
EXPENSIVE: **Praia das Fontes**, Av. Cel. Antônio Teixeira 1, tel. 338-1179, fax 338-1087, beautifully situated luxury beach hotel, good restaurants, pool, fitness center, large sports complex, room safes.
BUDGET: **Das Falásias**, Praia das Fontes, tel. 338-1018, pool, restaurant; **Pousada do Morro Branco**, Praia de Morro Branco, tel. 330-1040 (reservations: 223-3433), pool, restaurant.

SÃO LUÍS
Area Code 098
Accommodation
EXPENSIVE: **Sofitel São Luis**, Praia do Calhau, tel. 235-4545, fax 235-4921, park, pool, room safes.
MODERATE: **São Francisco**, Rua Luís Serson 77, tel. 235-5544, fax 235-2128, on the riverbank, pool.
BUDGET: **Pousada do Francês**, Rua da Saavedra 160, tel. 235-4844, fax 232-0879, all rooms equipped with TV.

179

THE NORTH – THE AMAZON

Endangered Paradise or Green Hell?

THE AMAZON RIVER
PARA / BELÉM
SANTARÉM
AMAZONAS STATE / MANAUS

THE NORTHERN REGION

Northern Brazil has a population of only 3.6 million, but accounts for 42 percent of the country's land area. This extensive *Região Norte* stretches from latitude 13°S to 5°N, encompassing seven states: Tocantins, Pará, Amapá, Roraima, Amazonas, Rondônia and Acre. The region is so large it contains three time zones: there is a two-hour difference between Belém, the capital city of Pará, and Rio Branco, the capital of Acre. The north is Brazil's least populous region: in an area roughly half the size of the contiguous United States live only about 10 million people, or six percent of Brazil's total population. The region's contribution to the gross domestic product can likewise be expressed in single digits, despite its wood exports, extensive mineral resources, gold deposits, and the industrial zone near Manaus.

The 7.2-million-square-kilometer drainage area of the Amazon extends beyond Brazil into Bolivia, Peru, Colombia, Venezuela, Guyana and Ecuador. The origin of the name of the world's largest

Previous pages: The Amazon rain forest is one of the most important sources of oxygen on earth. Left: A miner in Carajás using modern technology.

river system is a matter of some dispute, although it is widely believed that it stems from a Greek myth: The Amazons, heroic female warriors, had one of their breasts removed so that they could shoot more easily with bow and arrow. When he came to Ecuador in 1542 with 60 men in pursuit of the legendary golden city of *El Dorado*, Francisco Orellana, the Spaniard credited with discovering the Amazon, had such a strong desire to meet such women in the flesh that he wrote of encounters with "tall, fair-skinned women who fight like ten men." Another less dramatic, but plausible explanation for the name of the river and region is the Indian word *amaçunu*, which means "water-clouds-noise."

THE AMAZON
The River that Sweetens the Atlantic

Is this 6,500-kilometer-long river the longest in the world, or only the second longest after the Nile? The facts are open to various interpretations, since the river is only called "Amazon" for 3,700 kilometers, beginning in the Peruvian state of Iquito. The Amazon's total length is measured from the point where it rises in the Peruvian Andes to where it empties into the Atlantic. Its principal tributaries are the Apurimac, the Ucayali and the

183

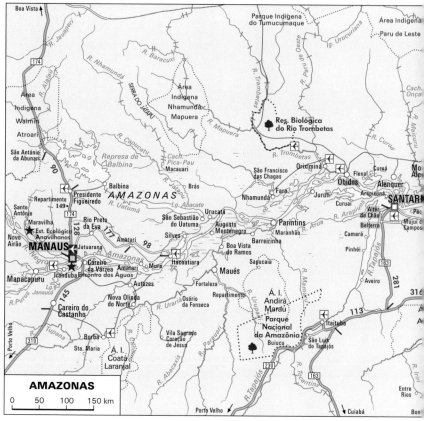

AMAZONAS

0   50   100   150 km

Marañón, all of which rise to more than 4,000 meters above sea level. At the place where the borders of Peru, Colombia and Brazil intersect, the Brazilians call their most important river the Solimões. It is only near Manaus, at the confluence of the Rio Solimões and Rio Negro, that Brazilian maps label this watercourse "Amazon" (in Portuguese: *Amazonas*). It is an undisputed fact, however, that the Amazon has the largest drainage area of any river in the world, which is why it contains two and a half times as much water as the Nile and twice as much as the Mississippi. It also has over 1,000 tributaries, 17 of which are longer than the Rhine, and it measures 100 meters at its deepest point. The river

is navigable for large ocean-going vessels as far as Iquitos, and for smaller freight and passenger ships over approximately 50,000 kilometers of Amazon basin watercourse. At its narrowest point it measures two kilometers (at Obidos) and at its widest 30 (at Belém).

At its 320-kilometer-wide mouth, 20 percent of all the Earth's fresh water empties into the Atlantic, spreading over a radius of up to 200 kilometers. Every year the river carries away one billion tons of silt that is in turn driven northward by strong currents and deposited on beaches in French Guyana, 800 kilometers away. Its rate of flow varies from 35,000 cubic meters to 160,000 cubic meters per second; as much as 310,000

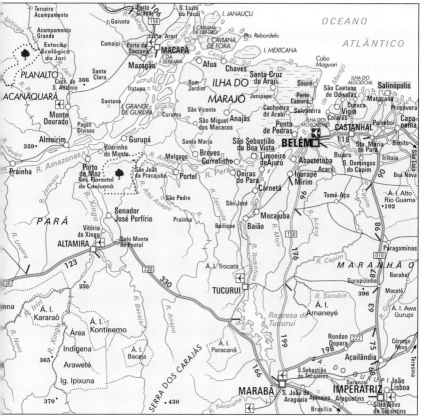

cubic meters per second has been measured at high water. This fluctuation can be clearly seen on the high-water mark in the floating harbor at Manaus – up to14 meters!

For many years it was a mystery why such denizens of the Amazon as sharks, rays, sole, prawns and even dolphins are able to survive thousands of kilometers away from shore. Geologists then discovered that 130 million years ago Africa and South America formed one large continent called Gondwana. During this period the original Amazon, which was even longer than the present one, flowed into the Pacific. After Gondwana broke up, the South American continental plateau drifted west and collided with the

Pacific tectonic plate. This collision gave rise to the Andes, which soon blocked the mouth of the Amazon, forcing the river to change direction and eventually cut its way through to the Atlantic. For marine life there was no turning back: they had to either adapt to the fresh water streaming down from the Andes or perish.

White-, Black- and Clearwater – Malnutrition vs. Malaria

The central and eastern Amazon basins are drained primarily by clearwater rivers, the largest of which are the Rio Tapajós and Rio Xingú. Clearwater is similar to distilled water in that both are virtually free of impurities. Clearwater is

185

transparent up to a depth of four meters and tends to have an "acidic" pH level.

Blackwater is found primarily in the northern part of the Amazon, for example in the Rio Negro, the "Black River." Such rivers flow through huge marshy areas, carrying humus away with them. The humus (earth) that is washed away colors the water amber. The water itself is nutrient-poor and high in huminous acids, with a pH value of 4. Such water is clear up to a depth of slightly over one meter. Blackwater and clearwater rivers drain the northern and southern Amazon basins, whose bedrock constitutes some of the most ancient on Earth. The soil in these areas is heavily weathered and depleted, and can no longer deliver nutrients. Mosquitoes cannot survive under such conditions, and are therefore rarely encountered in the Amazon. But this has

Above: The blackwater Rio Negro meets the whitewater Rio Solimões at Manaus (Encontro das Águas). Right: Latex is collected and transformed into rubber.

grave consequences from an agricultural standpoint: because hardly any humus is left, and the rivers bring no nutrients with them, the basic conditions are lacking that would allow the proud and self-sufficient *ribeirhinos* (people of mixed Indian and European ancestry living along Amazon) to survive.

By contrast, whitewater tributaries carry valuable nutrients from the geologically youthful Andes, depositing them as they flow through the riverbed. The waters of these rivers are pH-neutral, rich in minerals and suspension matter, and clear to a depth of up to half a meter. Small farmers prefer to live in the *várzea* (riverine floodplains) in which this fertile sediment is deposited – but this is also the preferred habitat of mosquitoes. Consequently, most inhabitants of this area have contracted malaria at least once, and often repeatedly, with some villages and indigenous settlements experiencing near-epidemic outbreaks. Wild game and fruit also abound around whitewater tributaries, as do fish and caimans.

In earlier times, it did not escape the attention of missionaries or of scientists on research expeditions (such as Alexander von Humboldt) that the more prosperous Indians groups were to be found along the banks of whitewater rivers such as the Napo, Marañon, Beni and Solimões, with their cloudier waters but more fertile soil. However, the price for nutritional variety is endemic malaria, a problem that at the end of the 20th century remains unsolved. This also explains why most tourist lodges in the Brazilian Amazon basin are near blackwater tributaries: there are few mosquitoes, but also little fauna.

PARÁ
Caoutchouc and Brazil Nuts

Nearly five million people of mostly mixed Indian and European ancestry live in Pará, Brazil's second largest state. The most important sources of income in this region include cattle raising and the growing of corn, rice, pepper and cassava, as well as the extraction of *caoutchouc* (rubber) and the gathering of Brazil nuts.

Caoutchouc is an Indian word that, like tomato, chocolate and cocoa, exists in many languages. It means "weeping tree" (*Hevea brasiliensis*), which is the tree from which caoutchouc (rubber) is obtained. The trees reach 20 meters in height and 75 centimeters in diameter, and can be tapped from the time they are six years old for as long as 30 to 35 years. The *seringueiros* (tappers) make a 10-centimeter-deep hole in the trees in the morning, and then place a bucket underneath, into which the latex drips at a rate of about seven grams per day. The sap is then dried, formed into hard balls over an open fire, and sent to a factory in Belém or Manaus for processing into rubber. The discovery of vulcanization by Charles Goodyear in 1842 led to a rubber boom in the entire Amazon basin. It also provided "rubber barons" in Iquito, Ma-

naus and Belém with the financial resources to send their children to European boarding schools and their dirty laundry to be washed in France or England, as well as to buy themselves every imaginable kind of luxury item from abroad.

In 1876, although he could have faced the death penalty had he been caught, an Englishman named Henry Wickham smuggled 70,000 rubber tree seeds out of Brazil to England and planted them in the Queen's botanical garden. The precisely 2,397 seedlings that sprouted were then cultivated in Britain's equatorial Asian colonies as an experiment – which worked – and the profitable monoculture of rubber that had never been feasible in the Amazon basin now became a success story in Ceylon and Malaysia. Although at the turn of the century all the world's caoutchouc was still being produced in Brazil, it has now been many years since Brazil figured among the world's top eight producers of natural rubber. In 1939, the country still had a 98 percent

share in worldwide production (e.g., for automobile tires), but by 1975 this figure had declined to 33 percent owing to the fact that by then most rubber was being manufactured synthetically. In recent years there has been a rising demand for natural rubber for products related to the prevention of AIDS, for example, for the manufacture of rubber gloves, condoms, and other products.

Brazil nut trees (*Bertholletia excelsa*) are found only in the Amazon region, and are not amenable to cultivation in any other part of the world. They can live to be up to 500 years old, can reach a height of 60 meters, and often grow at a distance of many kilometers from each other. They can only be pollinated by carpenter bees, and only the agouti can disseminate their seeds. This small rodent is the only forest dweller capable of cracking the hard, coconut shell-like seed capsule

Above: An agouti hunting for Brazil nuts.
Right: Carajás, where huge quantities of pure iron ore are mined.

containing the nut, which has a very high fat content. He then buries part of his winter provender, but often forgets where, and this absent-mindedness often results in the "birth" of a sapling. After growing for between 12 and 15 months, the tree begins to produce fruit (during the rainy season), as much as 150 kilograms per tree. Each capsule contains roughly a dozen triangular nuts encased in a hard shell. Some 46,000 tons of Brazil nuts are produced annually, all of them collected by Brazil nut gatherers called *castanheiros*, who, like the caoutchouc gatherers, have a stake in keeping the rain forest intact and are therefore making efforts to protect it.

Carajás – Enough Iron Ore for the Next Five Hundred Years

Carajás, situated 840 kilometers south of the city of Belém, is the site of one of the most extensive iron ore deposits in the world. It was accidentally discovered in 1967 by a geologist who was flying

over the area in a helicopter from which he happened to catch sight of unusual clearings in the dense jungle with reddish clumps of hematite lying on them. The mountains of the Serra dos Carajás, which range from 700 to 900 meters in height, are estimated to have a potential yield of 18 billion tons of ore containing 66 percent iron. The deposit also contains gold, manganese, copper, tin and bauxite in the strata from the Precambian era.

This huge opencut mine, known as *Projeto Grande Carajás*, is operated by the Brazilian government. It occupies 900,000 square kilometers; more than 10 percent of the land area of the state of Pará, whose topography and ecology are being irreversibly altered by the project. In 1986, 890 kilometers of railroad track were laid for Carajás' sole use, and the project currently sends three 160-car trains per day, each one carrying 15,000 tons of iron ore, to the Atlantic port of São Luís. The ironworks are powered by charcoal, for which 200,000 hectares of virgin forest are cut down each year; eu-calyptus trees are mainly used for "reforestation" because they grow rapidly. Rio Tocantins, one of the largest rivers in the Amazon basin, has been dammed at Tucuruí for hydroelectric power, and at the same time 2,400 square kilometers of forest have been sub-merged. The government-owned mining company *Companhia do Vale do Rio Doce* has made good-faith efforts to pro-tect the environment, including reduction in the volume of waste, reforestation, and enforcement of anti-hunting laws; even pets have been banned. But with the 23,000 workers in the region – some of whom have lost their jobs and have set-tled there permanently – have come the usual problems experienced by other Brazilian "pioneer" areas in the past: slash-and-burn, oversettlement, garbage, prostitution, crime and poverty.

In the 1980's, photographs were seen around the world of *garimpeiros* (gold miners) slaving away under inhuman conditions in a mine situated between the Tucuruí Dam and Carajás. Today the

area resembles a partly flooded lunar landscape – but the mine is gone.

BELÉM

Belém is located on the southern arm of the Amazon Delta and is separated from its northern arm by the Ilha do Marajó. The city, which has a population of 1.3 million, was founded in 1616, but because it was only accessible by sea or river, to a great extent remained isolated from the rest of Brazil until well into the 19th century. By 1900, Belém's population had reached 100,000, benefiting from both the rubber boom and its strategic position as the last river port on the Amazon before it flows into the Atlantic.

Visitors to Belém's harbor, **Porto de Belém**, cannot fail to take note of this city's economic affinity for the sea: the

Above: The butchers' hall in the Ver-o-Peso market in Belém was imported from Glasgow in the early 20th century. Right: Lundú – a Belémian dance.

Old Town, the market, and the most significant churches are all in close proximity to Belém's bay, Baía do Guajará. **Ver-o-Peso** is one of Brazil's most renowned and colorful marketplaces, and features a gargantuan selection of unusual and grotesque wares. Its name, which means "keep your eye on the scale," speaks for itself. Visitors will find mountains of cassava meal, coconuts, bananas, mangos, and a vast array of seldom seen tropical fruits. Salt- and freshwater fish can also be purchased, as can yellowish brown *dendê* (palm) oil, and *tucupi,* a cassava sauce that is used in numerous regional dishes. Copious quantities of vegetables, spices and herbs are also sold at Ver-o-Peso.

Probably of greatest interest to visitors to the market is the "pharmacological" section (qualifying it as a witch's or a herb market, although perhaps somewhat apt, would be stretching the truth). Visitors can peruse or purchase such substances as tree bark, whose decoction can be drunk as a tea or simply bathed in;

rosewood water against excessive perspiration; or the cadaver of a songbird, which is supposed to bring good fortune in affairs of the heart. Various herbs are said to combat impotence; the same properties are ascribed to the sex organs of a female river dolphin. Scorpions and snakes preserved in sugar-cane spirits, roots, feathers, sloth mummies, and countless other remedies for all kinds of ills can be purchased here. *Tias* (aunts), as these merchants of magic are affectionately called, will create custom potions to combat nasty neighbors, unfaithful wives or baldness. Difficult to miss across the way is the cast-iron butcher's hall, which was imported from Glasgow at the beginning of the 20th century and is covered with a grating to protect against the omnipresent vultures.

A short distance west of the market (towards the bay) lies **Forte do Castelo**, which was built in 1616 as a bastion against French troops – but under its more evocative original name of *Forte do Presépio de Belém* (Fort of the Manger of

Bethlehem). Rio Guamá flows into Baía do Guajar precisely at this point, and it was in order to defend the bay that the Portuguese chose this perfect strategic position.

The power of the military is now followed by that of the Church: just next to the fort, in a former Jesuit seminary, stands the Palace of the Archbishop. The Jesuit church, **Igreja de Santo Alexandre**, is one of the few well-preserved Jesuit churches in Brazil. Although it dates from the early 18th century, the structure is built in Portuguese Baroque style, and boasts vividly executed wood carvings and high pulpits. Also on this square, **Praça Frei Caetano Brandão**, is Bélem's 18th-century **Catedral da Sé**, which contains a remarkable painting, *The Virgin Mary at the Altar*, by the Portuguese artist Alexandrino de Carvalho.

In the **Cidade Velha** there are a number of other stately historic buildings worth visiting that feature azulejos and formal gardens. Between 1869 and 1875, during the height of the rubber boom, the

191

1,000-seat neoclassical **Teatro da Paz** was erected on **Praça da República**. The structure manifests the yearning for splendor that characterized the period: no expense was spared in outfitting and decorating this near-replica of a full-fledged Italian opera house in which, during its heyday (from 1905 to 1918), many famous Italian opera stars also performed. To this day, concerts and other events are still held on occasion in the theater.

The **Museu Emílio Goeldi**, two kilometers east of Praça da República on Av. Magalhães Barata, has not only botanical, ethnological, and mineralogical collections, but also an engaging park featuring a **zoo** and an aquarium, where visitors can see creatures of the deep and forest that are rarely caught sight of in their natural habitats. The unique and boldly geometric Marajoara pottery on

Above: Sunset on the Amazon – an unforgettable experience of nature's grandeur.
Right: A boat trip on the Amazon is leisurely, but not luxurious.

display in the archeological section of the museum is of considerable artistic and ethnological interest as well. Marajoara pottery combines modeling and painting with low relief carving. Some excellent examples have been unearthed, but the island has proven difficult to excavate owing to the fact that it is regularly flooded by the mouth of the Amazon.

Missionaries needed compelling images of sin to help them communicate Christian values to potential converts. Consequently, in the course of the 18th century, the Jesuits instituted a procession that nowadays attracts upwards of a million people: the festival of **Círio de Nazar** extends over 10 days and reaches a climax on the second Sunday in October. By boat, bus and car, pilgrims flock to this event, which begins at the cathedral and then wends its way through the city to the **Basílica de Nazar** (1908), which is a copy of St. Paul's Cathedral in Rome. The figure of Mary with the infant Jesus that the pilgrims carry at the head of the procession is by the south Tirolean

Jesuit Hans Treyer, who lived in Belém in the 18th century. The traditional post-processional banquet calls for *pato no tucupi*: duck in manioc stock with tropical herbs.

Boat Excursions from Belém

Belém's location makes it an ideal jumping-off point for boat excursions lasting anywhere from several hours to five days. Brief outings into the *igarapés* (canoeing channels) can be booked in any hotel, and schedules can be obtained from Paratur.

In **Icoaraci**, 23 kilometers north of Belém and accessible by either bus or boat, craftsmen produce replicas of Marajoara pottery. The crossing to **Ilha do Outeiro** can be made from here, although the riverside beaches are much frequented by local residents and are not terribly clean. **Ilha do Mosqueiro**, 85 kilometers north of Belém in Baía do Marajó, is favored by *Belenenses*, especially on weekends. The island, which can be reached either from the mainland or by river, offers the unbeatable combination of a fresh-water swimming beach with ocean breakers.

The idyllic **Ilha do Algodoal** (Cotton Island) can only be accessed by means of small fishing boats that depart from Marudá, which is 170 kilometers north of Belém. This Eden of an island has just the right mix of bliss-inducing beaches, dunes and lagoons. **Salinópolis**, an exclusive luxury resort recommended for the very affluent only, is located 220 kilometers north of Belém, and can be reached by bus. However, during the Brazilian school holidays in July and over New Year's, the city is as overcrowded as it is expensive, and should be avoided during these periods.

Visitors who would like to see **Santarém** or **Manaus**, but who would rather spend several days sailing slowly up the Amazon than fly there in a matter of hours, can book their tickets in Belém. The boat trip to Santarém, which is something of an adventure, takes 60 hours. To

Manaus you should figure on five days and nights: owing to chronic lack of funds, the catamarans operated by government-owned *Enasa* actually set sail only extremely rarely, and it is therefore advisable to book passage on a privately-owned vessel. All passenger ships travel the Amazon in a 14-day cycle. Tickets and reliable information regarding boats at anchor that are ready to set sail can be obtained from *Macamazônia* or other ticket agencies in the vicinity of the port.

Most boats provide hammock-hanging facilities (bring your own), and also offer two- and four-person cabins whose temperatures unfortuntately rise to discomfort levels during the day. The only boat with air-conditioned (and, naturally, more expensive) cabins is the *Nélio Corrêa*. Any visitor contemplating a trip up the Amazon à la *Fitzcarraldo* should inquire into the older, more open and airier ships called *gaiolas* (bird cages). Their names are *Wejard Vieina*, *João Pessôa Lopes* and *Cisne Branco*.

Ilha de Marajó

This immense riverine island has a population of 250,000 spread over 13 cities and towns, the most important of which, **Souré** (population 20,000), can be reached by boat or plane from Belém. The boat takes three hours to **Porto Camará**, from which it's a half-hour bus ride to Souré. The flight from Belém to Souré, on the other hand, is a quick 30 minutes. The broader, western part of the island consists mainly of dense forests, while the eastern plains are comprised primarily of savanna, which is usually covered by Amazonian floodwater during the first six months of the year.

Water buffaloes are important on Ilha de Marajó: herds of them (the largest in Brazil) roam the island, and buffalo

Right: In Souré on the Ilha de Marajó, life flows by tranquilly.

ranches also rent out guest rooms, which are accessible by boat from Souré or by plane from Belém. Wild animals abound too, including monkeys, sloths, capybaras, deer, turtles, and huge flocks of scarlet macaws; and the rivers teem with fish: in addition to catfish and perch, the dreaded piranhas also frequent these watercourses. The vegetation in the savannas (*campos* in Portuguese) consists predominantly of sage (*Cyperaceae*) and *caraná* palms; wetter areas are characterized by marshlands and mangroves. Among the plant life that thrives here is the mangle tree, with its tannic acid-yielding bark, and the poisonous *Strychnos blackii* liana plant.

A 24-hour boat trip around this substantial land mass includes a visit to **Macap**, the capital of the state of Amapá, located on the northern arm of the Amazon. The main attraction in this city of 180,000 inhabitants is **Forte São José**, which sits on a spit of land near the harbor and the town center. The fort was built by the Portuguese between 1764 and 1784 to protect the northernmost corner of their colonial possession. **Marco Zero**, the equatorial line situated five kilometers south of the city, is a well-liked locale for photographs, as it provides visitors with a unique opportunity to have their photo taken with one foot in each hemisphere. From **Porto da Santana**, which is 21 kilometers south of Macapá, there are boat excursions to the Amazonian islands as well as to the *igarapés*.

SANTARÉM

Upstream, about halfway between the Amazonian cities of Belém and Manaus and an hour's flight from both, lies the region's third-largest city, Santarém (population 280,000). Belém and Santarém are 956 riverine kilometers apart, but overland the distance is 1,369 kilometers. The city, situated at the confluence of the **Rio Tapajós** and the **Amazon**, was the site of

a highly developed Indian civilization from 1000 A.D. until the arrival of Europeans in the early 16th century. During the colonial era, Santarém was an important river port and military outpost, and the city has retained a fair amount of its colonial charm.

One museum well worth whiling away some time in is the **Museu dos Tapajós**, which features handicrafts by the Tapajó, Tapuio and Munducuru, all of whom are descendants of the Santarém culture. As in Manaus, visitors can observe the **Encontro das Águas** (see p. 197), which is best combined with a brief boat excursion. The contrasting clear and ochre-colored waters of (respectively) the **Tapajós** and the **Amazon** flow side by side for many kilometers before finally joining to make one river.

On the banks of the Rio Tapajós, 34 kilometers south of Santarém, lies the fishing village of **Alter do Chão**, whose snow-white sandbars are the most popular beaches in the area from July to December. The village also has an in-

triguing museum, the **Museu do Centro de Preservação de Arte Indígena**, whose collection encompasses 1,500 artifacts of 57 different groups from the Amazon and Mato Grosso regions. Visitors can also view, in its natural habitat, the Amazonian water lily *Victoria regia*, which grows wild in the vicinity of the village. Its leaves sometimes reach two meters in width and are sturdy enough to support the weight of a child without bending. Somewhat farther upstream lies the village of Belterra, where, in 1926, Henry Ford built **Fordlândia**. This agro-forest enterprise in the middle of the jungle was supposed to produce rubber, but once Ford realized this cannot be done in the Amazon region, the facility was closed.

Parque Nacional da Amazônia is situated 370 kilometers southwest of Santarém and during the dry season can be reached via the Transamazônica (BR 230), and at other times by boat in 18 hours. This 994,000-hectare nature preserve abounds with lush rain-forest vege-

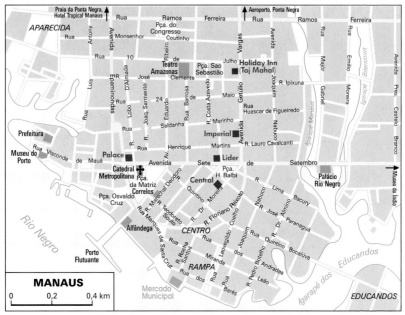

MANAUS

0   0,2   0,4 km

tation and wildlife. The permit that must be obtained from park officials prior to entering the park also entitles visitors to rustic accommodations for up to eight persons. The southern end of the preserve is traversed by the Transamazônica, which provides all too easy access to illegal prospectors, who often tramp through – and damage – the vegetation as they prospect for gold.

Upstream from the park on the opposite bank of the Amazon from Santarém lies the small colonial city of **Óbidos** (population 40,000). The trip here by river is particularly exciting, since the stream reaches its narrowest point at Óbidos, but is also up to 100 meters in depth. Of interest in the town are several stately colonial buildings, as well as the remains of **Forte Pauxi**, built in 1697.

AMAZONAS
The Largest State

Amazonas is the underpopulated giant among Brazilian states: with a land area of 1,564,445 square kilometers it is larger than Germany, Holland France and the Iberian peninsula put together, but has a population of only 2.5 million, half of which is concentrated in the capital city of Manaus. The state's economic base consists of the newly built industries in the duty-free zone near Manaus, metals such as tin and gold, and commercial fishing and agriculture. Meat processing and dairy farming are important economic mainstays, as are pineapples, cassava, rice and corn. Owing to increasing worldwide interest in the protection of the rain forest, ecotourism has also become a significant source of revenue.

The main problem faced by the region is its infrastructure. Both people and freight are transported mainly by river, and the only north-south link is from Porto Velho, the capital of Rondônia, via Manaus to Boa Vista (the capital of the northernmost state of Roraima), and from there to Venezuela. In the rainy season, the Transamazônica to Belém is impassable, and during the rest of the year is only marginally so, which is why so many travelers forego driving and opt instead for the long boat ride up the Amazon. The riverine distance from Manaus to Belém is 1,700 kilometers, but overland it is 3,445 dusty, solitary and seemingly endless kilometers. There are also daily flights from Manaus to Brasília, Rio, Salvador, Belém and other Brazilian cities, as well as to Iquitos (Peru), Santa Cruz (Bolivia), Caracas (Venezuela) and Miami (USA).

MANAUS

The capital of the state of Amazonas is located not on the river of the same name but rather on the Rio Negro, 18 kilometers upstream from the confluence of the aforementioned "Black River" with Rio Solimões, the two rivers flowing parallel to each other for a time and then joining to form the Amazon. This striking spectacle will be clearly visible to any traveler sitting by the window on a flight into Manaus on a cloudless day. Boat excursions to **Encontro das Águas** can also be booked in Manaus. The murky waters of the upper reaches of the Amazon (which is how Brazilians refer to Rio Solimões) flow next to the dark but clear waters of the Rio Negro for many kilometers before they come together. The contrasting coloration of the two rivers is determined by their flow rates, the quantity of suspended matter in the water, and their respective temperatures, the Rio Negro being about two degrees warmer.

The Treaty of Tordesillas (see p. 16) granted Spain dominion over the western Amazon basin. But owing to Spain's military and political weakness in the mid-17th century, the Portuguese took control of the entire Amazon region in the name of the Crown, and in 1669 founded São José da Barra do Rio, which, overshadowed by Belém, remained a rather unimportant city until the end of the 18th century. In 1791, the Viceroy made Manaus the seat of the *Capitania do Rio Negro*, and in 1848 granted it city status. The town was renamed Manaus in 1856, but economic growth only began in earnest nine years later with the advent of international maritime law on the Amazon.

During the rubber boom (1890-1920), Manaus became one of the most prosperous cities in the world, as well as the first in Brazil to have streetcars and the second to illuminate its streets with electricity. The height of the city's affluence-driven desire for recognition came with construction of the Teatro Amazonas (see p. 198). During the rubber boom, little thought was given to the future, and the rubber barons were not strong believers in investment. Instead, they grew rich by exploiting the labor of the *seringueiros* (latex gatherers), who were miserably underpaid and many of whom died in the jungle of malaria or other tropical diseases. The 50 percent decline in rubber prices in 1913 owing to competition from cheaper latex produced on Asian plantations was a rude awakening, as one company after another went bankrupt. To a certain degree, the gold prospecting mindset of the past still lingers on today: because production of basic foodstuffs in Manaus and the surrounding area is still not sufficient to feed the population, food staples must be shipped in from 4,000-kilometer-distant São Paulo, which of course drives up the cost of living.

In 1967, a hundred years after international maritime law went into effect, the military regime declared Manaus a *zona franca* (duty-free zone), and lured investors to the region with low real estate prices and tax advantages. Since then, over 400 high-tech businesses have come to the area, and in the space of three decades Manaus has again become a prosperous city, with all the contradictions that have accompanied such booms elsewhere in Latin America: on one hand, modern industrial plants, luxury hotels,

and shopping centers; and on the other slums called *palafitas*, which are unstable dwellings built on stilts.

Teatro Amazonas

The theater's opulent curtain with its *Encontro das Águas* (Meeting of the Waters) motif went up for the first time on a production of "La Gioconda" in 1896, following 12 years of construction. In its heyday, despite tropical temperatures, culture-hungry *Amazonenses* attended opera performances in tuxedos and plush gowns. The designers of the building went to great expense to prove to the world that a city situated in the middle of the jungle was the equal of any European metropolis. Everything but the tropical wood was imported: Murano glass chandeliers, Alsatian tiles, Carrara

Above: Teatro Amazonas – the pride of Manaus on Praça São Sebastião. Right: A young boy plays with a boa on the banks of the Amazon.

marble, furnishings from Paris, and seats with red velvet upholstery. Caruso and Sarah Bernhardt were invited, but leary of the climate and mosquitoes, demurred. The last opera performance, *The Jewess*, took place in 1907.

The jungle humidity subsequently caused severe damage to the interior of the building, which, in order to avoid the worst, was restored in 1929 and again in 1962; an unreliable air-conditioning system was also installed in 1974. But it was only at the end of the 1980s that a long-overdue top-to-bottom renovation of the structure was undertaken at a cost of US $15 million. The seats were found to be infested with termite larvae, and all the interior woodwork had to be sealed against possible reinfestation. The gala reopening was celebrated on March 17, 1990, with a performance of Georges Bizet's *Carmen*. A regular opera season now takes place, although tourists with cash to spare are lured in to fill seats that would otherwise go begging: the average price per ticket of US $100 is simply too

high for most citizens of Manaus. In April 1997, the city's first opera festival was held in the Teatro, of which no visitor to Manaus should miss an opportunity to take a guided tour.

The theater plaza, **Praça São Sebastião**, is covered in black and white paving stones in a wave pattern that symbolizes the confluence of the Rio Solimões and Rio Negro. Over the plaza presides a sizeable monument with four ships representing the four corners of the earth, i.e., Africa, the Americas, Asia, and Europe (Australia was a still colony back then). It was designed by Domenico de Angelis to commemorate September 7, 1867, the day international maritime law went into effect. Visitors who enjoy walking tours can comfortably reach the city's remaining sights from here on foot. The first stop, five blocks towards the river down Avenida Eduardo Ribeiro, is Praça da Matriz, where both the cathedral and main post office are located.

After crossing Rua Marques de Santa Cruz, look to your left for the customs building, **Alfândega**, an ochre structure that was brought from England brick by brick in 1906. Just in front of Alfândega bobs the floating harbor, **Porto Flutuante**, a masterful achievement of turn-of-the-century British engineering. In order to compensate for the up to 14-meter difference between water levels during the rainy and dry seasons in a given year, twin 150-meter-long quays were built that float on air tanks and are linked to the bank with movable bridges. The high-water mark is recorded every year on a wall in front of the bridge. The harbor is not always accessible to visitors, however: sometimes there is an entry fee, and at other times only passengers with tickets are allowed access.

Just 500 meters further to the southeast and a short distance from the riverbank stands the market hall, **Mercado Municipal**, an iron structure that was designed by Gustave Eiffel and whose components were shipped in from Paris. The marketplace is in **Rampa**, the most effervescent neighborhood in Manaus. From the mar-

ket, meander several blocks north to expansive Avenida Sete de Setembro,
where a right turn takes you across a wide
bridge to **Igarapé dos Educandos**, a
broad canal over which stand, on stilts,
numerous picturesque but extremely
poor dwellings known as *palafitas*.

A spit of land in the middle of the canal
is the site of the unfailingly freshly
painted Governor's Palace, **Palácio Rio
Negro**, which originally belonged to a
German rubber merchant. The third street
on the left after the bridge is Av. Duque
de Caxias, where the **Museu do Índio**
furnishes visitors with food for cross-
cultural thought. The museum, which is
run by the Salesian mission, provides an
overview of the ways of life of the
various indigenous groups that inhabit
the upper reaches of the Rio Negro.

Visitors in the mood for the beach
should catch the bus from here to **Praia**

*Above: Amazonian lodges are the most
common type of accommodations in the rain
forest.*

da Ponta Negra**. Located 18 kilometers
north of downtown, right next door to the
well-known luxury resort, Hotel Tropical, it is the most popular riverside beach
in Manaus.

Hotel Tropical Manaus

Guests staying in this 600-room hotel
located only five kilometers from the airport luxuriate in an oasis far from the
sound and fury of Manaus. Extending
over 450,000 square meters of Rio Negro
riverbank and nestled between river and
forest, the spacious (but only three-story)
hotel buildings blend harmoniously into
the surrounding landscape. The rooms
have modern furnishings and facilities,
and for the fitness-minded there is a
swimming pool complete with artificial
waves, a tennis court and an exercise
room. The science-minded have also
been provided for: the hotel's mini-zoo
and educational botanical pathways make
excursions into the virgin forest seem almost superfluous.

But all this comes at a price, especially since the Hotel Tropical is the only facility of its kind within a radius of a thousand kilometers. An enormous effort is required to keep this complex running smoothly. Because of the damp tropical climate, buildings need to be refurbished on an almost continuous basis. Staffing is another problem faced by hotels throughout the Amazon region, but particularly in a mega-resort like the Tropical. While management positions are held either by Brazilians from the coastal cities or by foreigners, the hundred or so hotel staff who wait on tables, clean the guests' rooms, and staff the kitchens are local *caboclos* who are much more accustomed to surviving in the rain forest than under the hectic working conditions of a modern luxury hotel. Moreover, the fact that many flights arrive in Manuas at night make employees' work schedules less than ideal. Bearing this in mind, guests are advised to be patient with the staff and to calmly enjoy their stay in this one-of-a-kind resort.

Excursions in the Amazon Region

Trips to **Encontro das Aguas** can be booked at the Hotel Tropical or any travel agency. **Lago Salvador**, a lake featuring *Victoria regia* (royal water lily), caimans and monkeys, is 35 minutes away by boat from the Hotel Tropical. Tours with cruise ships lying at anchor in the harbor should be avoided, as such outings are usually limited to marching down the paths in single file. Four hours away by boat is the 500-island river archipelago **Estação Ecológica Anavilhanas**, for which a visitor's permit is required. During the high-water period from November through April, most of the islands are submerged. This nature preserve lies northwest on the Rio Negro, and provides local fauna with a safe haven. The area can also be toured in a large or small boat, or by helicopter.

BELÉM
Area Code 091

Accommodation
MODERATE: **Belém Hilton**, Av. Pres. Vargas 882, tel. 242-6500, fax 225-2942, centrally located on Praça da República, quite a bit of traffic noise, best in the city. Pool, sauna, fitness room, non-smokers' rooms, good restaurant; **Novotel**, Av. Bernardo Sayão 4804, tel. 229-7111 and 0800-11-1790 (toll-free), fax 249-7808. Lovely location 5 km out of town on the Guamá River, pool, sauna, room safes; **Regente**, Nazaré, Av. Gov. José Malcher 485, tel. 241-1222, fax 242-0343, good hotel with a pool; **Parque dos Igarapés**, 14 km north of town, accessible via Rod. Augusto Montenegro, tel. 248-1718, fax 224-6241. Park, tidepools, excursions on weekends.
BUDGET: **Aviz**, Jurunas, Rua dos Mandurucus 1014, tel. 212-0500, fax 212-0143; **Ver-o-Peso-Hotel**, Rua Boulevard Castilho França 214, tel. 224-2267, opposite the marketplace, large rooms.

Restaurants
Lá em Casa/O Outro, Av. Gov. José Malcher 247, tel. 223-1212. The owner has been cooking superb regional dishes (e.g., *pato no tucupi*) in this locale for the past 20 years.
Círculo Militar, Praça Frei Caetano Brandão, tel. 223-4374. This is the only restaurant with a view of the bay, in Forte do Castelo, specializes in regional cuisine.
Panela de Barro, Av. Duque de Caxias 602, tel. 246-6145, seafood and shellfish in exotic sauces, on Sundays only open for lunch.
Cantina Italiana, Nazaré, Tr. Benjamin Constant 140, tel. 225-2033, Italian specialities.

Sights
Mercado Ver-o-Peso, Cais do Porto, daily 4 am to noon; **Forte do Castelo**, Praça Frei Caetano Brandão 117, tel. 223-0041, daily 8 am to 11 pm; **Teatro da Paz**, Praça da República, tel. 224-7355, Tue-Fri 9 am to 6 pm; **Museu Emílio Goeldi**, Nazaré, Av. Magalhães Barata 376, tel. 249-1233, Tue-Thu 9 am to noon and 2 to 5 pm, Fri 9 am to noon, Sat-Sun 9 am to 5 pm; **Basílica de Nazaré**, Praça Justo Chermont, tel. 223-9399.

Transportation
SHIPS: **Manaus**: *Macamazônia*, Rua Boulevard Castilho França 730, tel. 223-8635, fax 222-5604. **Santarém**: *Alves & Rodrigues*, tel. 225-1691. **Macapá**: Senava, tel. 225-1691, departures Mon at 10 am and Wed at 6 pm. **Porto Camaré, Ilha de Marajó**: Setran, tel. 243-3288, departures Mon-Sat at 7 am, Sun at 10 am.
BUS STATION: São Brás, Praça do Operério, tel. 228-0500.

RENTAL CARS: **Dallas**, tel. 225-2237; **Unidas**, tel. 241-3535.

TAXIS: **5 Estrelas**, tel. 249-0011; **RTP**, tel. 241-6224.

Post Office
Av. Presidente Vargas 498.

Tourist Information
Paratur, Praça Kennedy, tel. 212-6601.

SALINÓPOLIS
Area Code 091

Accommodation
BUDGET: **Gringo Louco**, at the canal, R. do Castelo, tel. 968-4120, lovely view, pool, sauna, jet-skiing; **Salinópolis**, Av. Beira-Mar 26, tel./fax 823-1239; **Atalaia Inn**, Praia Farol Velho, R. Caminho das Dunas 1, tel./fax 824-1122, beach hotel.

Restaurants
Gringo Louco, tel. 981-0749, hotel restaurant, excellent international cuisine; **Do Nicolau**, Av. Alm. Barroso 549, riverside seafood restaurant, closed Mondays and Thursdays.

Transportation
BUS STATION: Av. Dr. Miguel Sta. Brígida, tel. 823-1148.

ILHA DE MARAJÓ – SOURÉ
Area Code 091

Accommodation
BUDGET: **Ilha de Marajó**, Travessa entre 7 e 8 Rua, tel./fax 741-1315, riverside hotel with a beach and pool; **Pousada dos Guarás**, 6 km from Souré in Salvaterra, Av. Beira-Mar, tel./fax 765-1133, riverside beach hotel.

FAZENDAS (buffalo farms): **Fazenda Bom Jardim**, 40 minutes by plane from Belém and two and a half hours from Souré by boat, tel. 241-1859, accommodates 22; **Fazenda Jilva**, 45 minutes by plane from Belém, 40 km from Souré, tel. 212-6244, accommodates 18.

Transportation
SHIPS to **Belém** (the trip lasts 4 hours): the *Navio Barbacen* weighs anchor Mondays, Wednesdays, and Fridays at 4 pm, and Sundays at 6 pm. The *Navio Domingos Asmar* leaves from Camará, 34 km from Souré, Mon-Sat 1 pm, Sun 4 pm.

MACAPÁ
Area Code 096

Accommodation
MODERATE: **Novotel**, Av. Eng. Azarias Neto 17, tel. 223-1144, fax 223-1115, pool, sauna, safes.
BUDGET: **San Marino**, Av. Marcílio Dias 1395,

tel. 223-1522, fax 223-5223, pool; **Frota**, Rua Tiradentes 1104, tel. 223-3999, fax 222-4488.

Restaurants
Martinho's Peixaria, Sta. Inês, Av. Beira-Rio 140, seafood. On Sundays only open for lunch, Mondays only for dinner.

Tropeiro, Av. Pres. Vargas 456, tel. 223-3107, churrascaria with *rodízio*. On Sundays only open for lunch, closed Mondays.

Sights
Fortaleza de São José de Macapá, tel. 212-5118, daily 8 am to 6 pm; **Marco Zero** (equatorial demarcation), Estrada para Fazendinha km 5.

Transportation
SHIPS: **Belém**: *Senava*, tel. 223-9090, departures Tue 3 pm, Fri 10 am. **Santarém**, **Manaus**: *Enavi*, Porto de Santana, 21 km south of Macapá, irregular departure times.

BUS STATION: BR-150, km 5, opposite Polícia Técnica.

RENTAL CARS: **Localiza**, tel. 223-2799.

TAXI: **Marco Zero**, tel. 223-2639.

SANTARÉM
Area Code 091

TIME: Same as in the state of Amazonas, i.e., one hour earlier than in southern and eastern Brazil.

Accommodation
BUDGET: **Tropical**, Av. Mendonça Furtado 4120, tel. 523-2800, fax 522-2631, located near Rio Tapajós, large pool, garden, all rooms have a view of the river and a balcony equipped with a hammock; **Santarém Palace**, Av. Rui Barbosa 726, tel. 523-2820, fax 523-2826, all rooms have TV; **New City**, Tr. Francisco Corrêa 200, tel./fax 522-4719, restaurant.

Restaurants
Luar da Cidade, Tr. Silva Jardim 820, tel. 975-1808, seafood dishes are the speciality here.
Lumi, Av. Cuiabá 1683, tel. 522-2174, Brazilian-Japanese cuisine.

Museums
Museu dos Tapajós, Rua Adriano Pimentel, tel. 523-2434, Mon-Fri 7:30 am to 6 pm.
Museu do Centro de Preservação de Arte Indígena, Alter do Chão, Rua D. Macedo Costa, daily 8 am to noon and 1 to 5 pm.
Parque Nacional da Amazônia. Information: Ibama-Par, tel. 224-5899.

Transportation
SHIPS: Cais do porto, Avenida Tapajós.
BUS STATION: Vila Esperança, Av. Cuiabá km 3, tel. 522-1342.
RENTAL CARS: **Nobre**, tel. 522-2990M; **Yes**, tel. 523-2333.
TRAVEL AGENCY: **Amazon**, tel. 522-2620.

MANAUS
Area Code 092

TIME: One hour earlier than in Brasília, i.e., the same as in southern and eastern Brazil.

Accommodation
EXPENSIVE: **Tropical Manaus**, Estrada da Ponta Negra, tel. 658-5000, fax 658-5026, large pool, sauna, room safes (see pp. 200-201).
MODERATE: **Holiday Inn** (formerly the Taj Mahal), Av. Getúlio Vargas 741, tel./fax 633-1010, on the main thoroughfare in the center of town, expensive, pool, sauna, room safes; **Da Vinci**, Adrianópolis, outside of town, Rua Belo Horizonte 240-A, tel. 663-1213, fax 611-3721, pool, sauna, room safes, tennis.
BUDGET: **Imperial**, Av. Getúlio Vargas 227, tel. 622-3112, fax 234-1709, on a central thoroughfare in the center of town; **Mônaco**, Rua Silva Ramos 20, tel. 622-3446, fax 622-1415, rooftop pool; **Lider**, Av. Sete de Setembro 827, tel. 633-1326, fax 633-3393, centrally located, noisy, well managed; **Central**, Rua Dr. Moreira 202, tel. 622-2600, fax 622-2609, centrally located; **Palace**, Av. Sete de Setembro 593, tel. 234-5800, centrally located, behind the cathedral, formerly a luxury hotel.

Restaurants
Xalaco, Planalto, Av. Pedro Teixeira 300, tel. 238-1688. One of the best addresses in town, international cuisine, open only for dinner, closed Sundays.
Panorama, Av. Boulevard Rio Negro 199, tel. 624-4626, lovely view of the river, delectable seafood dishes.
Mouraria, Vieiralves, Rua Pará 440, tel. 233-1419, Portuguese cuisine, only open for dinner, on Sundays only open for lunch, closed Mondays.
Canto da Peixada, Rua Emílio Moreiera 1677, tel. 234-3021. As the name suggests, a wide variety of seafood is served here, closed Sundays.
Búfalo, Rua Joaquim Nabuco 628 A, tel. 633-3773, churrascaria with rodízio, in the center of town.

Sights
Teatro Amazonas, Praça São Sebastião, tel. 622-2420, Mon-Sat 9 am to 4 pm.
Mercado Municipal, Rua dos Barés, daily 6 am to 6 pm.
Museu do Índio, Rua Duque de Caxias 356, tel. 234-1422, Mon-Fri 8:30 to 11:30 am and 2 to 4:30 pm, Sat 8:30 to 11:30 am.

Transportation
SHIPS: Information: **Departamento Nacional de Transportes Aquaviários**, Av. Eduardo Ribeiro 520, 16. St., tel. 633-1224; **Lago Salvador**, **Amazon Ecopark**, tel. 658-5000, next to street 631; **Lago Janauacá**, info: Tel. 622-2577; **Estação Ecológica Anavilhanas**, permits from Ibama, tel.

237-3710. Various excursions: **Onzenave**, **Barco Dona Carlota**, 45 cabins, max. 155 persons, tel. 232-2481, fax 232-2480.
CHARTERED BOATS: **Tarumã Turismo**, **Amazon Clippes**, eight cabins for 16 passengers, tel. 642-2100, fax 642-2255; **Amazon Nut Safaris**, Iguana, two cabins for eight passengers, tel. 671-3525, fax 6711415. You can also embark right at the harbor: **Porto Flutuante**, Rua Marqués de Sta. Cruz.
HELICOPTER SIGHTSEEING FLIGHTS: Information, tel. 654-2673.
BUS STATION: Flores, 8 km outside of town, Rua Recife, tel. 236-2732.
RENTAL CARS: **Avis**, tel. 234-4440; **Nobre**, tel. 233-6056.
TAXIS: **Amazonas**, tel. 232-3005; **Coopertáxi**, tel. 621-1544.

Post Office
Praça da Matriz/corner of Rua T. Souto.

Tourist Information
Emantur, Av. Sete de Setembro 1546, tel. 633-2850; **Fumtur**, Estrada Torquato Tapajós 313, tel. 654-3265; **Aeroporto**, tel. 621-1120.

Lodges in the Surrounding Area

Ariaú Jungle Tower, 60 km west at Rio Ariaú (2.5 hours by boat), tel. 234-7308, fax 233-5615, reservations, tel. 092-800-5000. One of the best facilities in the Manaus area, 140 double rooms, 40-meter-high observation tower, pool, river beach from Sept. to March, museum, orchid garden. Guided tours included in price of accommodations, plenty of crocodiles, monkeys and parrots to marvel at.
Lago Salvador Lodge, 30 minutes west of town, Amazon Ecopark, tel. 658-5000, next to street 631, fax 658-3506, part of Hotel Tropical, 12 bungalows with space for three persons.
Green Land Lord, 50 km west of town on Rio Tiririca (90 minute drive via the AM-070 or 3 hours by boat), tel./fax 236-0833, at the mouth of Rio Negro, 12 bungalows that sleep 2-3 persons.
Amazon Village, 60 km north of town on Lago Puraquequara (two and a half hours by boat). Gran Amazon, tel. 633-1444, fax 633-3217, reservations, tel. 021-283-0802, on Eel Lake, 32 double bungalows. Founded by immigrants from Switzerland, well managed, popular with tour groups, cold water showers only.
Amazon Lodge, 80 km south of town on Lago do Juma (four hours by boat). Nature Safaris, tel. 622-4144, fax 622-1420, reservations, tel. 021-275-6544, more downscale subsidiary of Amazon Village, 12 double rooms in a floating hotel, good for wildlife-watching.

THE RAIN FOREST

"Joy is an inadequate word for the feeling the naturalist experiences when he first wanders through a Brazilian forest. The elegance of the grasses, the curious parasitic plants, the shimmering green of the leaves, and above all the richness of the vegetation filled me with wonder." Thus wrote Charles Darwin in his diary in 1831 after arriving on the northeast coast of Brazil. Today, however, few areas with protected rain forests remain along the country's 7,500-kilometer-long Atlantic coast, and nowadays, when people talk about Brazil and tropical rain forests, it is usually in connection with the Amazon basin in the Brazilian hinterland. Unlike "virgin forest," by which is usually meant an undisturbed forest in

Previous pages: Slash-and-burn clearing is a threat to man and beast. Samba in Salvador. Above: The tropical rain forest is an irreplaceable source of medicinal and crop plants. Right: A magnificent passionflower.

any climatic zone, "rain forest" is associated with certain very specific climatic conditions – although they are found outside the tropics as well, e.g., in northern Canada and southern Chile. The expression "tropical rain forest" refers to forests near the equator in the tropical climatic zone. These forests are always hot, humid and wet, with year-round average monthly temperatures of 18°C and mean annual precipitation of at least 1,800-2,000 mm. They generally lie at an altitude of less than 1,000 meters; where altitude increases they are replaced by cooler but equally steamy montane forests. Today, tropical rain forests cover roughly 10 million square kilometers, or seven percent of the earth's land mass. On this seven percent live 90 percent of all primates, 80 percent of all insects and 60 percent of all plant species.

A tropical forest is by no means an impenetrable "green hell," as some adventure films would have us believe: a maximum of three percent of the sunlight filters down to the forest floor, and consequently the vegetation on the forest floor is spare. Only at the edges of the forest, along river courses and in clearings does abundant sunlight allow for the growth of lush bushes and grasses.

Tropical rain forests can be classified into five different strata of vegetation: (1) ground vegetation; (2) bushes and shrubs; (3) undergrowth, i.e., plants that can reach a height of 15 meters; (4) trees of medium height whose crowns create a closed canopy beneath which many different animals can live; (5) the highest level: giant trees averaging 40-60 meters in height whose trunks are higher than the crowns of trees of the fourth stratum. These massive "supertrees" survive with the help of extensive systems of buttress roots that may reach 10 meters in height.

Rain Forest Flora

Trees: The earth's tropical rain forests are estimated to have approximately 10,000 species of tree, of which 3,000 are native to the Amazon. How prodigious this number is can be appreciated by comparing it to the no more than 50 indigenous species of tree in all European forests. Because there is little climatic variation, rain forest trees do not produce an annual ring, although it is known that their life span is an average of 200-250 years. Some trees lose their leaves over the course of the entire year, while others lose all their leaves; there is no definite time when the trees are in bloom.

Stranglers: They are the most insidious competitors for life-giving light. The seeds of strangler figs are dispersed to the branches of host trees by birds. The epiphytic seedlings develop long aerial roots that descend down the tree into the soil, sometimes becoming as big around as a human arm, and eventually grafting themselves together to form a lattice, which then wraps itself around the tree and eventually strangles it. Meanwhile, the strangler fig foliage prevents the host

tree from growing by robbing it of its canopy of light.

Lianas: These tropical forest "swinging" vines have evolved a highly specialized way of climbing from the dark at the bottom of a tree towards the sunlight above. Some types of liana wrap themselves around a tree trunk like a coat; others grow through the tops of the host tree, thereby condemning it to death; still other varieties grow no leaves until they creep up under the crown of the host tree and develop a secondary crown beneath the host's.

Epiphytes: This word of ancient Greek origin refers to air plants, the best known of which are the circa 25,000 species of orchid. The native South American bromeliads are also members of this genus. They grow on branches near the upper canopy but must survive without mineral nutrients from the soil. They compensate for this by gathering nutrients from rain water as it washes over their funnel-shaped leaves, which are fertilized by the metabolic waste of

specialized fauna (primarily frogs and insects) who make their home on the leaves.

Mammals of the Rain Forest

Many rain forest visitors are disappointed that the only living creatures they see are vultures and mosquitoes. There are several reasons for this. Rain forest mammals are inherently difficult to catch sight of, as approximately two-thirds of them are nocturnal, and half of those are arboreal. Moreoover, the wet climate of the rain forest makes it unnecessary for animals living there to move about a great deal in search of water – as, by contrast, animals in the African savanna must. An additional factor is that visibility on rain forest paths is considerably more restricted than the distance over

Above: These small owl monkeys, like two-thirds of all mammals living in the rain forest, are nocturnal. Right: The jaguar – king of the rain forest.

which animals are able to take flight. An interesting fact in this respect is that a number of mammal species, such as the puma, are thought to have migrated from North to South America only after the Mesoamerican land bridge was formed some three million years ago. Zoologists have identified as indigenous only 15 species (with 60 genera) of extant South American mammals of the tropical zone, whereas 13 species (64 genera) are of North American origin.

The largest native terrestrial mammal in South America is the lowland tapir (*Tapirus terrestris*), which can attain a weight of up to 150 kilograms. Despite the presence of a short trunk, the tapir is a relative of the rhinoceros, not the elephant, and like most Amazonian mammals, has adapted to a semi-aquatic life. Tapirs can swim as proficiently as the giant anteaters, which can reach 2.4 meters in length, including their tail. Even sloths are good swimmers when they take flight, although they usually hang motionless from trees, perfectly camouflaged by their stiff-haired brownish coats, and, during the rainy season, by the minute greenish alga that grows in their fur.

Monkeys in the rain forest have a great advantage over their relatives in the Old World – their prehensile tails, which make it much easier for them to climb to the crowns of rain forest trees. The most common species in the rain forest are the howler, capuchin, spider, owl and wooly monkeys. The warning cry of the howler monkey can be heard at a distance of five kilometers. The anteater, armadillo and porcupine also make use of their prehensile tails. The agoutis and pacas, both small rodents, are favorite prey of the big cats, as are the marsh deer. The capybaras reach a length of 1.2 meters and a weight of 70 kilograms. Although they are called "water pigs," they are not pigs at all but rather the largest rodents on earth. The *yapok* (water opossum) has webbed feet,

and is the only completely aquatic marsupial in the world.

Manatees, an endangered species, are stout and harmless mammals that can grow to two meters in length. They were intensively hunted in the past by Europeans and Indians for their oil and hides, but may soon have their revenge: manatees have a split upper lip that allows them to consume inordinately large amounts of vegetation, including the rampant and watercourse-choking *canarana* grasses and water hyacinths. Thus the manatee, the most cost-efficient river cleaner there is, may soon be missed in the Amazon basin. The people-loving dolphins have fared somewhat better: their meat tastes good, but is said to render men impotent.

Onça pintada, the jaguar, is the largest member of the South American cat family. Jaguars are solitary nocturnal predators whose numbers have been drastically reduced – as have those of the ocelot – by hunters desirous of acquiring (and selling) these animals' spotted coats. Peccaries are the wild pigs that are mostly found in small herds and whose tusks keep even the big cats at bay.

Caimans, Anacondas and Hummingbirds

The largest reptiles in the Amazon basin are the black caimans, which are virtually invisible as they glide through the rivers during the day, and who do most of their hunting on the riverbanks. At night, their eyes throw back an eery reflection in beams of light.

The *jiboa* (boa constrictor) can reach 4.5 meters in length. *Caboclos*, Amazonians of mixed Indian and European blood, traditionally favor them over cats as rat hunters. Many incredible stories are told about the non-poisonous large snake, the anaconda. There have been reports of lengths of up to 20 meters, although the longest specimen on record is 8.5 meters. These large snakes wrap themselves around their prey, killing them by constriction. They swallow their pray whole.

The profusion of fish species in the Amazon region – an estimated 2,000 in all – truly boggles the mind. Some 700 are found within a radius of 30 kilometers of Manaus alone, more than the total number found in all North American rivers and lakes. The only flying riverine fish in the world lives in the Amazon basin, and there are nine species of hatchetfish, which escape from their many predators by using their pectoral fins to propel themselves across the surface of the water. A refreshing swim in the Amazon is always a calculated risk: "only" four of the 18 species of piranha are dangerous for humans, and "only" when attracted by the scent of blood. Encounters with the stingray should also be avoided, as its tail can pierce a human leg with sword-like efficacy.

It's no wonder that the electric eel (*Electrophorus electricus*) fascinated the 19th century German naturalist Alexander von Humboldt: four-fifths of its body consists of tissue with an electrical charge of 600 volts that the eel – which can reach a length of two meters – can use to immobilze fish and other prey.

Orthinologists who come to the Amazon do so at the risk of feeling overwhelmed, as this is the habitat of approximately one-quarter of the world's 8,600 species of bird. The large harpy eagle preys primarily on monkeys and rodents. The tucans are remarkable for their oversized beaks, whose honeycomb-like structure makes the birds look heavier than they are.

No fewer than 319 species of hummingbird have been found; in Portugese they are called *beija-flor* (flower-kissers). Their ability to beat their wings up to 100 times per second allows these tiny aerial acrobats to suck nectar from flowers while remaining almost motionless in the air. All this exertion requires a daily intake of several times their body weight in food – the equivalent of 140 ki-

Above: Piranhas sometimes give tourists nightmares! Right: Leaf-cutting ants hauling heavy loads.

lograms of meat per day for a human being. Hummingbirds supplement their diet of flower nectar by eating small insects, and some species vigorously defend their feeding areas of approximately 2,000 square meters. Countless species of parrot, as well as heron, cormorant, scarlet ibis, and duck also feed from a bounteous Amazonian menu of fish, fruit, and above all insects.

The Leaf-cutting Ant

These industrious creatures (*Atta texana*) deserve to be described separately for two reasons. First, it is almost impossible for any visitor to the rain forest to overlook them; and second, they are the most numerous of the thousands of rain forest insect species, accounting for an estimated one-third of its animal biomass.

One hectare of rain forest can harbor up to 28 underground nests, each containing one million ants, which explains why they are able to strip entire shrubs and trees of their leaves in just one night. With their razor-sharp jaws, member of the species *attinae* cut leaves into pieces weighing several times their body weight, and carry the pieces from the crown of the tree down to their nest.

The ants do not eat their harvest, however, as many plants protect themselves with self-generated toxins. Instead, the workers cut up the leaves into small pieces, chew them until they become very soft, and then make the softened leaves into a kind of bed on which a fungus that the ants cultivate, *rhizotes gongylophora*, begins to grow. This fungus flourishes in the warmth and dampness of the ants' underground chambers, causing the leaves to become extremely moldy. The nodules that develop provide the ants with the bulk of their nourishment. As these fungus beds age, their chambers are abandoned. Tree roots eventually grow into these chambers – illustrating a paradigmatic symbiosis of ant and fungus that is beneficial to the tree as well.

The Endangered Rain Forest

Unlike European forests, many of which have been reduced to monocultures, the tropical rain forest has such a large variety of species that one hectare can contain up to 500 different species of tree. This biodiversity arises from the scarcity of basic nutrients such as phosphorus and calcium: the flora cannot allow any to go to waste, and consequently generate chemical substances that help protect against any loss of leaves due to insects, birds or parasitic plants. This also explains why the agricultural use of rain forest soil is problematic: pests appear as soon as a monoculture is planted, attracted by the sudden overabundance of food.

Rain forests have almost no humus layer to speak of. Most trees form sym-

Above: Brazil's valuable tropical woods are prized throughout the world. Right: Herds of cattle now graze where centuries-old trees once stood.

biotic mycorrhizal associations with fungi that grow in intimate contact with their roots. These fungi obtain energy from the tree, and in turn provide the tree with a direct source of nutrients. The high levels of precipitation leach out the soil, impeding humus buildup from fallen dead leaves and other organic litter. This is why clearwater and blackwater rivers contain such low levels of nutrients (see pp. 185-187).

Although the handful of areas in the Amazon region that are suitable for agricultural purposes were long ago mapped out, the map is universally ignored. The pointless slashing and burning – the "chainsaw massacre" of the rain forest – continues. Whereas at the turn of the 20th century 12 percent of the terrestrial surface was covered with tropical rain forests, the figure today is a mere seven percent. South America contains approximately 56 percent of the earth's remaining rain forests, but a tropical rain forest area as big as 30 football fields is being destroyed every minute of every

day. Researchers estimate that 50 plant and animal species are destroyed per day, many of them either not classified at all or incompletely studied.

Logging for timber is not big business in the Amazon, but it has repercussions nonetheless. Logging trails allow landless farmers to penetrate into the interior of the rain forest, where they manage to scrape by for a few years with slash-and-burn cultivation and small patch farming, after which the land is fully depleted. Long overdue land reform has been repeatedly postponed by the Brazilian government. In the meantime, both the rain forest and ecosphere are beginning to feel the effects. In areas where the forest dissapears, tropical rains wash away the topsoil, which has even caused huge dams to fill with silt. Ecological disaster leads directly to economic catastrophe.

Both ecologists and socially responsible economists have come to the conclusion that the only hope for saving the the rain forests lies in sustainable use of their recyclable resources. Practioners of these disciplines are trying to persuade the governments of the Brazilian states with rain forests within their borders to stop regarding the forests solely as a source of lumber, or as potential pastureland or cropland. About a dozen edible crops now account for roughly 90 percent of the world's food supply, and of these, half have tropical forebears (e.g., rice and corn). Experts estimate that making greater use of extant rain forest species could double the number of available crop plants that could be exploited commercially. Approximately one-third of all pharmaceutical drugs contain active ingredients derived from tropical plants, which means that many more discoveries remain to be made, including plants for the fragrances and essences used in perfumes. One study showed that within 50 years, three times more income could be generated through the ecological use of the rain forest than by overexploitation – but how many businessmen today make such long-term calculations?

215

THE INDIGENOUS PEOPLES

"The Indians believe that God must have been asleep, drunk or ill, or maybe even dead. Otherwise, such terrible things could never have happened to them." Thus has anthropologist Darcy Ribeiro, one-time Minister of Education and former President of the University of Brasília, described the attitude of the last remnants of the indigenous peoples of Brazil. Genetic analyses of the Yanomami have revealed that their forebears migrated across the Bering Straits from Asia thousands of years ago. When the first Europeans arrived, several million people were already living in the coastal areas, along the watercourses, and in the huge forests. These people were members of various ethnic groups, each of which had its own language. The Europeans encountered these vibrant cultures as they were undergoing a process of expansion; but they were either wiped out or acculturated.

Having scattered in response to the Europeanizing of the central Amazon region, Brazil's indigenous peoples live in a kind of diaspora. Estimates of their numbers vary greatly, depending upon the interests and point of view of the person compiling the statistics. The Society for Imperiled Peoples in Göttingen, Germany estimates that 220,000 Native Americans stemming from 180 language communities and 554 homelands currently live in Brazil, and that the territories they inhabit account for about 10 percent of Brazil's land area.

The status of the native peoples of Brazil in a "Christian" society in both the past and present is typified by the following quotes. In the 16th century, the highly respected Jesuit priest José de Anchieta from São Paulo wrote this about mission-

ary work: "When a Jesuit visits an Indian village and the Indian shows no sign that he is prepared to be catechized, then the Indian must be afflicted with the sword and the iron rod: there is no better sermon." Nearly 500 years later, in 1989, the Brazilian Minister of the Army Leonidas Pires Gonçalves expressed the view that Indian culture, "being one of the least developed, deserves little respect, and that Indians should integrate themselves once and for all into the mainstream of Brazilian society." But none of the many attempts to persuade Brazil's native peoples of their inferiority has succeeded. As Darcy Ribeiro put it: "Faced with a hopeless situation, they prefer to die by their own hand." And indeed, according to a report published in 1996, 238 Guarani, most of them young men, took their own lives over a 13-year period.

Brazilian government officials have never hesitated to pay abundant lip service to the importance of protecting native peoples. The SPI, the agency for the protection of Indians, was established as early as 1910, but after irrefutable evidence of corruption came to light in 1967, it was supplanted by FUNAI (Fundaçâo Nacional do Indio). This organization has turned out to be a refuge for has-been politicians and military officers who spend their time in air-conditioned offices in Brasília making policy decisions with regard to protective zones, supply flights, and the agendas of delegations – without ever having laid eyes on a real member of an indigenous group.

That FUNAI also acts as trustee for Brazil's native peoples only exacerbates the situation. The Brazilian constitution denies native peoples the right to vote, and allows them only restricted economic rights, thereby putting disenfranchised adults in the same ambiguous position as minors. Although intended to be a protective measure, in practice this policy gives free rein to corrupt officials.

Right: Madihans prepare manioc root, a staple for them as it is for most indigenous peoples of the Amazon.

What's more, since Indian territories are government property, native peoples have no control over the homelands they have lived in for centuries. The Brazilian constitution only grants them the right to make use of their mineral resources, rivers and lakes, but expressly forbids them to exploit these resources for industrial purposes: they are only entitled to attend meetings and to a share in the profits. Native peoples also have the right to *garimpagem* (pan for gold) in their own territories, but this has turned out to be a continuing source of conflict, as the *garimpeiros* (white panners) intrude into native territories, displacing their inhabitants and poisoning the lakes and rivers with the mercury they use while prospecting for gold.

In 1996, the "1775/1996" decree gave rise to protests by both the missionary council, CIMI, and international advocacy groups that concern themselves with the protection of native peoples' rights. The decree, promulgated in response to pressure from large landowners, called into question existing laws governing native peoples' land rights by stating that any Brazilian who wished to could both claim a right to their lands and raise objections to existing territorial borders. 1,749 such claims were filed by the closing date, thereby posing a renewed threat to many of the 210 officially recognized Indian territories. Why do the native peoples of the "melting pot" of Brazil have no lobby in Brazília? On the one hand, native peoples in Brazil comprise a far smaller percentage of the population than do their counterparts in neighboring South American countries; and on the other, they have no lobby in the capital.

The Way of Life of the Lowland Indians

The Amazon region is ideal for the hunter-gatherer way of life led by Brazil's ethnic tribes, many of whom also fish with harpoons or bow and arrow. Some also practice a combination of slash-and-burn agriculture – which, as it

Also grown are black pepper, pineapples, papayas, tobacco and cotton, as well as annatto, a plant from which the red *urucu* skin dye extensively used by many groups is derived.

In places where there has been little acculturation through contact with white people and no guns have been introduced, native peoples still hunt peccaries, monkeys, small animals and birds with bow and arrow or blowguns, which can be up to five meters long and are usually made from reeds and palms. Ammunition consists of a dart 40-50 centimeters in length with a twist of fiber at the base and a drop of curare on the tip. This paralysis-inducing alkaloid poison is prepared from the liana *Strychnos toxifera.* Recipes for curare vary and are for the most part closely guarded secrets of the few tribes who produce the substance, making it a valuable commodity.

The basic unit of tribal society is the extended family, which usually lives in a communal dwelling called a *maloka* that can provide shelter for up to 100 persons and in which the most important furnishing is the *rede* (hammock). The distance between the posts supporting the *maloka* is determined by the length of the hammock, which is not only for sleeping but is also the most important seat in the house. Its great advantage over beds or chairs is that crawling insects and creeping reptiles cannot climb up on it.

involves no chain saws, spares the largest trees – and small patch farming, whereby a small area is cultivated for several growing seasons after which the group moves on to clear a new field leaving the soil to replenish itself, sometimes returning to former sites after a number of years.

The staple food of most indigenous groups who inhabit the Amazon is manioc root. As this plant contains linamarin, which is high in prussic acid (i.e., toxic) and thus cannot be eaten raw, the root must first be boiled or roasted in order to neutralize the poison. A round, flat bread is made out of manioc meal. The main advantage of manioc root in a tropical climate is that since it can be stored in the ground, only the amount required for each meal need be harvested. Other crops widely cultivated include plantains, pumpkins, beans and yams.

Although the social structure of the ethnic tribes is distinctly patriarchal, hierarchy does not play an important role in their everyday lives, since all adults share equally the burden of assuring the economic survival and well-being of their clan. The men's sphere consists of hunting, farming and making war. The women see to the harvest, take care of the children, and prepare meals. Initiation rites are extremely important, although they vary greatly from one group to another. As a rule, men and women who marry must come from different tribes;

Above: Indian ceremonial ornamentation made of feathers. Right: A young Kulina practices hunting with bow and arrow.

dowries, which can give rise to war, are still quite common.

The Various Indigenous Groups and their Status Today

During the rubber boom at the turn of the last century, the Kuliná were especially hard-hit by persecution at the hands of the rubber barons. In response, they withdrew inland to the area around the upper Rio Negro, and eventually to Acre. Today, they number about 2,500. They have successfully resisted attempts to expel them from their land, and since 1991, in cooperation with the Kaxinawá, have taken charge of the surveying of their territory.

In 1996-97, a group of researchers from the Carl von Ossietzky University in Oldenburg, Germany, went on an expedition to study the Canela. The documentary made about this project brought the Canela fame after it was shown on German television. A custom unique to this group is a relay race (the men vs. the women) during which tree trunks weighing up to 150 kilograms are carried for hours at a stretch.

A geologist first stumbled on the Zoé in the northern Amazon in 1976. Since that time, owing to missionary activity, 45 members of this group have died from influenza, and today they number only 150. When the Zoé were discovered, they wore no clothing whatsoever, although some of the men and women adorn themselves with lip pegs that are up to 15 centimeters long and four centimeters wide.

In the state of Mato Grosso do Sul live the Guarani, who are divided into various subgroups. In recent years, they have been subjected to tremendous pressure from large landowners making claims on their reservations, an effort supported by local officials and judges. There have been numerous suicides and threats of collective suicide – despairing reactions to attempts to drive them off their land and resettle them.

North of Manaus live the Waimiri-Atroari who, in 1968, owing to construc-

tion of a highway through their territory that gave rise to harassment by the military, as well as an epidemic, saw their numbers reduced from 3,000 to 1,000 within a seven-month period. When the Balbina Dam was built in 1987, the last 300 Waimiri-Atroari were sent elsewhere to live.

The Parakana have been resettled 11 times within a 20-year period, most recently on a reservation that does not provide them with sufficient space to live in. Missionaries from various evangelist groups in North America continue to go about their ethnocentric business in the Amazon, and even study the languages spoken by the "poor savages" so as to be able to teach them the Bible in their own tongues. The Wai-Wai were "discovered" by missionaries and can now read St. Paul's letter to the Corinthinans in their own language. But will this really save their souls?

Above: Yanomami women ornament themselves by painting their skin.

The Yanomami

The Yanomami, who live in the rain forests of southern Venezuela and northeast Brazil, are the largest indigenous group in the South American lowlands. Estimates of their numbers vary. It is thought that about 15,000 of them live in Venezuela, and approximately 10,000 in Brazil – although borders have little meaning for such forest dwellers. Their equatorial homeland encompasses approximately 80,000 square kilometers, most of it dense tropical rain forest, except for a small area in the extensive Serra Parima savanna. It has been estimated that in order to practice their form of migratory agriculture, the Yanomami need about 64,000 hectares per 80 people. Their *shabonos* (villages), unlike those of most other groups, do not lie along the riverbanks, but are instead widely scattered across the forest. There are thought to be about 250 self-sufficient shabonos, each with between 40 and 250 inhabitants.

The shabono, or "clearing," constitutes the village square around which are built *malocas*, many of whose fronts are left open. The back walls of these thatched huts often form part of a palisade that some villages construct for protection, the entrance being closed at night. In each hut there is always a fire burning, over which objects (such as weapons) that might be damaged by moisture are hung, so as to keep them in working order in the humid tropical climate. At night, the Yanomami (who wear no clothing) gather around the fire for warmth. Three-quarters of their food supply is derived from the over 40 varieties of crop plants that they cultivate. During the dry season (December to March), they clear a patch of rain forest and plant the seedlings with a digging stick. The Yanomami's most important staple food crops are manioic and plantains, followed by taro, papaya and various types of palm.

The Yanomami women carry heavy loads with the aid of a strap secured around their chest. The Yanomami do not smoke, nor do they drink alcoholic beverages. They are of small stature: most of the men do not exceed 160 centimeters in height. Women comprise their only "wealth," and a successful hunter may have several. Many men have no wife, however, and in some cases brothers will share one woman. Beginning in early childhood, the Yanomami are taught the virtues of highly aggressive behavior, and abduction of women often leads to inter-tribal feuds.

The Yanomami's custom of endocannibalism is prone to misinterpretation. They believe that the *nobolebe* (soul of the deceased) can only reach the hereafter if the dead are properly prepared, the corpse cremated, and the charred and pulverized bones consumed by the next-of-kin in a banana mush. The Yanomami fear that if this is not done, the deceased relative will become a *bole* (ghost) and

will then threaten the living with evil and disease.

Paradoxically, the natural resources of the land they live on pose a serious threat to the Yanomami's existence. In the early 1970's, the systematic exploitation of gold, diamond, uranium, tin and titanium deposits began in earnest. And in 1973, a 600-kilometer-long highway was built through the Yanomami's homeland, bringing with it increasing numbers of irresponsible, illegal, and sometimes criminal gold diggers. They have spread influenza, measles, malaria, syphillis, tuberculosis and hepatitis B among the Yanomami, who lack defenses against such diseases. The overexploitation by gold diggers of the Yanomami's living areas, forests, and hunting grounds also constitutes a threat to their survival.

Every single gram of gold requires 1.5 grams of mercury as a binding agent for the gold dust; this pollutes the rivers, and poisons the fish who live in them. Since 1987, confrontations between gold prospectors and indigenous groups have become common. Such conflicts reached a climax in 1993 when a group of Yanomami women and children were massacred by *garimpeiros*, which caused the Yanomami to retaliate with a series of acts of revenge. With this, the government finally saw fit to take some action: illegal landing strips have been bombarded with propaganda, and some gold prospectors have been driven off. But the governor of Brazil's northernmost state of Roraima, who is a former general, approves of the *garimpeiros*. Moreover, this governor lives in the state's capital city of Boa Vista, where many of the gold dealers, pilots, and hotel and restaurant owners who have designs on the Yanomami's homeland also live.

In the spring of 1998, the Yanomami were confronted with a new threat: over 6,000 square kilometers of Roraima rain forest, including parts of the Yanomami reserve, were destroyed in huge forest fires that originated with slash-and-burn activities carried out by farmers and ranchers. Work on extinguishing the blazes was only undertaken after massive pressure was put on the Brazilian government by national and international environmental organizations, and by the UN; this delay severly reduced the efficacy of the helicopters. Some indigenous villages and farming areas were destroyed, and there were deaths from burns, serious cases of respiratory disease from smoke inhalation, and reports of famine among the approximately 20,000 indigenous inhabitants.

Alto-Xingu: A Positive Model

The **Parque Indígena do Xingu**, located in the state of Mato Grosso, is a 22,000-square-kilometer nature preserve that was founded in 1961. Named after the Xingu River, the affluent of the Amazon on whose upper reaches it lies, it houses 16 indigenous and four different language groups. In past centuries these tribes either migrated to this area from elsewhere in Brazil in order to escape European encroachment or, like the Kren-Akrore, were forcibly resettled. Until a road to the area was built in 1970, these groups were protected by rapids from the discontents of civilization.

Between 1946 and 1973, the Villas-Boâs brothers, two Brazilian businessmen who were neither anthropologists nor missionaries, made an invaluable contribution to the welfare of the indigenous communities dwelling along the Xingu River: they operated an administrative and trading center at Alto-Xingu that both helped maintain peace in the area and kept intact the homeland of the indigenous peoples whose cause these two men had decided to support.

Right: "Dance of the Negro Slaves" – the only form of entertainment available to slaves (17th-century watercolor).

Recently, the Xingu people have succeeded in integrating themselves into Brazilian society without sacrificing their cultural identity. They now use fishing hooks, radios and bicycles, and trade in timber and wild game. At the end of the 19th century about 3,000 indigenous people settled in the area, but by the middle of the 20th century, influenza, measles and malaria epidemics had reduced their numbers to no more than 1,000. The *Xinguanos* themselves estimate that approximately 3,500 people now live on their reservation, and that children under the age of 15 account for half that number.

Every year the Alto-Xingo stage an elaborate festival called the *Kuarup*. Shortly after the death of a chief or the member of a chief's family, the bereaved begin preparations for the event, which does not take place until August or September of the following year. *Kuarup* trees are cut down, decorated with red *urucu* paint and feathers, and are then displayed in the middle of the village square. The festival also includes dances, mock battles, games and a banquet. The *huka-huka* is a wrestling match between young boys who paint their bodies with red spots on a black background to resemble the anaconda.

In 1989, two members of the Kayapó tribe received worldwide media attention when, accompanied by ethnobotanist Dr. Darell Addison Posey, they protested to United States senators and World Bank officials in Washingon against proposed loans for a dam project that posed a threat to their entire homeland. The rock star Sting lent his support to their effort, and the government-owned company *Electronorte* temporarily gave up plans to follow through on the project. Shortly after their return to Brazil, both representatives of the Kayapó were forced to stand trial for treason, a travesty of justice that was only brought to a halt through international pressure.

MUSIC: SAMBA, CAPOEIRA AND CANDOMBLÉ

Brazil without music is unthinkable; to Brazilians, music is as vital as life itself. Brazil is the third-largest record market in the world, and over 60 percent of the music played on the media is "MPB": *Musica Popular Brasileira*.

Hardly any other culture in the world encompasses as wide a spectrum of music as Brazil's does. Nor have many other countries so successfully and creatively woven such a variety of ethnic strands into the fabric of their musical life. In Brazil, the mixture of indigenous, African and European elements generates boundless innovation.

The Portuguese colonists brought with them their Iberian musical tradition, mainly liturgical music, which was also their primary form of entertainment. The African slaves who came to Brazil were "allowed" to dance. And the indigenous peoples learned the Baroque music of the Jesuits. The manifold ways in which these cultures have enriched each other is endlessly fascinating: choro, chula, frevo, maracatu, capoeira, carimbo, toadas, forro, axé, sambareggae and samba constitute only a few facets of this enchanting musical kaleidoscope.

It would be a gross oversimplification to resort to the cliché that music helps the poor forget their troubles, because almost everywhere you go in Brazil you find music interwoven with every aspect of daily life. The joy of spontaneous singing and dancing, or of beating out rhythms on any object at hand, is inextricably bound up with the people themselves. In short, MPB is an attitude towards life that permeates every socioeconomic class.

Brazil without samba? Thinkable, yes, but then this aspect of the musical tradition would perhaps be called conga or chula. Because samba is only one of many names for an unpressured leisure-time social activity. Samba can be, for example, a birthday party at which the guests regale each other with singing and dancing, and through improvisation get everyone into the swing of things. Grand-parents, two-year-old children, pretty young women, a taxi driver, the neighbor who just dropped in, the acquaintance invited at a moment's notice, an awkward foreigner – each contributes whatever he can. And that's samba!

The first phonograph recording of samba ever made was a performance by what sounds like four musicians. The sound technology of the time only allowed voice and guitar to be pressed into the wax cylinder, which is why *Pelo Telefono* ("On the Telephone") lacks percussion. By contrast, when modern-day *samba enredos* (stories set to music) are performed at samba schools, hundreds of percussion instruments resound while the guitars play quietly in the background.

Baroque Music in the Rain Forest

Although the cultures of Brazil's indigenous peoples have gained recognition only relatively recently, their considerable musical gifts, humor, and spontaneity in the realms of both dance and music constitute a vibrant presence in Brazilian culture. Living in harmony with nature, these tribes were too unprejudiced and tolerant an ingredient in Brazil's melting pot. The Christians – and in particular the Jesuits – were another "ingredient," busy preaching the gospel of peaceful missionary work. When, in 1549, the Jesuits included the Indian tribes in their plans for a City of God, they quickly noticed how important music, dance and song were to them, and how simple it would be to use music to sweeten the pill of doctrine. The Indians, no strangers to complex rituals, enriched their own repertoires with songs from the Christian liturgy, whose rhythms were monotonous, but which still contained

Right: Capoeira – a combination folk dance and mock fight brought to Brazil by Angolan slaves – being performed in Salvador.

some engaging new melodies. And the Jesuits saw that their "little sheep" were singing along during Mass, apparently with fervor.

It is difficult to say to what extent the indigenous peoples of Brazil (whose percussion instruments bear a marked similarity to their African counterparts) have influenced modern day MPB. Then again, the imprint of indigenous groups is clearly discernible on the *xaxados* (shepherd's songs) of the northeast, as well as on the *carimbo* music of the north. And there is little doubt that the Brazilian composers Carlos Gomes and Heitor Villa Lobos (see p. 225) drew upon the indigenous musical tradition in their work.

Boi-bumbá, an important folk festival that draws heavily on indigenous rituals, is celebrated every July in Parintin, 400 kilometers east of Manaus. In atmosphere and scale, this musical and theatrical event in the middle of the Amazon region is beginning to rival Carnival in Rio! Taking as its themes the economic and ecological traditions of indigenous groups, the three-day event involves up to 500 percussionists, as well as hundreds of masked extras, performing a type of music called *toadas*.

Hot Accordion Playing

Religious holidays were the principal cultural events for the Portuguese colonists. And because festivals were the most important social events in the vast and isolated reaches of the northeast, the ecclesiastical calendar was expanded *ad hoc* to include the traditional pageant *Bumba-meu-boi* (see p. 176). The Europeans brought with them their recorders, as well as stringed instruments such as the mandolin, *cavaquinho* (a flat four-string guitar), and Spanish and seven-string guitar. The courtly love songs and poems of the Iberian troubadours were refined, and artists called *troubadoures*,

violeiros and *repentistas* gave (and in a few areas in the northeast still give) astonishingly polished improvised musical accounts of recent events and gossip.

The exotic melange of indigenous peoples, Portuguese and Africans in this tropical area gave birth to an idiosyncratic musical form. The Scottish country dance, originally the province of the upper classes, became the *xote*, the quadrille became the *quadrilha*, an aboriginal dance became the *xaxado*, and the *forró* was created for everyone. This highly popular musical form is a favorite throughout Brazil. For the *forró* all that's needed is an accordion, a triangle and a *zabumba* (a drum beaten on both sides), and then it's time to dance: everybody up for the *forró*! The lyrics are intensely accusatory or risqué – so passionate, in fact, that the highly erotic samba called the *lambada* pales in comparison. Hotter and more virtuosic accordion playing would be difficult to find anywhere.

Choro (weeping) is yet another Brazilian interpretation of European music, one that has been in existence since 1880. The *pandeiro* (a tambourine with bells) beats out a samba-like rhythm, while in the background the *cavaquinhos*, recorders and seven-string guitars play variations on complex virtuso motifs.

Classical Music in Brazil

Because the Brazilian empire only began showing an interest in theater and classical music in 1850, this genre has been somewhat short-changed in the nation's musical life. However, there have been two pearls in the treasury of Brazilian classical music – Carlos Gomes (1836-1896) and Heitor Villa Lobos (1887-1956). Gomes' opera *O Guarani* was highly successful at La Scala in Milan. And in 1870, with the support of Villa Lobos, the Indian version of Romeo and Juliette became the most celebrated work ever written by a Brazilian composer. Villa Lobos became famous in Paris in the 1920's for such works as *Bachianas Brasileiras*. Curitiba and

225

Campos do Jordão (near São Paulo) each hold annual international festivals of classical music. And Professor Hans Joachim Köllreutther from Germany has been a professor at the music conservatory in Salvador since 1954. In 1990, one of his students, Lindemberg Cardoso, created *Lidia de Oxum*, the first Brazilian opera to take slavery as its theme.

Capoeira in Bahia

There is little doubt that Salvador da Bahia, the first "black" capital of Brazil, constitutes the hub of 20th-century Brazilian musical life. For decades now, Bahia has been a worldwide symbol of progressive music. Once a port for the slave trade, the influence of African culture has been felt in Bahia more than in any other Brazilian city, and many internationally renowned stars regularly come here in search of new ideas.

Slaves were allowed to dance, but at the same time honed their fighting skills behind their masters' backs by means of the *capoeira*, a dance of ritualized fighting that was brought to Brazil by slaves from Angola, but which was later banned by slave-owners fearful that it might be used against them. Two muscular men gyrate through the air, stopping their kicks just before they land, as in karate but without the martial cry.

The dance is accompanied by increasingly rapid drum beats on the *atabaques*, *pandeiro* (a type of tambourine with bells) and *berimbau* (musical bow). This Angolan instrument consists of a curved stick with a hollowed-out gourd and a single string that is struck rhythmically with a rod. One of the world's outstanding percussionists, Nana Vasconcelos, rose to international fame playing the *berimbau*.

Right: For Western tourists, a mysterious and exotic world – a member of the Candomblé religion in a trance.

Candomblé – West African Ancestor Worship

The Yorùbá and Bantu brought their gods with them from West Africa. As the Candomblé ceremony unfolds, more and more of the assembled join in, until they have sung and danced themselves into a trance. The Candomblé have a strong sense of tradition, but their ability to adapt has allowed them to develop into the most powerful religious and cultural force in Bahia, despite restrictions imposed on them by the state's religious and cultural powers-that-be. But the statistics speak for themselves: Salvador has between eight and ten thousand Candomblé places of worship, but only 180 colonial churches. The African divinities (*orixás*) have their own feast day calendar. *Oxalá* is the head of the family of gods and at the same time the Lord of Peace and Creation. *Yemanjá* is the Goddess of the Sea and Mother of All *Orixás*. Amazingly, all Bahian art is derived from this one ancient and inspiring source.

Each year, the 5,000 white-clad members of the *Afoxé* ("Children of Gandhi"), which was founded in 1949, are lead in the Carnival procession by the massive drums of the group Olodum. The world of Candomblé pervades everything that makes Bahia unique, creative and famous: the motifs of the painter Caribé, the novels of Jorge Amados and the poetry of Dorival Caymmis. One of the most delightful songs – almost an anthem – about the city of Salvador is called *Toda Cidade é de Oxum*, or "The Whole City Belongs to Oxum" (the goddess of fresh water).

In 1964, following the momentous changes in cultural life brought about by the advent of a military dictatorship, Bahians returned to the limelight with *tropicalismo*. Gilberto Gil, Gal Costa, Caetano Veloso, Maria Bethânia, Raul Seixas and Tom Xé wrote lyrics on predominantly political themes for a heady musical

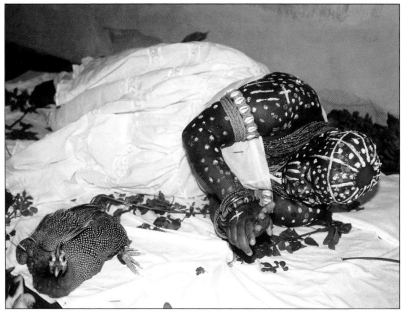

cocktail of samba, bossanova, candomblé, capoeira and rock. After some success, Gil and Veloso were imprisoned and then deported. Since their return in 1970, they have been leading practioners of *tropicalismo* along with Chico Buarque, Milton Nascimento and Djavan – to this day the most interesting composers and performers of Brazilian popular dance music.

During the 1970s, the music of Carnival groups such as Ilê Aiyê, Muzenza and especially Olodum went to the top of the charts. Jamaican reggae also made a highly successful comeback in Bahia, which led to the birth of sambareggae. Like samba, this musical form tries to bring about social and political change through cultural action – and does so with astonishing success. Groups like Ilê Aiyê and Projeto Axé (*axé* means "positive energy") have built social infractures through the creation of schools, kindergartens and job training centers.

Today, Bahians of all socioeconomic classes and ethnic backgrounds are proud of their Afro-Bahian culture, which though once only tolerated at best, has become an export product. The famous Montreux Jazz Festival now features a Bahia evening, and the International Music Festival in Tübingen, Germany features performances each year by the likes of Daniela Mercury. The Olodum group regularly goes on tour in Europe, and in 1996 made a music video with Michael Jackson. Such Axé (Bahian Carnival music) stars as Banda Mel and Timbalada have also gained international renown.

And through it all, Salvador's unique Carnival, which many regard as far more authentic than Rio de Janeiro's, goes its own thrilling way. Rehearsals begin in October, and in the days leading up to Ash Wednesday, upwards of two million people dance their way through the streets behind *trios électricos* – mobile stages equipped with hellishly loud sound systems. And right in the middle of the tropical summer, the city glows white hot with bedlam and uproar.

EATING AND DRINKING

Apart from the excellent fruit juices (*sucos*), it is above all the aperitifs that make a trip to Brazil so memorable. The best known, *caipirinha*, is made with *cachaça* or *pinga* (sugar-cane spirits) with added limes, ice and sugar. Thirsty travelers wishing to imbibe a less intoxicating drink can order a *caipiríssima*, which is made with rum rather than cachaça. Vodka fans, on the other hand, should request a *caipirosca*. Cachaça is also mixed with various fruit juices to make *batidas*, a palate-pleasing but alcoholically potent cocktail. Inviting, too, are *batidas de côco* with coconut milk, *batidas de maracujá* with passion fruit, *batida de limão* with lime, and as many other variations as there are types of fruit.

Because Brazilians, like most people living in southern countries, eat a small breakfast, a snack known as *cafezinho* (small coffee) has evolved, which is available everywhere at a fixed, government-regulated price. *Salgadinhos*, obtainable in *padarias* (bakeries), are salty rolls that come in various forms such as the perennially popular *pão de queijo*, literally a cheese roll, but in reality a pie with a manioc meal and cream cheese filling. Also available throughout the country are *coxinhas*, a dish made of a potato-based dough with chicken filling, and *empadinhas*, a pie with a crab or meat filling.

All Brazilian cities have corner bars and *lanchonetes*, both of which are fast-food restaurants that serve juice, coffee and beer as well as light meals including hamburgers, hot dogs (*cachorro quente*) and warm sandwiches like *misto quente* (ham and cheese). A variation on the latter (with added tomato) is called *bauru*, a dish which, when served with a fried egg

Right: One of Salvador's female "street chefs" selling her mouth-watering specialities.

and lettuce, becomes an *americano*. *Prato feito* (PF) is a tasty and inexpensive meal consisting of beef, black beans, rice, French fries and salad.

Pizzerias have also come to Brazil, especially to São Paulo and the southern part of the country. In more formal restaurants, however, they are served with a bit more fanfare (and at a higher price) – with bread, butter, olives, a raw vegetable platter, etc. Most foreigners are surprised at the large portions that are brought to their tables; but conspicuous waste (i.e., leaving some food on your plate) is regarded as "chic."

A viable and economic alternative to fast and high-calorie foods are the self-service restaurants that have sprung up in Brazil in recent years, where the bill is calculated according to weight. Salad, meat, vegetables, and dessert all cost the same (i.e., in the neighborhood of US $1 to 2 per 100 grams) – so go easy on those weighty potatoes!

Visitors who would like to sample more elaborate meat dishes (mad cow disease is not a problem in Brazil) should try a *churrascaria*, where most Brazilians order *rodízios*: What seems like armies of waiters serve meat on long skewers from a trolley, which they keep bringing back until you're full to bursting and wave them away. This isn't easy as it sounds, since meat, side-dishes, salad, and dessert are all included in a fixed price. Besides *coração de galinha* (chicken hearts) and *frango* (grilled chicken), everything is beef, which is sometimes prepared by first salting and then grilling it. The feast begins with a filling salami called *calabresa*, which you shouldn't eat too much of lest you have no appetite left for the best morsels, which are still to come. Next arrives the *picanha* (loin roast), then *contra-filé* (tenderloin), *filé-mignon* and finally *alcatra* (rumpsteak). Another specialty is *cupim*, meat from the hump of the zebu. Side dishes include cheese croquettes

made with manioc meal, *aipim frito* (fried manioc root) and baked bananas.

Feijoada, which enjoys the status of a Brazilian national dish, is primarily served for Saturday lunch. Its ingredients include the Brazilian staples, rice and black beans; beef, and several cuts of pork, including the loin, tongue, knuckles, ear and tail; and *linguiça* (sausage), bacon and *carne seca* (dried meat). The meats are marinated overnight and the beans simmer for hours until the broth thickens. Feijoada is served with *couve mineira* (kale), *farofa* (manioc meal), orange slices, and *molho carioca* (a spicy sauce).

On Sundays, southerners traditionally eat *cozido*, a casserole that is cooked over a wood fire. In addition to various types of meat, it is made from beans, chick peas, potatoes, and *xuxú* (a type of small pumpkin). *Tutu de feijão*, the nourishing regional specialty of Minas Gerais, is a kind of pureed stew that combines black beans, kale, pork chops, fried eggs, rice and pig crackling.

Throughout Brazil you can order a tasty chicken soup called *canja* that is flavored with rice, tomatoes and onions.

Bahian Cuisine: The Taste of Africa

The most distinctive and fascinating food you will find in Brazil is the exotic cuisine of Bahia. Unless you are fasting, it is virtually impossible to sit down to a meal in this state without meeting up with such delicacies as *óleo de dendê* (a reddish brown palm oil), coconut milk, fresh coriander, dried shrimps, fresh peanut butter, and various spices including the treacherously hot *malagueta* pepper. On many street corners in Brazil, and particularly in Salvador, *baianas* (dark-skinned female chefs dressed in white) sell *acarajé*, croquettes made of dried beans and shrimps; or *abará*, the same combination boiled and then wrapped in a banana leaf. Other Bahian specialities include *vatapá*, which is chicken or fish combined with shrimps, coconut milk, palm oil, bread, nuts, pepper and other spices, the whole concoction served with *caruru*: okra with dried shrimps and cashew nuts fried in palm oil.

Fish or shellfish are prepared in *moqueca*, a broth of coconut milk and dendê oil, onions, garlic, peppers, tomatoes, coriander and bay leaf. Variations include *moqueca de peixe* (with fish); *de camarão* (with shrimps); *de siri* (with crab); *de sururu* (with mussels); and *de polvo* (with calamari). *Camarão à baiana* is the name of a mouth-watering dish made of steamed shrimps with tomato paste, onions, dendê oil, coconut milk, lemon juice, spices and herbs, and served with rice.

Ximxim de galinha is chicken braised in palm oil with peanuts and dried shrimps. In addition to rice, the most common side-dishes include various types of manioc such as *pirão*, a paste made with spices and fish or fish stock. Sweet potatoes (*batata doce*) should be tried at least once, as should plantains (*banana da terra*), which are prevalent in the northeast and north. *Ensopado de peixe* is a tasty fish soup made from a coconut milk base, and *caldo de sururu* is a mussel soup.

Amazonian Pleasures

The Amazon region bears the imprint of the culinary practices of its indigenous inhabitants: the staples are fresh-water fish, manioc and bananas. The tuberous edible plant manioc (native to Brazil but now also an African staple) grows to be 30 centimeters in length under an up to three-meter-high bush, which is cultivated by simply planting a stalk in the ground. A cyanide-producing sugar derivative called linamarin occurs in most varieties. The poison is removed through a process that involves soaking and boiling the tubers.

Right: Acarajés, croquettes made of beans and shrimp – a Bahian specialty.

Pato no tucupi – duck in *tucupi* stock – is a festive dish common in the north. *Tucupi* is made from the juice of grated manioc root. *Jambu* is a vegetable used to make a sour soup; *tacacá* is a spicy okra casserole.

Turtles can also be found on menus, although hunting them was banned long ago. No visitor to the Amazon should forego the pleasure of sampling its fish, which, owing to a lack of refrigerated ships, are rarely found in restaurants in southern Brazil. *Dourado* and *filhote* are spiny catfish whose meat is delicious. *Tucunar tambaqui* and *pacu* are large fish with almost boneless meat. The heftiest fish of them all is the *pirarucú*, which can reach a length of two meters and a weight of over 200 kilograms. *Piranhas* – whose meat is flavorful but whose reputation as man-eaters makes them difficult to sell – are eaten smoked by some indigenous groups. *Peixada* is a fish specialty flavored with coconut milk.

Brigadeiros and Carambolas

Brazilian desserts and sweets could hardly be described as low in sugar, the maxim being the sweeter the merrier. Truly delicious confections are chocolate balls called *brigadeiros*, and *cocadas* – a sweet flavored with coconut. Common to the whole country is *goiabada com queijo* (guava preserves with fresh cheese), also called "Romeo and Juliette," because the two ingredients are inseparable.

There are also exotic-tasting cakes made of manioc meal (*bolo de mandioca*) or cornmeal (*bolo de milho*). Visitors looking to put on some weight should sample such rich delights as *quindim* (an egg and coconut cream) or *doce de leite* (crème caramel) or *pudim de leite* (pudding made with condensed milk and caramel sauce).

When it comes to fruit, Brazil is a veritable treasure trove: the number of tropi-

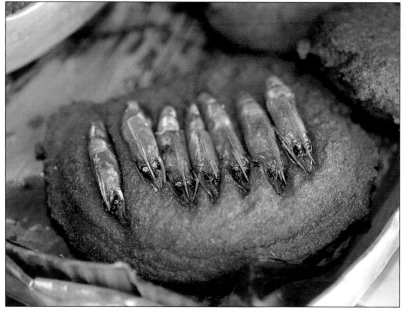

cal fruits available, some of which make their way into delicious but sometimes very sweet *sorvete* (ice cream), truly astonishes. Take bananas, for example, of which there are four different varieties: *banana de água* (water banana), which is the kind exported to the northern hemisphere; *banana-prata* (silver banana); *banana-ouro* (golden banana) which is very small and tasty; and *banana maça* (apple banana), which does in fact have an apple-like flavor.

In southern Brazil, the descendants of European immigrants primarily grow apples, pears, grapes, strawberries, honeydew melon and watermelon. A tasty fruit treat in early summer in Minas Gerais is the *jabuticaba*, a variety of cherry. Papayas (*mamão*), pineapples (*abacaxi*) and mangos (*manga*) are ubiquitous. The fields of northern and northeastern Brazil yield exotic fruits such as carambola, *jaca* (jackfruit), and *graviola* (soursop), the latter a type of custard apple (*annona*) that can weigh up to three kilograms.

Guaraná has become a fashionable drink at European discos in recent years owing to its stimulating (in all senses of the word) properties. In Brazil, the fruit of the climbing vine, *Paullinia cupana*, which contains caffeine, is available in soft drink (*refrigerante*), powder or tablet form for its purported aphrodisiacal properties. More convenional drinks such as rum and cachaça are made from sugar cane, as is freshly squeezed *caldo de cana*, a favorite among children.

From Rio Grande do Sul comes soothing *mate* tea, as well as Brazilian wine, which is not world famous but is nonetheless eminently drinkable, the red wines from *Forestier* and *Chandon* being the ones most worth trying. Internationally-renowned Argentian and Chilean wines are available in most good restaurants, and are only slightly more expensive than the native beverage. The Portuguese word for that essential thirst-quencher, beer, is *cerveja*; draft beer, served at Arctic temperatures in this hot country, is simply *chopp*.

LITERATURE

"My country, this part of me outside of me, that seeks me out relentlessly" is a line from the poem *Brazilian Song* (1987), by the late **Carlos Drummond de Andrade**, written when he was 85 years old. The search for one's own Brazilian identity has been the central theme of 20th-century Brazilian literature. **Euclides da Cunha** wrote *Os Sertões* in 1902 (published in English as *Rebellion in the Backlands*). As a reporter, he accompanied the army to Canudos, a village in the backlands of Bahia state, where the messianic Antônio Conselheiro and his followers had established their own "empire." Five successive government expeditions were required to subdue the rebels, who resisted to the last man. Cunha makes a plea for Brazil to commit itself to assimilating its countrymen into mainstream society.

In the 1930s the literary movement called Regionalism – an interest in the unique characteristics of a particular geographical area – predominated. Important writers in this genre include Jorge Amado and **João Ubaldo Ribeiro**. Born in 1941 on the island of Itaparica, Ribeiro wrote the ground-breaking epic *Viva O Povo Brasileiro* (published in English as *An Invincible Memory*), replete with bloody historical legends and parodies of Jesuit missionaries preaching Catholicism to cannibals. The plot involves the *caboclo* Capiroba and his women, and how they escape from the monk's tiresome preaching and take to hunting Dutchmen for the tenderness of their flesh – when cooked. In *The Lizard's Smile,* Ribeiro takes as his theme genetic experiments: children on the writer's native island find a lizard with two tails. In an interview, Ribeiro expressed the view that between 30 and 40 million Brazilians

Right: Outsiders figure significantly in the works of Jorge Amado.

have the educational level of people in developed countries, which means they are potential purchasers of books.

Jorge Amado, Brazil's most renowned author internationally, was born in Bahia in 1912 (he is now almost blind). Most of his nearly 100 novels and short stories have been translated into 40 languages, and some have been made into films. He sees himself as "a chronicler of courtesans and vagabonds." His protagonists live on the margins of society; they are the poorest of the poor. Prostitutes, scoundrels, and various kinds of losers are depicted as profoundly human individuals who are worthy of love. At the age of only 18, Amado began writing his six-volume cycle of novels about life in Bahia, of which *People from Bahia* and *Jubiabá* are the most successful. In *The Golden Harvest*, Amado depicted plantation life in the area around his home town, and in *The Violent Land* he described the struggle for survival of emigrants from the Sertão. He is best known as the author of *Gabriela, Clove and Cinnamon*, in which Gabriela, a mulatto woman, drives men crazy and creates disarray in high society. Several film versions (in various languages) have been made of Amado's short story *Tieta, the Goat Girl.*

Literatura da Cordel is a highly popular folk art of the northeast that is displayed at marketplaces hanging from a string (*cordel*). Approximately 20,000 of these rhymed verse narratives in pamphlet form have been published, and there are said to be approximately 5,000 poets living in Pernambuco alone, some of whom perform their lyrics with guitar accompaniment, since many of their customers are unable to read. The inhabitants of the Sertão learn of war, inventions, assassinations, the first men on the moon, and everything else under the sun through this medium, which they believe more readily than television or radio. Public health officials also hire the *cordel*

bards to inform their fellow Bahians about drugs, leprosy, AIDS, and even the use of *camisinhas* (condoms). As singers, they spontaneously compose songs on diverse subjects, such as Brazil's soccer team, inflation and corrupt politicians.

A typical *cordel* theme runs through *This Land* by **Antônio Torres**, a novel about the stark contrast between urban and rural life in Brazil. It tells the story of a young *Baiano* who returns to his native village after trying in vain for 20 years to make a life for himself in São Paulo. In *No Land like this One: Signs of the Future*, a novel that harks back to Orwell's *1984*, **Ignácio Loyola Brandço**, who was born in São Paulo in 1936, created an apocalpytic work about the city of his birth in the year 2020.

Born into a landowning family in Minas Gerais, **Joço Guimarães Rosa** went to Hamburg in 1938 as a diplomat, was interned by the Nazis, and in 1942 released in exchange for German diplomats. In his work, he combines regionalism with modern Brazilian narrative techniques. His masterpiece *Grande Sertão: Veredas* (published in English as *The Devil to Pay in the Backlands*), contains a 100-page monologue in which the first-person narrator talks about his extraordinary life. Before becoming a novelist, **Darcy Ribeiro** published works on anthropology and folkore in the Amazon. *Maíra* (1976) is about an Indian named Ava who, after studying for the priesthood in Rome, returns home to his tribe, where he meets a jaded upper-class Brazilian woman named Alma.

Some female authors from Brazil have also established international reputations, among them **Clarice Lispector**, born in the Ukraine in 1925 and raised in Recife. Lispector, whose work has been likened to that of Virgina Woolf, brilliantly explores the tension between outer reality and spiritual experience. Her first novel, *Perto do Coração Selvagem* (published in English as *Near to the Savage Heart*) appeared when she was 19 years old, winning critical acclaim for its sensitive depiction of adolescence.

METRIC CONVERSION

Metric Unit	US Equivalent
Meter (m)	39.37 in.
Kilometer (km)	0.6241 mi.
Square Meter (sq m)	10.76 sq. ft.
Hectare (ha)	2.471 acres
Square Kilometer (sq km)	0.386 sq. mi.
Kilogram (kg)	2.2 lbs.
Liter (l)	1.05 qt.

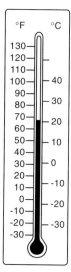

BEFORE YOU GO

Climate / Best Time to Travel

Owing to the fact that 90 percent of Brazil's land area is situated between the Tropics of Cancer and Capricorn, the climate is characterized by tropical temperatures, humidity and precipitation. Only the south has distinct seasons, which occur at opposite times of the year to those in North America and Europe, that is to say, summer is from December to March and winter from June to September. Winter temperatures in Rio Grande do Sul and Santa Catarina sometimes go below freezing, and there is occasionally snow, which, being a rarity in Brazil, is treated as news by the media.

The Northern, Southeastern, and Amazon Regions, as well as Rio and Minas Gerais, receive most of their precipitation during the summer months. In Brasília and Mato Grosso the rainy season lasts from November to March, and in the Northeast, from April to July. Average annual precipitation is unevenly distributed. In the dry inland regions of the Northeast it is 500 mm; in Rio 1,050 mm; 1,350 mm in Porto Alegre; 1,500 mm in Belo Horizonte and Brasília; 1,900 mm in Salvador and Manaus; and an average of 2,440 mm per year in Belém. Average annual temperatures range from 19°C in Porto Alegre to 27°C in Manaus. Visitors can expect to experience the nationwide highs of 35-45°C anywhere from the southeast to the north, at the higher elevation obtained in Brasília included. South of the equator in Foz do Iguaçu temperatures of up to 48°C in the shade have been recorded – but so have temperatures close to freezing, when the Antarctic wind blows in from the south.

Is there an ideal time to visit Brazil? The figures seem to indicate that there is not, especially for itineraries involving stays in various parts of the country. Are some times of the year better than others for being a tourist? This is an easier queston to answer. If possible, avoid coming during the Brazilian summer, as it is high season for the Argentian and Brazilian middle and upper classes, who fill airline flights, hotels, and especially beaches, and then have their numbers exponentially added to by sunshine-starved Europeans and North Americans seeking a respite from winter.

The long school holidays in Argentina last anywhere from Christmas to the end of March; and in Brazil from the beginning of December until Carnival. As holidays occur at similar times in other South American countries, you should count on booked-solid flights and hotel rooms from Christmas until the end of February at a minimum.

What to Wear

The tried and true layering system is perfect for Brazil: the best garments to bring are those that lend themselves to being worn over and under others. It is also advisable to carry protection against rain and sun at all times. Comfortable shoes are a must, as is at least one sweater for higher altitudes, cold fronts, or air-conditioning. A good supply of light and loosely-fitting clothing is recommended and, of course, a bathing suit. It goes without saying that visitors planning a trip into the Amazon or Pantanal regions need to outfit themselves somewhat differently. The most important items to bring are water-resistant outerwear, protection against mosquitoes, and footwear appropriate to the topography your feet will be treading upon. Formal clothing is hardly ever needed in Brazil, although some of the fancier restaurants do require men to wear a tie and jacket.

Nude beaches and topless bikinis are virtually nonexistent in Brazil: you have to cover up... at least a little bit. If you want your beach attire to blend in with that of the thousands of Brazilians you will doubtless enounter as you soak up the sun, you might want to consider purchasing your swimming suit after you arrive in the country.

Entry Requirements

Tourists from the UK and Ireland can enter Brazil for a stay of 90 days without a visa. On the other hand, visitors from the United States, Canada, Australia and New Zealand need to obtain a visa prior to entering the country; the visa is valid for a 90-day stay, which can be prolonged by application for a maximum of one 90-day period. For a list of embassies and consulates, see pp. 240-241.

Besides a valid passport, visitors also need to have with them a return ticket or credit card in order to enter the country. In addition, when crossing the border or while flying to Brazil, a landing card must be filled out in duplicate with the exact information that appears in your passport, including all middle names. When you enter the country, the customs official will stamp the carbon copy and hand it back to you, and you are required to keep it until you leave the country.

Airport Taxes

The airport tax for international flights is US $36 and is payable in cash at the ticket counter. In emergencies, credit cards and local currency at the current exchange rate are acceptable.

Currency / Changing Money

Brazil was plagued by high inflation for years. But the *Plano Real*, which went into effect on August 1, 1995, was instituted to create a new, stable currency, the *Real* (plural: *Reais*), that would have one to one parity with the US dollar. As of October 1999, the rate was 1.94 *Reais* for US $1. The rate of exchange for traveler's checks is usually lower than for cash. It is simplest, but also least advantageous, to cash traveler's checks in a hotel. Currency-exchange services and automatic cash machines offer the most favorable rates. Not all banks change money, and if they do the process often consumes patience-trying quantities of time and paper.

When in Brazil, regardless of the currency of your country of origin, it's best to use US$ (cash or traveler's checks) or a common credit card: Visa and American Express are accepted everywhere. Neither Diners Club nor Mastercard are as common, and Eurocheques and EC cards cannot be used at all.

It is both disadvantageous and unnecessary to obtain *Reais* from your bank prior to your departure, since using US$ when you first arrive (and most other times) presents no difficulties whatsoever. Unspent *Reais* can be exchanged at any bank (including at the airport) before you leave the country, but you must show your receipt from the original transaction in order to exchange your surplus Brazilian currency.

Staying Healthy

There are no regulations in Europe or North America requiring immunization prior to departure. However, innoculation against yellow fever is required for travelers who are entering Brazil within six days of having been either in a part of Africa in which yellow fever is endemic; or in Columbia, Ecuador, Bolivia or Peru. This is of particular importance for travelers who are touring South America.

Brazil, like some of its neighbors, is in an area of the world threatened with outbreaks of cholera. An innoculation against cholera exists, but it is no longer recommended by the World Health Organization. Cholera is a disease of the poor that tourists rarely contract (although it has happened); the chances of this occurring are estimated to be 1 in 500,000. The WHO and institutes of tropical medicine around the world generally advise all travelers to Brazil to be inoculated against tetanus and hepatitis A and B, and that those planning to spend time in the Amazon be immunized against yellow fever.

The greatest concern of most travelers to the tropics is malaria, and with good reason, as a vaccine against this disease has yet been found. However, such protection is by no means necessary everywhere in Brazil, and it is best to discuss your itinerary with a specialist in tropical medicine before leaving home. The entire south, southeast and northeast coasts of Brazil as far as Recife are free of malaria, which means that you can travel without risk throughout the southern and southeastern states, including Rio, from Bahia to Pernambuco, as well as to Brasília. If you are planning to visit any other areas, it is best to consult an institute of tropical medicine beforehand. The Amazon basin has the highest level of malaria

pathogenes in Brazil. The best way to avoid contracting malaria is, of course, to avoid being bitten by a carrier *anopheles* mosquito in the first place, although, as mentioned earlier (pp. 185-187), not every area of the Amazon is infested with them. Travelers who find themselves in such an area should take the following protective measures: Wear clothing that covers the entire body; spray exposed skin with mosquito repellent every four to six hours, as sweat reduces its effectiveness; use mosquito netting; and stay in accommodations protected by mesh window and door screens.

When in the tropics, the potentially devastating effects of the sun should never be understimated. Consequently, a hat or other head covering, as well as suntan lotion with a protective factor of at least 12, are indispensable.

The drinking of tap water and water from melted ice should be avoided, and ice cream and fruit juices should only be consumed in good restaurants and hotels with high standards of hygiene. Inasmuch as virtually all tropical fruits have peels or skins, there is no health risk involved in eating them after peeling them.

The US Centers for Disease Control and Protection recommend the following precautions to help you stay healthy:
-Wash your hands frequently.
-Drink only bottled or canned water and other beverages. If this is not possible, filter water through an "Absolute 1-Micron or Less" filter (available in camping stores) and add iodine tablets.
-Make sure food is thoroughly cooked.
-If you are visiting a malaria-risk area, take your anti-malarial drugs before, during and after travel as directed.
-Do not go barefoot (to prevent the risk of fungal and parasitic infections).
-Don't swim in fresh water; salt water is generally safe, though.

For more tips and information, check out the Centers for Disease Control website at: www.cdc.gov.

TRAVELING IN BRAZIL

By Air

Travelers who will be visiting more than one region of Brazil, but who plan to spend spend four weeks or less in the country, will probably want to move around by airplane. Although bus connections, at least between major cities, are quite good and buses are comfortable, the rule of thumb is that one inflight hour is the equivalent of one on-bus day.

The other drawback to long-distance buses is that the main highways they travel on tend to be montonous and of little visual or scenic interest. It's advisable to both plan your itinerary and purchase a Brazil Airpass before leaving home, as the Airpass cannot be purchased either in Brazil, or by individuals who are permanent residents of Brazil.

Flights within Brazil are expensive. For example, a one-way ticket from Rio to Ignaçu costs US $300, and to Manaus US $530 – which is approximately the price of the Airpass. All inland flights are subject to an airport tax which ranges, according to airport, from US $5 to 7.

Brazil Airpass

Available from Transbrasil, Vasp and Varig, this money-saver can only be purchased in conjunction with a flight originating outside the country, and is only valid within Brazil on flights offered by the issuing carrier. All Airpasses come with coupons, each of which is valid for one flight to a destination of the passenger's choice. The price of an Airpass, which varies according to season (and sometimes region), includes five such coupons, with the right to purchase up to an additional three flights at a discount, but only at the time the Airpass is issued.

In addition to an Airpass for all their respective routes, ranging in price from US $490 to $540, Transbrasil and Varig both offer streamlined versions. For example, one formula allows up to five

flights within the Northeast for US $290 (low season) and US $340 (high season). Children aged two years and older pay full fare, and infants under two pay 10 percent of the full fare. Regardless of the region or airline, all Airpasses are valid for a maximum of 21 days, and refunds are given only in the event no coupon has been used. Varig (but not Vasp) allows passengers to use coupons for routes serviced by its subsidiaries, Nordeste and Rio-Sul, making it possible to visit the Atlantic island of Fernado de Noronha.

For full details on conditions of purchase for Brazil Airpasses, contact your local travel agent or the airlines themselves. *TRANSBRASIL:* **UK**: Tel. (0171) 976-7994 (London). **US**: Tel. 1-800-872-3153 (toll-free). *VARIG:* **UK**: (0171) 629-5824 (London). **US**: Tel. 1-800-468-2744 (toll-free).

By Rail

Pressure from the large automobile manufacturers during the 1960's has made long-distance passenger train service a relic of Brazil's past. Visitors wishing to travel by train – for which they will want to have a lot of time on their hands – can do so on the various regional routes described in the travel section of this book.

By Long-Distance Bus

Brazilian long-distance buses are a comfortable and inexpensive means of transportation, the equivalent in some respects of European trains – except for the distances, which are proportionately much greater. Bus stations (*estações rodoviárias*) in every city have numerous companies competing for passenger patronage. Both economy (*convencional*) and first-class (*exekutivo*) buses have restroom facilities on board. Ticket prices are regulated by the government. For longer trips, the first-class *onibus leito* (night bus) is the best choice. These buses are equipped with rest rooms, and the reclining seats are comfortable to sleep in. Passengers receive a claim check for larger pieces of luggage, which are stowed in the bays beneath the bus. Stops are made at a self-service restaurant a minimum of once every four hours. It is advisable to purchase a ticket in advance for any trip via night bus, as well as for any bus trip undertaken during holiday periods or on weekends.

By City Bus

Owing to the dearth of trams, streetcars, and subways in its urban areas, buses are the main form of transporation within Brazilian cities. They are inexpensive, but also overcrowded, and thus a pickpocket's paradise. The network of routes is incomprehensible for visitors, and even most Brazilians know only the route they ride every day. Visitors who move around on urban buses should try to obtain information either from local residents (not necessarily policemen), or from hotel staff, who almost invariably are patrons of mass transit.

You always enter the bus from the back, buy a ticket from the cashier you find there, and then pass through a turnstile into the passenger section.

By Ship

Ships are an indispensable means of transportation in the Amazon. Travel options are described the in chapter "The North – The Amazon" (see pp. 194-195), but there are few inland passenger ships in the rest of Brazil.

By Car

Foreigners who drive in Brazil are required to have an International Driver's License, which must also be validated by *Detran*, the state road and traffic authority, which has an office in every state capital (e.g., Rio, Recife, Salvador). As throughout the Americas, cars are driven on the right side of the road. While traffic laws are similar to those in Europe and

North America, Brazilians tend to pay little heed to the rules of the road. Passengers sitting in the front seat are required to buckle up. In most cases, the official speed limit outside of towns and cities is 80 kmh.

Vehicles run on either *gasolina*, which contains 20 percent ethyl alcohol as a substitute for lead; *alcool*, pure ethyl alcohol; or diesel, which is used almost exclusively by trucks and buses.

Brazil has approximately 1.5 million kilometers of roads – but only eight percent of them are paved! Drivers should also bear in mind that many major through roads are subject to tolls.

Car Rental

Foreigners must show their passport, a valid International Driver's License and a credit card. Prices are relatively high, although regional and seasonal differences do exist. Other car rental options besides the ubiquitous Avis and Hertz agencies are the national companies, such as Localiza, Interlocadora, Nobre and Unidas, as well as local agencies. The relevant phone numbers can be found in the *Guidepost* sections of this book.

PRACTICAL TIPS FROM A TO Z

Accommodation

Hotels: Categories more or less correspond to the international one through five star rating system, whereby hotels with two, one or no stars provide only minimal comfort. Motel rooms are rented to couples by the hour, and are therefore not suitable for those traveling by car.

Pousadas (guest houses) are found primarily in rural areas and are often extremely pleasant places to stay.

Fazendas are working farms that also offer accommodations to tourists. They constitute the most widespread kind of lodging in the state of Pantanal.

Lodges, the most common form of accommodation in the Amazon, are simple private bungalows, usually with no hot water or electricity.

Prices vary greatly according to season and region, and have risen sharply since the insitution of the *Plano Real*. "Special" rates go into effect during Carnival (especially in Rio and Salvador de Bahia), and in most cases the week preceeding it. During these periods hotel rooms cost three times the normal price, and the minimum stay ranges from four to seven nights. Despite these rates, hotels are invariably booked up months in advance.

Banks

Business hours are generally from 10 a.m. to 4 p.m., although in major shopping areas and international airports banks stay open longer. Not all banks have currency-exchange windows, and cash advances with a credit card can only be obtained from a bank that has a contract with your credit card company. American Express has offices in Rio and São Paulo; they will also replace lost or stolen American Express traveler's checks. Their address in Rio is: Praia de Botafogo 228, tel. 021-552-3854, 552-3655; in São Paulo, tel. 011-800-5040.

Beaches

Information regarding the cleanliness of the water is posted at the most frequented beaches: *propria* means "suitable for swimming" and *impropria* means the opposite. Local newspapers also publish reports on pollution levels. Brazilians love spending time at the beach, and beaches overflowing with vacationers don't bother them a bit – on the contrary: they want to be seen and have a great time. The most popular (and populated) locales have certified lifeguards (*salvidas*) on duty, which in view of the ubiquity of high breakers and treacherous currents can be a matter of life and death.

Beach cleanliness is a vexed and recurring problem. The unpleasant habit many Brazilians have of simply leaving behind every kind of refuse, from food and cigarette butts to bottles and cans (often within a few steps of a trash can), forces municipal governments to expend enormous sums to keep beaches clean. Media campaigns aimed at altering this behavior have been unsuccessful. It is therefore wise to bring sandals or other footwear to the beach as protection against both litter and the sand, which can become very hot in the intense afternoon sun.

Bribery

Suborno in Brazil, as in all of Latin America, is an irksome, but often unavoidable strategy for getting around absurd rules and Kafkaesque red tape. However, visitors to Brazil are strongly advised to avoid such practices, or only to resort to them in dire emergencies. Brazilian civil servants and police usually act quite reasonably in most situations, and when dealing with tourists do not immediately put out their hand for money. The language barrier can also be of some assistance in such cases. The best policy is always to remain calm and polite: Be patient and keep smiling is the watchword!

Bribery Brazilian style is an extremely subtle and complex phenomenon, and therefore not easily fathomed by visitors. For example, there exists in Brazil an institution known as the *jeitinho* – a person whose function it is to mediate between unreasonable regulations and the people who have to deal with them. *Jeitinhos* are found in all socioeconomic classes. They use humor and common sense to help citizens overcome such annoying obstacles to everyday life as "no parking" regulations, government offices that don't stay open long enough, and the lack of an advance reservation.

Business Hours

The opening hours of businesses vary according to type, region, neighborhood, and other factors. Most stores are open from 9 a.m. to 7 p.m. In smaller cities, businesses tend to close at noon for one or two hours. Some stores only open at 10 a.m., but then don't close until 8 or 9 p.m. There are also 24-hour supermarkets and drugstores to be found. Popular shopping centers have longer opening hours. They tend to attract many customers partly because their parking lots have security guards; some are also open on Sundays. Essential items can always be purchased at airports and bus stations, as well as at many gas stations.

Carnival

Carnival is celebrated with enthusiasm not only in Rio but throughout Brazil. The most important days are from the Saturday before Lent until the Tuesday before Ash Wednesday. For weeks previous to this, however, rehearsals featuring dancing on the beaches and in town and city squares are ubiquitous, especially on weekends; the *bateristas* (drummers) also practice their samba rhythms – a sound that has truly universal appeal!

Customs

Personal possessions brought into Brazil for private use do not incur any customs duties. Each visitor is allowed to bring one still or video camera, radio, cassette recorder and laptop computer. However, since the institution of changes in regulations governing importation of goods (including expensive ones) within the framework of the Mercosur Custom Union Treaty, tourists entering Brazil are rarely checked for these items.

Each adult is allowed 600 cigarettes, 25 cigars, 280 ml of perfume, and 700 ml of toilet water.

Drugs

Illegal narcotics can easily be obtained in Brazil, but it's just as easy to end up embroiled in the country's criminal justice system! And no intelligent person would ever confuse a Brazilian prison with a hotel: they are extremely unpleasant places, and visitors are strongly advised to steer clear of any involvement with any kind of illegal substance during their stay in the country. Possession of even an infinitessimal quantity of an illegal narcotic is a crime. Moreoever, getting caught is even more fraught with hazards for foreigners, as Brazilian police expect non-Brazilians to spend large sums of money to buy their way out of trouble. Also, some drug dealers work hand in hand with the police.

Electricity

110 Volts are in use through most of Brazil, except in Brasília, Salvador and Recife, where the current is 220V. A few hotels provide sockets for both. Plug adapters often come in handy, but are not always easily obtainable.

Embassies (Brazilian Embassies and Consulates Abroad)

AUSTRALIA: Embassy of Brazil, 19 Forster Crescent, Yarralumla, Canberra Act 2600, G. P.O. Box 1540, **Canberra City** 2601, tel. (6) 273-2372, fax (6) 273-2375; General Consulate of Brazil, St. Martins Tower - L17, 31 Market Street, **Syndey**, NSW 2000, tel. (9) 267-4414, fax (9) 267-4419.

CANADA: Embassy of Brazil, 450 Wilbrod Street, **Ottawa**, Ontario K1N 6M8, tel. (613) 237-1090, fax (613) 237-6144; General Consulate of Brazil, 2000 Mansfield, Suite 1700, **Montreal**, Quebec H3A 3A5, tel. (514) 499-0968, fax (514) 499-3963; General Consulate of Brazil, 77 Bloor Street West, Suite 1109, **Toronto** M5S 1M2, tel. (416) 922-2503, fax (416) 922-1832.

IRELAND: Embassy of Brazil, Harcourt Centre - Europa House, 5th Floor, Harcourt Street, **Dublin**, tel. (1) 475-6000, fax (1) 475-1341.

UK: Embassy of Brazil, 32 Green Street, **London** WI1Y 4AT, tel. (0171) 499-0877, fax (0171) 493-5105; General

Consulate of Brazil, 6 St. Alban's Street, **London** SW1Y 4SQ, tel. (0171) 930-9055, fax (0171) 839-8958.

US: Embassy of Brazil, 3006 Massachusetts Ave. N.W., **Washington, D.C.** 20008, tel. (202) 238-2700/2805, fax (202) 238-2827; General Consulate of Brazil, 410 N. Michigan Ave., Suite 3050, **Chicago**, IL 60611, tel. (312) 464-0244, fax (312) 464-0299; General Consulate of Brazil, 8484 Wilshire Blvd., Suites 711/730, **Beverly Hills**, CA 90211, tel. (213) 651-2664, fax (213) 651-1274.

Foreign Embassies in Brazil (Brasilia)

AUSTRALIA: SHIS QD 1-9, cj16, casa 1, tel. (061) 248-5569.
CANADA: SES av das Nações, It 16, tel. (061) 321-2171.
UK: SES av das Nações, QD 801, cj K, It 8, tel. (061) 225-2710.
US: SES av das Nações, It 3, QD 801, tel. (061) 321-7272.

Holidays

Banks and most business are closed on the following legal holidays:
January 1: *Ano Novo*
Shrovetide (the three days preceeding Ash Wednesday): *Carnaval*
Good Friday: *Paixão de Cristo*
April 21: *Dia de Tiradentes*
May 1: *Dia do Trabalho*
Corpus Christi (about eight weeks after Easter Sunday): *Corpus Cristi*
September 7: *Independência do Brasil* (Independence Day)
October 12: *Nossa Senhora da Aparecida* (Feast of the Annunciation)
November 2: *Dia dos Finados* (All Souls' Day)
November 15: *Proclamação da República* (Proclamation Day)
December 25: *Natal* (Christmas)

Medical Services

The most important precaution to take in terms of medical care while traveling is to be sure you have an insurance policy that covers any medical bills you might incur while abroad. Private hospitals in large cities are extremely modern, sometimes even border-ing on the futuristic. There is usually at least one English-speaking doctor in every hospital. State-run hospitals should be avoided. Although as a cash-paying foreigner you will be taken ahead of Brazilians, waiting times can be lengthy, and hygiene tends to fall far short of state-of-the-art.

The better hotels usually have a contract with an English-speaking doctor who is on call at all times. If a doctor who speaks English is not available, ask at the desk if there's a guest or staff person who would be willing to translate for you.

Pharmacies

Brazil has an extensive network of *farmácias* that take turns providing night and weekend emergency service, which means that a pharmacy is always open either in, or in close proximity to, a city or town. As a rule, medication can be obtained without a prescription: most drugs for which you would expect to need a doctor's prescription at home can be procured over-the-counter, providing of course they are paid for in cash. And since most large pharmaceutical companies have production facilities in Brazil, the most common medications are readily available, albeit under slightly different names. If you have the information leaflet containing the exact chemical names of the active ingredients of a given drug, a Brazilian pharmacist can easily provide you with the product you need. Prices are generally lower than in Europe and North America, but you should always be sure to check the expiration date on the package before paying.

Phone Calls

The country code for Brazil is +55. When making a call to a foreign country from Brazil, you dial 00 plus the country code: For the US and Canada dial 001; Australia, 0061; the UK, 0044; Ireland, 00353; New Zealand, 0064.

It is simplest to make a call directly from your hotel room, but more expensive than in a public *postos de serviços* operated by one of Brazil's telephone companies, which have different names in each state.

Public telephones accept cards (*cartão telefônico*) or *fichas* (tokens), both of which can be purchased at kiosks or bars. Because of their shape, public telephones are called *orelhões* – "big ears" – by the Brazilians.

Photography

With the exception of a mere handful of museums and churches – particularly in Ouro Preto – there are virtually no restrictions on the use of cameras in Brazil. The common brands of film (with the exception of Agfa) are available everywhere, although slide film is sometimes difficult to come by and is more expensive than in Europe and the United States. Be sure to check the expiration date before paying!

Postal Services

Post (*correio*) offices are generally open Monday through Friday from 8 a.m to 5 p.m., and on Saturdays from 8 a.m. to noon. Post offices at the international airports in Rio de Janeiro and São Paulo are open 24 hours a day. Smaller branch offices often do not have stamps on hand; letters and postcards (only if they already have a message on or in them!) are run through a franking machine instead. Letters can take up to 10 days or more to reach Europe or North America from post offices in major cities and airports, and about a week longer from smaller inland cities.

Travelers who ask the hotel reception desk to send their mail for them should be aware that their vacation greetings may never reach their destination, as hotel staff are not a hundred percent reliable in this respect.

Security

Tourists stand out in Brazil, regardless of their complexion. Moreover, to those Brazilians with a predilection for criminal activities, tourists, including Brazilian ones, are the embodiment of wealth. Despite the fact that crime, and especially crime against personal property, constitutes a serious problem in this otherwise agreeable country, tourists should resist the urge to panic. As a rule, visitors who take certain basic precautionary measures will avoid the inconvenience of being relieved unexpectedly of their money or personal property.

In Brazil, as in most places in the world, thefts and muggings occur far more frequently in large cities; and some neighborhoods and districts are safer than others. The following security measures apply throughout Brazil, however:

1. Immediately upon arrival, deposit all your valuables, documents and money that you will not be needing for the day in the hotel safe.

2. Passports can also be left in the hotel safe. As long as you do not leave the city you are staying in, a photocopy of your passport is sufficient identification.

3. When going to the beach bring no valuables; just your bathing suit and a towel, and whatever money you might need for drinks and snacks.

4. If someone approaches you and demands your money and your watch, comply immediately, and above all do not try to argue or negotiate. It's a good idea to carry a small amount of "mugging" money with you at all times in order to avoid surrending a large sum or – worse yet – finding yourself in a situation of not being able to hand over anything, which could prompt an assailant to take "revenge."

You should never take valuable jewelry, watches or camera equipment with you on a walk or to the beach. Handbags or shoulder bags that dangle loosely are an open invitation to pickpockets, as are wallets in back trouser pockets. Money bags worn around the neck are not ideal, as they are easily spotted by thieves who might be tempted to remove them violently from their owner's body; an act which can lead to physical injury. If you must carry a large sum of money or important documents with you, use a wallet that can be carried inside your trousers or, alternatively, a money belt that can be worn around either the waist, abdomen or calf.

You should never try to act like a hero when confronted with a mugger: they are usually extremely nervous and are prone to reach for a weapon that can do you much more harm than the loss of any money or property ever could.

Shopping

Brazil does not offer as wide a variety of crafts to visitors as do the Andean countries or Mexico, with their more prevalent indigenous (Indian) cultures. There are nonetheless high-quality and regionally differentiated crafts to be found.

The South is known predominantly for leatherwork, Minas for decorative objects made of soapstone, and the Northeast (mostly Recife and Fortaleza) for embroidery, as well as intricately beautiful lace. A range of hand-made products from the indigenous Amazonian peoples in the North are available throughout the country, including necklaces made of dried seeds, bows and arrows, batiked fabrics, pottery, hammocks and jewelry.

Many different kinds of precious stones are also a temptation to the traveler in Brazil. Such polished products of the earth as agates, amethysts, emeralds and diamonds are available in every imaginable variation. However, buyers should resist seduction by the alluring wares and unbelievable rock-bottom prices of street vendors, especially in Ouro Preto and Brasília. To some extent, visitors to Brazil purchase jewelry on trust, and should therefore do their jewelry shopping in a reputable store. Numerous such establishments are to be found both in Rio and Ouro Preto.

Taxis

At the airports, travelers will find taxi cooperatives with their own counters at which you pay the flat rate fare to hotels or specific districts of a given city. A similar service is also offered by the larger hotels. The aforementioned taxis, as well as the numerous *radio-táxis*, are the safest and best bet; the latter conveyances are also listed in the yellow pages. The cheapest cabs are the ones that can be flagged down in the street, but caution should be exercised, especially at night, when dishonest taxi drivers tend to come out of the woodwork. The meter must be running, otherwise the fare should be agreed upon in advance.

The conversion tables that were common during the time of high inflation are no longer valid. Therefore, passengers should only pay the fare indicated on the meter. Taxis that wait for potential customers outside of discos and nightclubs should be avoided, as their drivers tend to lie in wait for passengers unfamiliar with the city, whom they then overcharge unscrupulously.

Television

In Brazil, satellite and cable TV are even more widespread than they are in many European countries. The vast majority of hotels, including the moderately priced ones, provide access to numerous programs in Portuguese, Spanish and English. Visitors who spend even an hour watching programming on *Globo*, the largest media outlet in South America, will gain invaluable insight into the Brazilian way of life; even without the slightest knowledge of Portuguese.

Time

Brazil extends over four time zones, all of which lie west of Greenwich, and are therefore behind Greenwich Mean Time (GMT). Time in Brazil is set according to the capital of Brasília: the *hora legal do Brasil* is three hours behind GMT, and applies to the entire Southern, Southeast and Northeast Regions, the states of Goiâna, Tocantins, and Macap, the Distrito Federal (Brasília), and eastern Pará, including all of Belém.

The following are four hours behind GMT: Western Pará, Mato Grosso, Mato Grosso do Sul, Rondônia, Roraima and most of the state of Amazonas, including Manaus.

Western Amazonas (beginning at the Tabatinga Line), Porto Acre, and the state of Acre are five hours behind GMT.

The Atlantic islands of Fernando de Noronha and Trindade are only two hours behind GMT.

Important note: During the summer months in Great Britain and North America, the time difference increases by an hour, whereas during the Brazilian summer (from mid-October to mid-February), the difference decreases by the same amount. For example: At noon on December 25 in London it is 10 a.m. in Rio (-2 hours); at noon on March 8 in London it is 9 a.m. in Rio (-3 hours); at noon on July 1 in London it is 8 a.m. (-4 hours) in Rio.

Tipping

The standard tip in restaurants is 10 percent. In hotels, fifty cents to one dollar (US) per day for the chambermaid and the same amount per piece of luggage for the hotel bellhop are the norm. Porters at the airport usually charge a flat rate; taxi fares are usually rounded off to the nearest *Real*. Brazilians are by and large generous, and almost never accept payment down to the last fraction of a *Real*. In restaurants, the norm is for the waiter or waitress to bring one check for the whole table; he or she will be extremely embarrassed if separate checks are requested.

Weights and Measures

Brazil uses the metric system for all weights and measures. Sizes for shoes and apparel are the same as those used in Western Europe, although the American system – small, medium, large, and X-large – is often found on T-shirts, shirts, caps, etc.

GLOSSARY

Aldeia: A small settlement with a church typical of the early colonial period.

Azulejos: Derived from the Arabic word *az-zuleycha* ("mosaic stone"); Spanish, and later principally Portuguese tiles produced from the 14th century onward. Beginning in the 19th century these tiles were used in Brazil to decorate church façades and the interiors of bourgeois homes.

Basílica: In Brazil, the term for a church granted certain liturgical privileges by the Pope.

Bandeirante: Literally "standard bearers," these were adventurers and conquerors who pushed far into the interior in search of slaves and mineral wealth during the colonial era.

Berimbau: A single-string musical instrument of African origin made of a hollowed-out gourd that resonates when the string is struck with a bow. The berimbau is used to beat out the cadences and rhythms of the *capoeira*, which is the ritualistic martial arts dance brought to Brazil by African slaves.

Bloco Afro: A group of Afro-Brazilians who participate in Carnival.

Bumba-meu-boi: A pageant with dancing, traditional in the northeast; the principal figure is an ox.

Caboclos: Simple country folk, mestizos of mixed white and Indian ancestry.

Cachaça: Sugar-cane spirits.

Caipirinha: A drink made with *cachaça*, limes, ice and sugar.

Candomblé: An Afro-Brazilian religion.

Carioca: Literally "house of the whites"; a resident of Rio de Janeiro.

Capoeira: Literally "cock fight." A ritualistic "fighting" dance brought to Brazil by slaves from Angola. It was used by Brazilian slaves as a form of self-defense.

Chafariz: Public fountain with a basin.

Churrasco: Argentinian expression for meat grilled on an open fire.

Escunas: Two-masted schooner, e.g., in Búzios.

Favela: Shantytown; slum.

Fazenda: Farm.

Gaiola: Birdcage; also a word for boats on the Amazon.

Garimpeiro: A prospector for gold.

Jagunço: Adventurer and vagabond, often used to refer to hired killers.

Lavagem: Ablution; a folk tradition involving symbolic cleansing of the steps leading up to the church.

Mata: Forest; bush.

Muxarabi: A Moorish word for the wood paneling used in the bay of a church.

Orixás: A Yorùbá god.

Paço: A former residence of the King, now used in Brazil as seat of the municipal government.

Paulista: A resident of São Paulo.

Praia: Beach.

Quilombo: A community of escaped slaves.

Retábulo: Altarpiece; retable.

Rodízio (from Portuguese *rodar*, "revolve"): Waiter in a churrascaria who offers a large variety of different kinds of meat to guests – as often and as much as they would like – on a *rodízio*.

Rodoviária: Bus station.

Sambaqui: An archaeological site of the coastal culture with piles of mussel shells.

Saveiro: A broad wooden sailing ship used for fishing.

Sé (from Latin *sedes*, seat or throne): Jurisdiction (e.g., diocese or province) of a bishop; cathedral.

Seringueiro: Latex gatherer (tapper).

Solar: Mansion belonging to a wealthy family.

Taipa: A building material made of clay and plant fibres.

Terreiro: Candomblé temple.

Trio eléctrico: Mobile stage with loudspeakers used during Carnival in Bahia.

Umbanda: Afro-Brazilian religion prevalent in the Southeast.

Vila: During colonial times, an *aldeia* (small settlement) that grew and which was then granted the status of *vila* by the colonial government.

USEFUL WORDS AND PHRASES

Cardinal Numbers

0	*zero*
1	*um, uma*
2	*dois, duas*
3	*três*
4	*quatro*
5	*cinco*
6	*seis*
7	*sete*
8	*oito*
9	*nove*
10	*dez*
11	*onze*
12	*doze*
20	*vinte*
21	*vinte e um*
30	*trinta*
40	*quarenta*
50	*cinquenta*
60	*sessenta*
70	*setenta*
80	*oitenta*
90	*noventa*
100	*cem*
101	*cento e um*
200	*duzentos*
1000	*mil*
2000	*dois mil*

100,000	*cem mil*
1,000,000	*um milhão*

Ordinal Numbers

1	*primeiro/a*
2	*segundo/a*
3	*terceiro/a*
4	*quarto/a*
5	*quinto/a*
6	*sexto/a*
7	*sétimo/a*
8	*oitavo/*a
9	*nono/a*
10	*décimo/a*
11	*undécimo*
20	*vigésimo*

Fractions

1/2	*meio, meia*
1/3	*um terço*
1/4	*um quarto*
1/5	*um quinto*

Time and Dates

date	*data*
second	*segundo*
minute	*minuto*
hour/time of day	*hora*
day	*dia*
week	*semana*
month	*mês*
year	*ano*
time	*tempo*
watch/clock	*relógio*
What's the time?	*que horas são?*
today	*hoje*
yesterday	*ontem*
tomorrow, morning	*manhã*
afternoon	*tarde*
evening	*noite*

Days of the Week

Monday	*segunda-feira*
Tuesday	*terça-feira*
Wednesday	*quarta-feira*
Thursday	*quinta-feira*
Friday	*sexta-feira*
Saturday	*sábado*
Sunday	*domingo*

Months

January	*Janeiro*
February	*Fevreiro*
March	*Março*
April	*Abril*
May	*Maio*
June	*Junho*
July	*Julho*
August	*Agosto*
September	*Setembro*
October	*Outubro*
November	*Novembro*
December	*Dezembro*

Greetings – Forms of Address

Hello; good morning	*Bom dia*
Hello; good afternoon	*Boa tarde*
Good evening; good night . .	*Boa noite*
Familiar greeting	*Tudo bem?*

(= How are things? The response to this is also *tudo bem/tudo bom*, i.e., "Everything's fine")

See you later	*Até logo*
Goodbye	*Adeus*
How is everything? . .	*Como est você?*
Okay, thanks	*Bem, obrigado/a*
Please	*Por favor*
Thanks . . .	*Obrigado/a* (man/woman)
What's your name? .	*Como é seu nome?*
My name is...	*Meu nome é...*
Nice to meet you	*E' um prazer*
Do you speak English? . . .	*Você fala inglês?*
I don't speak Portugese	*Eu não falo português*
To your health!	*Saúde*
Excuse me	*Desculpe*
May I	*Com licença*
Yes/No	*Sim/Não*

At the Hotel

single room . . .	*apartamento solteiro*
double room	*apartamento casal*
double bed	*cama de casal*
bathroom	*sala de banho*
key	*chave*
suitcase	*mala*
bag	*bolsa*
manager	*gerente*

chambermaid . . . . . *criada do quarto*
hot water . . . . *água quente*
shower . . . . *chuveiro*
towel . . . . *toalha*
light . . . . *luz*
lamp . . . . *lâmpada*
air-conditioning . . . *ar condicionado*
trash can . . . . *balde de lixo*
elevator/lift . . . . *elevador*
stairs . . . . *escada*
breakfast . . . . *café da manhã*

In a Restaurant

appetizer . . . . *entrada*
soup . . . . *sopa*
main course . . . . . . *prato principal*
dessert . . . . *sobremesa*
lunch . . . . *almoço*
dinner . . . . *jantar*
reservation . . . . *reserva*
waiter . . . . *garçon, moço*
menu . . . . *lista*
table . . . . *mesa*
smoker . . . . *fumador*
ashtray . . . . *cinzeiroc*
cutlery . . . . *talheres*
plate . . . . *prato*
knife . . . . *faca*
fork . . . . *garfo*
spoon . . . . *colher*
cup . . . . *xícara*
glass . . . . *copo*
bottle . . . . *garrafa*
salt/pepper . . . . *sal/pimenta*
sugar . . . . *açucar*
bill/check . . . . *conta*
tip . . . . *gorjeta*
change . . . . *troca*
receipt . . . . *recibo*

Menu

Drinks . . . . *bebidas*
mineral water . . . . . . *agua mineral*
carbonated/non-carbonated . *com/sem gás*
beer . . . . *cerveja*
draft beer . . . . *chopp*
non-alcoholic beer . *cerveja sem álcool*
soft drink . . . . *refrigerante*
fruit juice . . . . *suco*

red wine . . . . *vinho tinto*
white wine . . . . *vinho branco*
sparkling wine . . . . *champanhe*
coffee with milk . . . . . *café com leite*
tea . . . . *chá*

Meat . . . . *carne*
beef . . . . *de boi*
pork . . . . *de porco*
veal . . . . *de vitela*
lamb . . . . *de borrego*
chicken . . . . *de frango*
duck . . . . *de pato*
turkey . . . . *de peru*
grilled . . . . *grelhado*
boiled . . . . *cozido*
fried . . . . *frito*
roast . . . . *assado*
cutlet . . . . *milanesa*
salami . . . . *salsicha*
sausage . . . . *salsichas*
ham . . . . *presunto*

Fish . . . . *peixe*
seafood . . . . *mariscos*
salmon . . . . *salmão*
sole . . . . *linguado*
trout . . . . *truta*
tuna . . . . *atum*
dried cod . . . . *bacalhau*
fresh cod . . . . *bacalhau fresco*
carp . . . . *carpa*
squid . . . . *lula*
shrimps . . . . *camarão*
crab . . . . *caranguejo*

Side orders . . . . *suplemento*
bread . . . . *pão*
butter . . . . *manteiga*
eggs . . . . *ovos*
vegetables . . . . . *legumes, hortaliça*
salad . . . . *salada*
lettuce . . . . *alfaca*
potatoes . . . . *batatas*
rice . . . . *arroz*
pasta . . . . *massas*
beans . . . . *feijão*
corn . . . . *milho*
manioc . . . . *mandioca*

mushrooms . . . . *fungo*
peppers . . . . *pimentão*
cucumber . . . . *pepino*
tomato . . . . *tomate*
hearts of palm . . . . *palmito*
avocado . . . . *abacate*
onions . . . . *cebola*
garlic . . . . *alho*
olives . . . . *azeitonas*
vinegar . . . . *vinagre*
oil . . . . *óleo*
mustard . . . . *mostarda*
dressing . . . . *molho*
broth . . . . *caldo*

Fruit . . . . *fruta*
pineapple . . . . *abacaxi*
apple . . . . *maçã*
banana . . . . *banana*
pear . . . . *pêra*
strawberry . . . . *morango*
rasperry . . . . *framboesas*
mango . . . . *manga*
melon . . . . *melão*
orange . . . . *laranja*
papaya . . . . *mamão*
peach . . . . *pêssego*
watermelon . . . . *melancia*
grapes . . . . *uva*
lemon . . . . *limão*

Sweets . . . . *doces*
ice cream . . . . *sorvete*
pancake . . . . *crepe, panquequa*
crème caramel . . . . *flan*
cake . . . . *pastel*
jam . . . . *marmelada*
honey . . . . *mel*

Health

doctor . . . . *médico*
blood . . . . *sangue*
inflammation . . . . *inflamação*
cold . . . . *resfriamento*
first-aid . . . . *pronto socorro*
fever . . . . *febre*
cough . . . . *tosse*
insect bite . . . . . *picada de insecto*
headache . . . . *dor de cabeça*

hospital . . . . *hospital*
medication . . . . *remdio*
emergency . . . . *emergncia*
unconscious . . . . *desmaio*
adhesive bandage . . . . *emplasto*
sunburn . . . . . *queimadura do sol*
suntan lotion . . . . *creme de
protecção solar*
parasol . . . . *guarda-sol*
accident . . . . *acidente*
bandage . . . . *atadura*

On the Road

traffic light . . . . *semáforo*
car . . . . *carro, automóvel*
auto mechanic . . . . *oficina
de automóveis*
railway station . . . . *ferroviária*
postage stamp . . . . *selo*
bridge . . . . *ponte*
multi-colored . . . . *multicolor*
bus station . . . . *rodoviária*
ferry . . . . *balsa*
colors - . . . . *cores*
- blue . . . . *azul*
- brown . . . . *castanho*
- yellow . . . . *amarelo*
- green . . . . *verde*
- red . . . . *vermelho*
flight . . . . *vôo*
airport . . . . *aeroporto*
airplane . . . . *avião*
drivers license . . *carteira de motorista*
place to leave luggage . . . . . *depósito
de bagagens*
straight ahead . . . . *a direito*
border . . . . *fronteira*
size (clothing) . . . . *tamanho*
harbor . . . . *porto*
busstop . . . . *parada*
house . . . . *casa*
building . . . . *edifício*
island . . . . *ilha*
church . . . . *igreja*
coast, coastline . . . . . . *costa, litoral*
left . . . . *esquerda*
parking space . . . . . *estacionamento*
square, plaza . . . . *praça*
right . . . . *direita*

tires . . . . *pneu*
city . . . . *cidade*
street/highway . . . . *rua/rodovia*
gas station . . . . . . *posto de gasolina*
customs . . . . *alfândega*

AUTHORS

Anton Jakob has traveled extensively in Latin America over the past 20 years, and also spent five years there working as a journalist and restaurateur. Since 1985, he has been a free-lance leader of educational tours and has traveled extensively through South America, especially in Brazil and the Amazon region.

As an active member of Amnesty International, The Society for the Protection of Threatened Peoples, and the organization Pro Regenwald ("For the Rain Forest"), he has become involved with the current plight of indigenous peoples in Brazil as well as the problem of the destruction of the rain forests.

Fernanda Cordoeiro is the author of the "History and Culture" section of this book. She lives in Porto, Portugal, where she works free-lance leading educational trips, mostly to the Iberian peninsula and Brazil. Her main interests include bringing about cultural exchanges between the former motherland of Portugal and the ex-colony of Brazil, as well as investigating the special linguistic features of Lusitanian countries.

Claus Jäke wrote the "Music" feature in this guide. After completing his musical training at the Mozart-Konservatorium in Augsburg, Germany and the Swiss Jazz School in Bern, he traveled extensively in the Carribbean and Brazil. Fascinated by the enormous creativity and rich musical culture Salvador da Bahia has to offer, he has been living there since 1979.

He appears regularly at jazz festivals and has produced a CD entitled *Conspiração Baiana*, which is distributed by Tropical Music in Marburg, Germany.

PHOTOGRAPHERS

Archiv für Kunst und Geschichte,
  Berlin   17, 19, 21, 22,
                            23, 24, 27, 223
Bauer, Rudolf (Silvestris)   84
Beck, Joseph   cover
Frangenberg, Johannes   53, 62, 63
Franz, Dr. Roger (Silvestris)   29
Frommer, Robin Daniel   8/9, 30, 75,
        100, 104, 106, 108, 109, 111,
        140, 145,150, 164, 168, 191,
        193, 195, 206/207,227,
                            229, 231
Gross, Andreas M.   42/43, 59,
                         148, 149, 225
Harding, Robert (Silvestris)   220
Heil, Günter   15
Heine, Heiner (Silvestris)   14, 187,
                            217, 219
Hoffmann, Per-Andre   151, 192
Holzbach, R. / Bénet, P.   39
Janicke, Volkmar E. 33, 37, 44, 49, 64,
    65, 68, 72, 82, 89, 90, 91, 93, 107, 110,
    124, 128, 138/139, 162, 170, 198, 199
Jennerich, Herbert   55
Kirst, Detlev   112
Kötter, Ricardo   54, 76, 77, 144,
                         154, 190, 200
Lacz, Gerard (Sunset, Silvestris)   211
Legler, Peter (Silvestris)   173, 174
Lyons, David (Event Horizions) 98/99,
                         105, 115, 117
Nill, Dietmar (Silvestris)   158
Nollmann, Felix   79
Ohlbaum, Isolde   233
Posey, Darell (Pro Regenwald)   218
Schramm / Lenk   58
Schulz, Günther   214
Vautier, Mireille   12, 35, 36, 38, 88,
     94, 126, 129, 157, 159, 165, 169,
      171, 176, 182, 189, 204/205, 215
Walz, Uwe (Silvestris)   122/123, 136
Wendler, Martin (Silvestris)   10/11,
        48, 52, 57, 78, 134, 186, 208
Wirz, Dominique   40/41, 209
Ziesler, Günter (Tierbildarchiv
  Angermayer)   114, 135, 180/181,
                      188, 210, 212, 213.

A

A Dama Branca, dune 68
Abricó, beach 63
Acre 183, 219
Alagoas 141, 142
Alcântara 176
Aleijadinho 85, 88, 89, 90, 91, 92, 93, 94, 95
Alencar, José de 174
Alexander VI, Pope 16
Alter do Chão 195
  Museu do Centro Preservação de Arte Indígena 195
Amado, Jorge 144, 148, 149, 159, 226, 232
Amapá 183, 194
Amazonas 37, 183, 196
Amazon Region 25, 35, 183, 187, 197, 201, 208, 211, 212, 214, 215, 216, 217, 219, 230
Amazon River 183-187, 194, 195, 197
Anchieta, José de 73
Andrade, Carlos Drummond 232
Angra dos Reis 64, 71
Aparados da Serra National Park 105
Aquiraz 175
Aracati 175
Araújo, José Soares de 87
Armação 107
Armação dos Búzios 68, 71
Arraial d'Ajuda 159
Axé, music 146

B

Bahia 23, 25, 36, 142, 226, 229
Bahia, Salvador de 17
Bandeirantes 22-23, 76, 95
Barra da Lagoa 107
  Nossa Senhora da Conceição, church 107
Barra de Tabatinga 172
Baturite 175
Bautista, João Gomez 88
Beberibe 175, 179
Belém 19, 187, **190-192**, 201
  Catedral da Sé, church 191
  Cidade Velha 191
  Forte do Castelo 191
  Museu Emílio Goeldi 192
  Porto de Belém 190
  Santo Alexandre, church 191
  Teatro da Paz 192
  Ver-o-Peso, market 190
Belo Horizonte 45, 46, 60, **83-84**, 96
  Estádio Mineirão 83
  Museu de Arte 84
  Museu Mineiro 83

  Palácio das Artes 83
  Pampulha 83, 84
  Parque Municipal 83
  Praça da Liberdade 83
  São Francisco de Assis, church 84
Bethânia, Maria 156, 227
Blumenau **107-108**, 119
  Museu da Família Colonial 108
Boa Vista 221
Bragança Dynasty 23-25, 66
Brandão, Ignácio Loyola 233
Brasília 32, 36, 45, **125-130**, 131
  Catedral 128
  Congresso Nacional 129
  Eixo Monumental 128
  Jardim Zoológico 130
  Lago Paranoá 130
  Maquete da Cidade 130
  Ministério da Justiça 129
  Palácio da Alvorada 130
  Palácio do Itamaraty 129
  Palácio Planalto 129
  Pombal 129
  Praça dos Três Poderes 129
  Santuário Dom Bosco 130
  Supremo Tribunal Federal 129
  Teatro Nacional 130
  Torre de Televisão 128
Brecheret, Victor 76
Brito, Francisco Xavier de 58, 91, 92
Brito, Manuel de 58
Buarque, Chico 227
Bumba-meu-boi, folk pageant 176, 224
Búzios 172

C

Cabo Frio 68
  Forte São Mateus 68
  Nossa Senhora da Guia, church 68
Cabral, Pedro Álvares 13, 159
Cachoeira **156-157**
  Capela da Ordem Terceira do Carmo 156
  Casa da Câmara e Cadeia 156
  Convento Nossa Senhora do Carmo, convent 156
  Museu Hansen Bahia 156
  Nossa Senhora do Rosário, church 156
  Ponte Dom Pedro II 157
  Praça Teixeira de Freitas 157
Cachoeira da Fumaça, waterfall 158
Cachoeira do Caracol, waterfall 105
Câmara, Helder 168
Caminha, Pero Vaz de 13

Campo Grande 133, 137
Campos do Jordão 226
Camurupim 172
Canasvieiras 107
Candeias, beach 166
Candomblé 35, 142, 154, 223, 226, 227
Canela **104-105**, 118
  Parque Caracol 105
  Pinheiro Multisecular 104
Canela, indigenous group 219
Caoutchouc 187, 190, 192, 195, 197
Cannibals 15
Capitanias 16-17
Capoeira 21, 142, 148, 223, 226, 227
Capoeira Dancers 151
Carajás 188
Cardoso, Fernando Henríque 34, 37, 39
Cardozo, Joaquim 128
Carneiro, Francisco Xavier 94
Carnival 33, 49, 142, 150, 224, 227
Carvalho, Alexandrino de 191
Cascata do Imbuí 67
Castro Alves, Antônio de 150
Caymans 135
Caymmis, Dorival 226
Ceará 173, 174
Congonhas do Campo 88, **93-94**
Corcovado 49, 53, 55
Corumbá 133
Costa Athayde, Manuel da 83, 90, 92, 94
Costa Coelho, Caetano da 58
Costa, Gal 227
Costa Lisboa, Manuel Francisco de 88, 90, 91, 92
Costa, Lucio 128
Cuiabá 133, 137
Cunha, Euclides da 29, 232
Curitiba **110-112**, 120, 226
  Cathedral 111
  Largo da Ordem 111
  Museu de Arte Contemporânea 111
  Museu Paranaense 111
  Passeio Público 111
  Rua das Flores 111
  Solar do Barão 111
  Torre Mercês 111

D

Darwin, Charles 208
Dedo de Deus 67
Diamantina **85-87**, 96
  Casa de Chica da Silva 86
  Casa do Antigo Forum 86

Casa do Intendente Câmara
86
Casa do Juscelino Kubitschek
86
Mercado dos Tropeiros 86
Museu do Diamante 86
Nossa Senhora do Carmo,
church 86
São Francisco de Assis, church
86
Dias, Antônio 90
Dias, Francisco 168
Distrito Federal 125, 126
Don Bosco, Pater 126
Drinking 228-231

E

Eating 228-231
Eiffel, Gustave 199
Embu 79, 81
Nossa Senhora do Rosário do
Embu, church 79
Praça 21 de Abril 79
Encontro das Águas 195, 197
Estação Ecológica Anavilhanas
201

F

Favelas 35, 39, 73
Fazenda 17, 21
Feira de Santana 157
Fernando de Noronha, island 16
Ferreira, Alexander Rodrigues 25
Filhos de Gandhy 148
Florianópolis 106, 119
Museu de Antropologia 106
Palácio Cruz e Sousa 106
Praça 15 de Novembro 106
São Francisco da Ordem
Terceira, church 106
Fonseca, Andrade 62
Fonseca, Deodoro da 28
Fordlândia 195
Fortaleza 19, 141, **173-175**, 179
Mercado Central 174
Theatro José de Alencar 174
Foz do Iguaçu 117, 121
Franco, Itamar 34, 130
Franz I, Emperor **27**
François I, King (France) 16
Franciscan 18, 57, 89, 168
Freyre, Gilberto 165

G

Garganta do diabo, waterfall 116
Geisel, Ernesto 33
Genipabu 173, 179
Gil, Gilberto 227
Goiás 23, 36, 125

Gold 23, 25, 46, 48, 64, 65, 83,
86, 92, 95, 125, 142, 221
Gomes, Carlos 224, 225
Gonçalves, André 48
Goulart, João 31, 32
Graçandu 173
Gramado 105
Gruta Azul 68
Gruta da Lapinha 85
Gruta de Lapão 158
Guarani, indigenous group 219,
220

H

Habsburg, Leopoldine von 26
Heyn, Pieter 19
Hidrovia 136
Humboldt, Alexander von 187,
212

I

Icoaraci 193
Igarassu 170
Santo Antônio, convent 170
São Cosme e São Damião,
church 170
Iguaçu 35, **113-117**
El Camino Inferior, hiking trail
116
El Camino Superior, hiking trail
116
Hotel das Cataractas 115
Macuco Safari 115-116
Ilha Campeche 107
Ilha da Areia Vermelha 171
Ilha de Itacuruçá 64
Ilha de Itaparica 155
Ilha de Santa Caterina **106-107**
Ilha de São Francisco 109
Ilha do Algodoal 193
Ilha do Cabo Frio 68
Ilha do Marajó 190, 194, 202
Ilha do Mel 109, 113
Forte Barra 113
Ilha do Mosqueiro 193
Ilha do Outeiro 193
Ilha Grande 64
Ilhéus **158-159**, 161
Museu Regional do Cacau 159
Indigenous Peoples (see Indians)
Indians 14, 18, 24, 25, 34, 35, 230
Isabel, Princess 28, 174
Isla San Martin 116
Itacuruçá 63
Itaimbezinho, canyon 105
Itaipu 66
Itaipu dam **117**
Itamaracá, island 170
Itaparica 160
Itaúna 176

J

Jacumã 173
Jaguanum, island 64
Jesuits 18, 22, 25, 68, 73, 113,
191, 192, 224
João III, King 16, 73
João V, King 92
João VI, King 26, 27, 56, 59, 60
João Pessoa 170, 178
Capela de Ordem Terceira de
São Francisco 171
Convento de Santo Antônio,
convent 171
Parque Sólon de Lucena 171
São Francisco, church 171
Joaquina, beach 107
Jobim, Antonio Carlos 53
Joinville **108-109**, 120
Cemitério do Imigrante 109
Museu Arqueológico do
Sambaqui 109
Museu Nacional da Imigração
109
Jurerê, beach 107

K

Kaxinawá, indigenous group 219
Kayapó, indigenous group 222
Kren-Akrore, indigenous group
222
Kubitschek, Juscelino 32, 83, 85,
126
Kuliná 219

L

Lagoa da Conceição 107
Lagoa de Abaeté, nature preserve
155
Lagoa de Pitangui 173
Lagoa Santa 85
Lapa 112
Largo São Francisco 89
Lençóis 157, 161
Leopoldine, Empress 58, 76
Lisboa, Antônio Francisco (see
Aleijadinho)
Lispector, Clarice 233
Literature 232-233
Literatura de Cordel 165, 232
Locatelli, Aldo 102
Loronha, Fernão de 16
Loyola Brandão, Ignácio de 74
Lucena 171

M

Macapá 194, 202
Fort São José 194
Marco Zero 194

Porto da Santana 194
Mãe Luisa 172
Manaus 37, 185, 187, 193, 196, **197-201**, 202, 203, 220
Alfândega 199
Hotel Tropical Manaus 200
Igarapé dos Educandos 199
Mercado Municipal 199
Museu do Índio 200
Palácio Rio Negro 199
Porto Flutuante 185
Praça São Sebastião 198
Praia da Ponta Negra 200
Rampa 199
Teatro Amazonas 37, 197
Mangaratiba 64
Manioc 13, 15, 17, 24, 101, 187, 196, 218, 221, 230
Marajó, island 15
Maranhão 141, 175
Maria Anna, Queen 92
Maria Farinha 170
Maria I, Queen 26
Mariana 87, **92-93**
Basílica da Sé 92
Casa de Câmara e Cadeia 92
Casa do Conde de Assumar 92
Mina de Passagem 93
Museu Arquidiocesano 92
Nossa Senhora do Carmo, church 93
Praça Cláudio Manoel 92
São Francisco de Assis, church 93
Maricá 68
Marx, Roberto Burle 128
Mata Atlântica 78
Mato Grosso 23, 36, 125, 133, 222
Mato Grosso do Sul 36, 125, 133, 219
Matos, Antônio Fernandes 163
Mello, Collor de 34
Mercosur 136
Minas Gerais 23, 24, 25, 36, 45, 46, 48, 64, 83, 97, 229, 231
Moraes, Vinicius de 48
Morais, Prudente de 28
Moreno, Martim Soares 173
Morro da Babilónia 50
Morro da Urca 55
Morro do Careca, dunes 172
Morro do Pai Inácio 158
Morro dos Cabritos 51
Morro Santo Antônio 57
Morro São João 51
Music 223-227

N

Nascimento, Milton 227
Nassau-Siegen, Moritz von 19, 20, 163
Natal 172, 178

Barreiro do Inferno 172
Câmara Cascudo 172
Casa de Dentenção 172
Forte dos Reis Magos 172
Praia do Forte 172
Neblina, Pico da 35
Neves, Tancredo 34, 95
Niemeyer, Oscar 60, 63, 76, 83, 84, 128, 129, 169
Niterói 65, 66, 68
Nóbrega, Manuel da 73
Nova Friburgo 67

O

Óbidos 195
Forte Pauxi 196
O Cajueiro, tree 172
Olinda 19, 163, **166-170**, 177
Alto da Sé 168
Convento de São Francisco, convent 168
Igreja da Misericórdia, church 169
Mercado da Ribeira 169
Mosteiro de São Bento, monastery 169
Museu de Arte Contemporânea 169
Museu de Arte Sacra de Pernambuco 169
Nossa Senhora da Graça, church 168
Nossa Senhora das Neves, church 168
Nossa Senhora do Carmo, church 166
Palácio Governadores 169
Praça do Carmo 166
São Salvador do Mundo, cathedral 169
Oliveira, Manuel de 75
Olodum 146, 226, 227
Orellana, Francisco 183
Ouro Preto 25, **87-92**, 97
José Joaquim da Silva Xavier, statue 88
Museu da Inconfidência 88
Museu de Arte Sacra 91
Museu de Mineralogía 89
Museu do Aleijadinho 90
Nossa Senhora da Conceição, church 90
Nossa Senhora do Carmo, church 88, 91
Nossa Senhora do Pilar, church 92
Nossa Senhora do Rosáriodos Pretos, church 92
Ponte de Marilia 90
Praça Reinaldo Alves de Brito 91

Praça Tiradentes 88
Rua Conde de Bobadela 91
Santa Efigênia 90
São Francisco de Paula, church 88
São Francisco, church 88, 89
Teatro Municipal 91

P

Pantanal 133-136
Paul II, Pope 56, 62
Pará 183, **187-189**
Parakana, indigenous group 220
Paraná 35, 101, 110
Paranaguá 112-113, 121
Museu de Arqueologia e Etnologia 113
Nossa Senhora do Rosário, Kathedrale 113
Palácio Visconde de Nácar 113
Rua da Praia 113
Paratí 64-65, 65, 71
Santa Rita de Cássia, church 65
Parque Indígena do Xingu 222
Parque Nacional da Amazônia 195
Parque Nacional da Chapada Diamantina 157-158
Parque Nacional de Brasília 130
Parque Nacional da Serra do Cipó 85
Parque Nacional da Serra dos Orgãos 67
Parque Nacional do Iguaçu 115
Parque Nacional do Pantanal 133
Pau Amarelo 170
Paulista, village 170
Pedra do Sino 67
Pedro I, Emperor 26, 27, 59, 76
Pedro II, Emperor 27, 28, 56, 66, 109, 176
Pernambuco 19, 25, 163
Petrópolis 66-67, 71
Casa de Santos Dumont 66
Museu Imperial 66
Palácio de Cristal 66
Palácio Imperial 66
Quitandinha Complex 66
São Pedro de Alcântara, cathedral 66
Philipp II, King 18
Pico do Barbado 158
Pico da Caledônia 67
Pico da Tijuca 49
Piedade, beach 166
Pipa 173
Pirangi do Norte 172
Piranhas 135

Pirenópolis 131
  Nossa Senhora do Rosário,
    church 131
Planaltina 131
Pombal, Marquês de 24, 25
Pomerode 108, 119
  Museu Pomerano 108
Ponta do Seixas 171
Ponta Negra 172
Ponte Negra, beach 68
Porto Alegre 102-104, 118
  Cathedral 102
  Lagoa dos Patos 102
  Mercado Público 102
  Palácio Piratini 102
  Praça Marechal Deodoro 102
  Teatro São Pedro 102
Porto de Galinhas, beach 166
Porto Seguro 13, 159, 161
  Igreja da Misericórdia, church
    159
  Nossa Senhora da Penha, church
    159
Posey, Dr. Darell Addison 222
Post, Frans 168, 170
Praia da Redinha 173
Praia do Forte 155, 160
Praia do Poço 171
Praia dos Ingleses 107
Prestes, Luís Carlos 30

Q

Quadros, Jânio 31, 32
Quilombo 21, 22

R

Recife 19, 141, 163-166, 177
  Capela Dourada 163
  Casa da Cultura 165
  Catedral de São Pedro dos
    Clérigos 164
  Convento de Santo Antonio 163
  Forte das Cinco Pontas 165
  Igreja do Carmo, church 164
  Ilha Joana Bezerra 163
  Mercado São José 165
  Museu do Estado de
    Pernambuco 165
  Museu do Homem do Nordeste
    165
  Nossa Senhora dos Prazeres,
    church 166
  Palácio das Princesas 163
  Parque Histórico Nacional dos
    Guararapes 165
  Praça da República 163
  Santíssimo Sacramento, church
    164
  Santo Antônio 163
  Teatro Santa Isabel 163

Rain Forest 78, 196, 208-215
Recôncavo 155-158, 161
Refúgio Ecológico Caiman 133
Ribeiro, Darcy 37, 216, 233
Ribeiro, João Ubaldo 232
Rio Aquidauana 133
Rio de Janeiro 20, 24, 26, 36, 45,
  46, 48-63, 69
  Aqueduto da Carioca 62
  Assembléia 60
  Barra da Tijuca 55
  Biblioteca Nacional 61
  Centro Cultural do Banco do
    Brasil 59
  Christ, statue 49
  Cinelândia 60
  Confeitaria Colombo 58
  Convento Santo Antônio 57
  Copacabana 51-53
  Copacabana Palace 51
  Costa Verde 63
  Cultural Center, postal service 59
  Dois Irmãos 62
  Historic Quarter 57
  Ilha de Paquetá 63
  Ilha Fiscal 60
  Ipanema 52, 53, 54
  Jardim Botânico 56
  Lagoa Rodrigo de Freitas 54
  Largo da Carioca 57, 61
  Largo do Boticário 56
  Leblon 52, 54
  Maracaña Stadium 56
  Museu Nacional de Belas Artes
    60
  Nossa Senhora da Candelária,
    church 58
  Nossa Senhora da Glória do
    Oteiro, church 62
  Ordem Terceira de São
    Francisco da Pemitência,
    church 58
  Paço Imperial 59
  Palace of Culture 60
  Praia de São Conrado 54-55
  Praia de Vidigal 54
  Praia do Arpoador 53
  Praia do Botafogo 50
  Praia do Flamengo 49
  Praia do Leme 50, 52
  Praia da Urca 50
  Praia Vermelha 50
  Sambódromo 62
  Santa Luzia, church 60
  Santa Teresa, district 61, 62
  Santo Antônio, church 57
  São Sebastião, cathedral 62
  Sugar Loaf, peak 53, 55, 56
  Teatro Municipal 61
  Tijuca, forest 56
Rio Grande do Sul 25, 35, 101,
  231

Rio Negro 184, 186, 197, 219
Rio Paraguai 134
Rio São Francisco 142
Rio Solimões 184, 197
Rio Tapajós 186, 194, 195
Rio Xingú 186
Riserio, Antonio 145
Rondônia 183
Roosevelt, Anna 15
Roraima 183, 221, 222
Rosa, João Guimarães 233

S

Sabará 84-85
  Museu do Ouro 85
  Nossa Senhora da Conceição,
    church 84
  Nossa Senhora do Carmo,
    church 85
  Nossa Senhora do Ò, church 84
Salinópolis 193, 202
Salvador 18, 18, 26
Salvador da Bahia 141, 142-155,
  160, 226
  Beaches 152
  Boa Viagem, church 152
  Campo Grande 150
  Casa do Benin 149
  Catedral Basílica 145
  Cidade Baixa 151
  Elevador Lacerda 144, 151
  Farol da Barra 153
  Forte de São Diogo 153
  Forte de São Pedro 150
  Forte São Marcelo 144
  Fundação Casa de Jorge Amado
    148
  Gabinete Português de Leitura
    150
  Igreja do Bonfim, church 152
  Igreja do Carmo, church 149
  Ilha de Itaparica 145
  Largo da Piedade 149, 150
  Largo Tereza Batista 146
  Mercado Modelo 152
  Museu Abelardo Rodrigues
    148
  Museu de Arte Sacra 150
  Museu Hidrográfico de Salvador
    153
  Nossa Senhora da Conceição da
    Praia, church 151
  Nossa Senhora do Monte Serrat,
    church 152
  Nossa Senhora do Paço, church
    149
  Nossa Senhora do Rosário dos
    Pretos, church 149
  Ordem Terceira do Carmo,
    church 149
  Paço Municipal 144

Palácio Rio Branco 144
Pelourinho, district 146
Peninsula Itapagipe 152
Praça Anchieta 145
Praça Cairu 151
Praça Castro Alves 149, 150
Praça da Sé 145
Praça Tomé de Souza 144
Rua Gregório de Matos 148
Santa Teresa, church 150
Santo Antônio da Barra, church 153
São Domingos, church 145
São Francisco, church 145
São Marcelo, fort 152
São Pedro dos Clérigos, church 145
Senac 148
Terceira Ordem de São Francisco, church 146
Terminal Marítimo 152
Terreiro de Jesus 145
Salve Floresta 78
Samba 150, 223, 224, 227
Santa Catarina 35, 101, 105
Santa Rita 173
Santarém 193, **194-196**, 202
Museu dos Tapajós 194
Santiago, Antônio 163
Santo Amaro 156
Nossa Senhora da Purificação, church 156
Santos 19, 78, 79, 81
Guarujá 79
Ponte dos Práticos 79
Rampa do Mercado 79
São Felix 157
Centro Cultural Dannemann 157
São João del Rei 95, 97
São Francisco de Assis, church 95
Solar da Baronesa de Itaverava 96
Solar do Barão de São João del Rei 95
São Leopoldo 104, 118
Casa do Imigrante 104
Museu do Trem 104
Visconde de São Leopoldo 104
São Luís 19, 175, 179, 189
São Paulo 26, 36, 39, 45, 46, 49, **73-77**, 80
Biblioteca Mário de Andrade 75
Capela Imperial 76
Casa Anchieta 73, 74
Casa do Grito 76
Edifício Copan 75
Edifício Itália 75
Estação da Luz 78
Instituto Butantã 77

Monumento da Independência 76
Monumento das Bandeiras 76
Museu de Arte Contemporânea 76, 77
Museu de Arte de São Paulo 77
Museu de Arte Sacra de São Paulo 77
Museu Paulista 76, 77
Parque da Independência 76
Parque do Ibirapuera 76
Patio do Colegio 74
Praça da República 74, 75
Praça da Sé 74
Predio Martinelli 74
São Bento, monastery 74
São Francisco da Penitência, church 75
Teatro Municipal 75
Viaduto do Chá 74
São Vicente 16, 17
Saquarema 68
Sarney, José 34
Seixas, Raul 226
Sepúlveda, João de 164
Sergipe 141, 142
Serra do Espigão 109
Serra do Mar 35, 49, 65, 73
Serra Gaúcha 104
Serra Pelada 189
Serro 85
Sertão 141, 142
Silva Xavier, José Joaquim da (Tiradentes) 25, 60, 88, 96, 126
Silva, Chica da 85, 86
Simões, Mário 15
Slave Republic 21-22
Slave Trade 18, 21, 22
Slavery 39, 141, 174
Slaves 23, 24, 25, 28, 48, 86, 90, 142, 146, 149, 223, 226
Sopher, Eva 102
Souré 194, 202
Sousa, Martim Afonso de 16, 73
Sousa, Tomé de 17, 142
Staden, Hans 14
Sto. Antônio de Lisboa 106
Nossa Senhora das Necessidades, church 106
Street Children 39
Sugar Cane 17, 18, 38, 48, 65, 83, 141, 142, 155, 163, 231

T

Tamandaré, beach 166
Tambaba 171
Tambaú 170
Teresa Cristina, Empress 27
Teresina 141
Teresópolis 67, 71
Tibau do Sul 172

Tiradentes, city 96, 97
Casa da Cultura 96
Museu Padre Toledo 96
Santo Antônio, church 96
Tocantins 183
Torres, Antônio 233
Trancoso 159
Treaty of Tordesillas 16, 197
Trem da Serra 78
Treze Tílias **109-110**, 120

U

Umbanda Rites 50

V

Vargas, Getúlio 30, 31, 32
Vasconcelos, Nana 226
Vauthier, Luis 163, 165
Veloso, Caetano 156, 227
Vespucci, Amerigo 14, 142
Via Graciosa 112
Vila Velha 112
Villa Lobos, Heitor 224, 225, 226

W

Wai-Wai, indigenous group 220
Waimiri-Atroari, indigenous group 220

X

Xé, Tom 227
Ximenez, Ettore 76

Y

Yanomami, indigenous group 37, 216, 220-222
Yemanjá 50, 154, 226

Z

Zoé, indigenous group 219
Zweig, Stefan 56, 67, 152